AN ORCHESTRA BEYO…

AN ORCHESTRA BEYOND BORDERS

ELENA CHEAH

London • New York

To the memory of Edward Said and the future of the West-Eastern Divan.

First published by Verso 2009

1 3 5 7 9 10 8 6 4 2

Verso
UK: 6 Meard Street, London W1F 0EG
US: 20 Jay Street, Suite 1010, Brooklyn, NY 11201
www.versobooks.com

Verso is the imprint of New Left Books

ISBN-13: 978-1-84467-408-4

British Library Cataloguing in Publication Data
A catalogue record for this book is available from the British Library

Library of Congress Cataloging-in-Publication Data
A catalog record for this book is available from the Library of Congress

Typeset in Fournier by Hewer Text UK Ltd, Edinburgh
Printed in Sweden by ScandBook AB

Contents

Foreword
by Daniel Barenboim

The West-Eastern Divan Orchestra is of course incapable of bringing peace to the Middle East. We are musicians, not politicians. My late friend Edward Said and I founded this orchestra in 1999 as an experiment for people who believe that politics should serve humanity and not vice versa. We wanted to create a human solution in the absence of a political one.

Today, after ten years of this continuing experiment, I am delighted that this book has given individual members of the West-Eastern Divan the opportunity to narrate their own personal development, often in their own words. Other stories have been succinctly and eloquently related by Elena Cheah, who has lived and played with the orchestra over the last three years. These individual stories run parallel with the orchestra's development and tell its history in human terms.

It is my sincere wish that these personal stories open the minds and hearts of all the peoples of the Middle East, and I imagine Edward Said would have felt the same way. Stories alone are obviously unable to bring about peace, but they might at least serve to awaken the reader's curiosity about the history of the Middle East. We Middle Easterners are all great artists when it comes to abusing historical knowledge in order to demonstrate our victimhood and wallow in self-pity. It would be far more productive to allow our curiosity and knowledge to help us imagine and create the conditions for a better future.

Middle Eastern readers may be positively surprised by some of the atypical opinions expressed here by their geographical neighbors. Edward Said and I believed in letting opposing voices be heard at the same time; we were not interested in providing a line of thought to be followed by all. We based this principle on musical counterpoint, where a subversive accompanimental voice can enhance a melody rather than detract from it. To this day, we do not try to diminish or soften our differences in the orchestra: we do the opposite. By confronting our differences, we attempt to understand the logic behind the opposite position.

I am very proud of the maturity of the musicians portrayed here, and full of respect for their courage.

Introduction

An orchestra is a microcosm of society. This particular orchestra is a microcosm of a society that has never existed and may well never exist. The West-Eastern Divan Orchestra, founded in 1999 in Weimar, is an ensemble made up of musicians from Israel, Palestine, Jordan, Lebanon, Syria, Egypt, Turkey, Iran, and Spain. It meets every summer for about a month to discuss Middle Eastern issues, rehearse, and play concerts. A month may not seem like a long time, but it is a month of extremely strenuous rehearsal and performance, constant social contact, and very little sleep. Every moment is invested with an extraordinary energy; time is not merely stretched but takes on a different quality. For a month, the musicians work and live together in very close quarters with their colleagues, who may come from countries they will never be able to set foot in.

Every year there are auditions for new members, but many musicians have been invited to return again and again, and this has allowed the orchestra to develop and mature both musically and socially over the years. The musicians who have chosen to tell their stories in this book are not any more or less important than all the other musicians of the orchestra, past, present or future. Each musician simply opens a window into the soul of the orchestra, which is something unimaginable to an outsider: the soul of the orchestra is a constantly changing original composition being collectively written by all of its members, who can tell its story better than anyone else.

I feel very fortunate to have spent so much time with the West-Eastern Divan Orchestra. I became involved with it through a series of coincidences. I do not come from any of the countries listed above; I was born in the United States. In 1999 I was already living in Germany, but did not hear of the orchestra until 2005, when I took on a one-year contract as principal cellist of the Staatskapelle Berlin, the orchestra of the German State Opera. Many of my new colleagues had been enlisted by Maestro Daniel Barenboim to coach the young musicians of the Divan, and they told me about the orchestra. I was fascinated by the idea and hoped to be able to visit the workshop someday to hear the orchestra and meet the people in it.

In 2006, my wish was granted through an unfortunate circumstance. A week before the workshop was set to begin, war broke out between Israel and the Hezbollah in Lebanon. The Lebanese musicians were suddenly trapped inside their country, and several other Arab musicians found it impossible to attend the workshop under the circumstances. All in all, fifteen musicians were missing, a considerable percentage of an ensemble of about eighty or ninety. At the beginning of the workshop, there was still hope that a ceasefire would soon be negotiated and the missing musicians would be allowed to return. As the days and weeks went by, however, it seemed less likely that this would be the case. The rehearsal period was nearly over, the tour was about to begin, and the orchestra was still incomplete. It was decided that the tour would proceed anyway with the help of a few professional outsiders. Since I had expressed interest in the project, I was one of the musicians contacted by Tabaré Perlas, Barenboim's personal assistant and administrator of the West-Eastern Divan Orchestra.

There were still Arab musicians at the Divan workshop in 2006 from Palestine, Egypt, and Jordan, but there was obviously a disturbance in the equilibrium. The handful of professional musicians who filled in at the last moment may have rescued the musical balance of the orchestra, but it soon became clear to me that they could not restore the social balance.

On the afternoon of August 6, 2006, I arrived in Pilas at the Lantana guest house, site of the Divan workshop. A former convent, the place is structured like a miniature university campus with dormitories, rehearsal spaces, and a cafeteria in separate buildings. Lemon trees create enough shade to sit on the prickly grass lawns between the buildings, and there is an Olympic-sized swimming pool behind the parking lot.

The spartan, linoleum-tiled room I was assigned had a view of the parking lot, and I could see waves of heat rising from the pavement. I didn't have much time to unpack my things, because there was an orchestra rehearsal scheduled that evening in the bullfight arena of Seville, where the orchestra would be performing two days later. I looked around the campus, getting my bearings and feeling as if I'd arrived late for summer camp and all the other kids knew how to get around better than I did. As I walked down the hall, I saw through the open doors of a few other bedrooms that the other kids had all removed the mattresses from their metal frames and put them on the floor. Sitting down on one of the creaky old twin beds in my room, I realized why.

I arrived at the bullfight arena early; I wanted to look around, since I had never been in one before. It was not the most obvious choice of location for a performance of Beethoven's Ninth Symphony, but it had the advantage of being large enough to accommodate several thousand people. A stage had been built right in the center of the arena, where the bullfights ordinarily took place. Soon the orchestra buses arrived, and the musicians began to unpack, leaving their instrument cases lined up against the bulls' stalls.

There were an odd number of cellists in the orchestra before I arrived, which left one young girl from Ramallah sitting alone in the last stand. I sat next to her and we began to talk. She had been playing the cello for only one and a half years, but had managed to learn the Beethoven symphony well enough to be able to go on tour with the orchestra. She was fourteen years old and had played the violin for a while before switching to the cello, but she was not terribly serious about music: she wanted to become a doctor.

Before I joined the orchestra, there had been considerable discord in the cello section because of a pendant she wore around her neck in the shape of present-day Israel. The word "Palestine" was written across the map-pendant. There were more Israeli than Spanish or Arab cellists in the section that year because of the war, and they were deeply offended by the necklace. They insisted that she remove it.

By the time I met her, there was no more pendant, but the memory of it obviously lingered in the minds of the cellists. It seemed like some of the others were grateful that there was now an outsider who could sit next to her.

Soon the rehearsal started, and I observed my stand partner closely. It would have been more interesting to listen to the whole orchestra, which I was hearing for the first time, but the lack of a natural acoustic made it difficult to hear anything but the instruments immediately surrounding me. At the same time, I was curious to see how a relative beginner would cope with Beethoven's Ninth Symphony, a challenge I could hardly imagine.

She did extraordinarily well. It was clear that certain passages were beyond her skills on the instrument, but she knew exactly when to play out and when to play a little less so as not to disturb the group by playing wrong notes. She never got lost, either.

After we played through the symphony, Barenboim presented an anti-war declaration that he had written together with Edward Said's widow Mariam. He explained that he felt it was necessary for the orchestra to make a statement to be printed in their concert programs as long as the war went on. He read it aloud to the orchestra:

> This year, our project stands in sharp contrast to the cruelty and savagery that denies so many innocent civilians the possibility

> to continue living, fulfilling their ideals and dreams. Israel's destruction of life-giving infrastructure in Lebanon and Gaza, uprooting a million people and inflicting heavy casualties on civilians, and Hezbollah's indiscriminate shelling of civilians in northern Israel are in total opposition to what we believe in. The refusal to have an immediate ceasefire and the refusal to enter into negotiations for resolving once and for all the conflict in all its aspects goes against the very essence of our project as well.

As he read it, I looked around, trying to gauge the musicians' response. I could not detect any obvious immediate reaction. After reading the statement, Barenboim asked the orchestra to consider whether it should be printed and let him know if they wanted any changes made. He took the ensuing silence as a sign of consent and dismissed the orchestra for the evening. It was quite late already, and some people were anxious to get on the bus and go back to Pilas, where dinner would be served. As I left the stage, though, I saw a cluster of musicians standing around Barenboim, engaged in heated discussion. I found out only later that these were the Israelis.

The next day at lunch, the statement was still being passionately discussed. One Israeli boy felt pushed into a corner: "I don't agree with this statement, but my only alternative is to leave? I don't want to miss out on the whole concert tour just because of this!" Another Israeli girl told me, "But I'm not against the war, I support my government!"

I silently wondered how it was possible to support a war against one's own colleagues; furthermore, to continue to support the war even while participating in a workshop whose sole statement regarding the Israeli–Palestinian conflict is that there is no military solution. It was only the first of many personal contradictions I would discover among the members of this most unusual of orchestras.

Immediately after lunch and while still arguing about the declaration, everyone headed for the rehearsal hall, where we were to rehearse the encore: Wagner's Prelude and *Liebestod* from the opera *Tristan und Isolde*. Waltraud Meier was sitting in the hall among a small audience of visitors. A strong supporter of the project, she was with the orchestra to rehearse and perform the Beethoven symphony with them. Judging by the expression on her face as we began to play the Prelude, she had not been told what we were going to play. It was a look that began with shock, as if she had stepped into a stranger's living room by mistake; it then slowly progressed to disbelieving acceptance and an apparent struggle with tears. Sitting in the orchestra next to an Israeli girl, I too had to hold back tears while the tension steadily mounted.

I had played the whole opera many times before, with Christian Thielemann at the Deutsche Oper Berlin and with Barenboim at the Berlin State Opera, and each time had been powerfully memorable, but this time was different. "Why?" I asked myself as I played and listened to the ever more voluptuous harmonic waves. Was I projecting my own sentimental ideas of peace and cooperation onto the orchestra and the music? Was I introducing a non-musical dimension to my consciousness of the music, thereby willing myself to hear something that was not really there? As we continued to play, I realized that the answer was no. I heard in the orchestra's playing a certain unity of purpose in each phrase, an understanding of the cumulative effect of so much unresolved tension, a sensual relationship to the never-ending, continually sustained sound, and an audible comprehension of the harmonic turning points of the piece. I was not imagining all this; it was real. It was overwhelming enough without adding any non-musical sentiment.

Then Waltraud Meier began to sing. She faced the orchestra and opened her arms to us, as if to embrace all of us with her voice. In the opera, it is always a moment of breathtaking emotion, if not relief, to hear the *tremolo* chords at the beginning of the *Liebestod* and the singer's voice rising up out of them. In the opera, though, I had only ever heard this from the pit, and no matter how wonderful the singer was, it was something far away, above our heads and directed toward an audience in the dark. Now I was facing perhaps the greatest Isolde of all time, who was singing with us, to us, and for us. *Us*: in that instant I began, unconsciously, to identify with the group of Israeli, Arab, and Spanish musicians playing around me.

There was no way not to identify with a group of people making such sublime music. Playing with them, I naturally felt at one with them musically. Waltraud Meier's voice did indeed embrace our sound, blending with the orchestra and yet remaining above it, riding the crest of each crescendo and forestalling each diminuendo. The totality was like nothing I had ever heard before. When it was over, I was grateful for the presence of the small audience who started to applaud after a respectful silence. Applause was the only sound that could have broken the spell of the music painlessly.

After this rehearsal, I knew I had arrived in the West-Eastern Divan. I was part of it all now, whether I liked it or not.

In 2007, the workshop took place in Austria as part of the Salzburg Festival, and the Divan was at the center of many of the festival's events. I returned to the orchestra that summer to teach a group of Palestinian children who came from Nazareth, Ramallah, and other areas of the West Bank. The children's group was an adjunct to the "big kids'" workshop; it was an opportunity for them to have intensive lessons while watching the orchestra rehearse and perform. At one point there was a podium discussion with eight or nine members of the West-Eastern Divan Orchestra, and each member said a few words about their cultural backgrounds and their involvement in the workshop.

As they went along the line introducing themselves and answering questions from the audience, I saw a very beautiful picture begin to emerge: the tapestry woven by so many individuals from mutually hostile nations who had learned to live with each other in some way, always seeking the right balance between honesty and diplomacy, confrontation and forgiveness, emotion and logic. In addition to the musicians on stage, I thought of all the other musicians who were not on stage at that moment, each of whom had his or her own story of the West-Eastern Divan. That was when I decided that these stories had to be told.

I started out by speaking to the musicians I knew had a lot to say, and whenever possible I have allowed them to speak for themselves here. In some cases, the stories lent themselves to a third-person narration, which had the advantage of allowing me to describe events from the inside and the outside at once. Some of the musicians are born storytellers; others are not. By shifting the perspective accordingly, I was able to include everyone who had something to contribute.

Naturally it was not easy for many of the musicians to let their constantly changing ideas and opinions be printed in a "final" version when they themselves may have since strayed a great distance from the perspectives presented here. The reader may therefore take it for granted that any particular opinion expressed by any particular musician may have been supplanted by another by the time of printing, or that many new opinions have grown in its place. This book is simply a snapshot of something fluid and transient; the story of the West-Eastern Divan Orchestra continues to be spun, and will hopefully continue for a long time to come.

Daniel Cohen was the first person I spoke to about his experiences in the Divan, and he made everything very easy for me. For one thing, he had moved to Berlin after completing his conducting studies in London, and had very conveniently found an apartment five minutes' walking distance from my own. For another, as we sat in his small, orderly kitchen sipping *nana* (mint) tea, he unleashed a passionate and humorous torrent of tales, from his early childhood until the most recent summers with the Divan. Daniel is himself an Israeli West-Eastern mixture: his mother is of European Jewish descent, and his father was born into an Iraqi Jewish family in Baghdad.

I had printed out a list of questions I wanted to ask him, which lay folded and untouched on the kitchen table as he told me about things I never would have thought of asking. Daniel was my best possible preparation for speaking to the rest of the musicians I met; he recounted all the major events of the workshop from 2003 to the present, and touched on many of the inevitable contradictions inherent in being a patriotic Israeli *and* having an outsider's view of the Middle East. I was impressed by his candor and willingness to speak about sensitive and sometimes painful issues with me, a person he knew only casually from two summer sessions.

When I visited Daniel for the first time, he was reading *The Iron Wall* by Avi Shlaim, a book that presents Israel's history from quite a different perspective than the one preferred in Israeli textbooks and schoolrooms. Shlaim had visited the Divan, and this was the first book of his that Daniel had read. It was obvious from the way he talked about it that the book was equally fascinating and disturbing for him. He seemed to be in a state of controlled turmoil, enduring a painful collapse of old beliefs without yet having constructed a stable structure to support the new ones. Meanwhile, he poked fun at his own agony with his characteristic sense of humor. In the past, I would have called it Jewish humor, but after having spent two summers with both Jews and Arabs, I can only call it Divan humor.

Daniel Cohen

The Divan is so intertwined with my life that I don't even know how to approach it, how to start telling. When I first came to the Divan in the summer of 2003, things were different. Today there is a core group of musicians who know each other and have been returning every year for many years, and there is a certain basic trust that allows us to discuss things maturely. My first year, things were different. Over time, we have gradually developed some sort of sensitivity to what the "other side" finds offensive. In the beginning we were not so attuned to this.

The confrontations in the beginning were painful, horribly painful. I remember storming out of one of them shaking violently; I was so full of rage that I was inconsolable. It was not a discussion but a film, and I think all, or at least most of the Israelis left. It was a documentary called *Route 181* co-directed by an Israeli and a Palestinian. In it, they walked along the 1949 Green Line (which was intended to separate Israeli from Palestinian territories) and talked to people they met along the way. The line between intellectually provocative cinema and propaganda is very fine but very tangible. I think all we Israelis sat there thinking, if we had wanted to listen to propaganda, we wouldn't have come to the Divan. We were all very upset.

I don't think many of us had any major objections to the general line of thinking in the film, which was that the human rights of Palestinians living under the occupation were being violated. I think it's safe to say that most people who come to the Divan probably think along those lines anyway. I think that's a safe assumption, because if you don't, why would you go to the workshop? There are exceptions, of course. It's not that you have to have specific political views to be a part of the Divan, you can just come for the music; but it stands to reason that if you don't think that all human beings have equal rights, you would probably not find yourself at the workshop. In the film, though, the only Israelis they interviewed were right-wing settlers, and when you ask such a person a loaded question, you know what kind of an answer you will get. The film was not a fair representation of general Israeli opinion.

Another thing that upset us very much was the use of images in the film. There was an image in the movie of a barbed-wire fence between watchtowers running along train tracks, which is exactly the image that you see over and over again in Israel in reference to the Holocaust. These images are burnt into your memory: they have become icons, almost. Even I, who had no living memory of it in my family, have seen these images every year since I can remember. I'm not saying there are no watchtowers or checkpoints in the West Bank—of course there are—but to use exactly this image says something. And to me, as much as I am unable to live with the occupation, as much as I denounce it and disagree with it, analogy between the occupation and the Holocaust is at best unhealthy, and at worst manipulative and wholly unjust. It was the kind of provocation that made you dig your heels deeper into the ground because it played on the instincts of your indoctrination as a child: don't touch the Holocaust!

Nevertheless, I think the intentions in planning the discussions and guest lecturers for the orchestra were always good. Not every visit was great, and some of them, like this one with the film, went terribly wrong. Others, though, were provocative in a very positive way. I remember Mustafa Barghouti's visit three or four years ago in Pilas: he was very fiery. This Palestinian doctor and former politician and the founder of the organization Medical Relief came when the wall in the West Bank was in the process of being constructed. He showed us some maps and I remember seeing them, finding them very disturbing, and thinking they could not possibly be true. He was showing us the 1967 borders on the one hand, and, on the other, the places where the wall was going to be constructed.

This wall fragmented the West Bank into small islands completely detached from each other, leaving the Palestinians no chance of forming a unified national identity or striving for any sort of viable statehood. I remember thinking back then: "I can't listen to this kind of propaganda. This is horrible, this has to be false because what I have read and heard in books and in the news must be true." The strange thing is that no one actually lied. Each faction just presented the part of the truth it wanted to present. But I think that the greatest shock I got from Mustafa Barghouti was that he said, "All you Israelis"; I remember he started the sentence with this phrase: "All you Israelis talk to us as if we want something of yours, and you give it to us as if we have no right to it, you give it to us like a handout." I think this statement was a response to someone saying, "But in the Oslo agreement we wanted to give you this and we wanted to give you that . . ." You could see that he was truly agitated. He has a very pleasant character and he's a very charismatic speaker, but he can get very agitated. He said, "You always want to give it to us as if it were yours to give."

It suddenly hit me that I had been taught that the Palestinians wanted to take something away from us. I wasn't told that they thought they had a right to something. Whether they have that right or not is not the point here, although I obviously think that they do. The way that the truth is presented from the Israeli standpoint leads to a way of thinking that cannot resolve the conflict with the Palestinians. As far as Mr. Barghouti was concerned, even if I were to *give* him 80 percent of the territory, it would not be acceptable. The only thing that would be acceptable would be my coming to terms with his *right* to govern any percentage of that territory. That had a huge effect on me and my way of thinking. At the time I really didn't like him very much, and when I went to speak to him one-on-one, I got very upset with him and he got very upset with me, but afterward he sat next to us at the table and we ate together.

He's actually a lovely man and a very talented politician. He knows how to provoke and how to resolve a conflict: he knows how far he can push things, which is an ability not many politicians in our region have. As an Israeli, I had to come to terms with the idea that Palestinians do in fact comprise a nation, and that their claims are based on the rights of nations in general. That's something that I didn't grow up with. If you ask people today, almost all of them will say they are left-wing, because it's very trendy to be left-wing. We're all good people on the left. Nevertheless, it's very easy, when you grow up in Israel, not to let things register.

Unfortunately I heard only one of Edward Said's lectures: his last lecture to the Divan before he died. It was a formidable event lasting a mere four hours. He didn't really speak about the Israeli–Palestinian conflict as such. He spoke about it in order to make larger, deeper points about human nature and the rights of human beings. At least in that one particular lecture which I heard, the conflict was simply a starting point for him. He was virtuosic. You could see that the man was a thinker, not a politician. He had no interest in discussing what percentage of the land goes where. He wanted to get to deeper issues: to the rights of the human being, the rights of a person under occupation and the duties of nations.

In general, I had contact with many intellectuals and politicians in the Divan before really knowing who they were or understanding what they were saying. It wasn't that I was too young, I was just not aware or interested enough. It is definitely something I very much regret. They made me think, but not enough to actually make use of their visits. When we had people in front of us like the Palestinian human rights activist, writer, and lawyer Raja

Shehadeh, I had no instruments I could use to pick his brain. I could only sit and listen and be more or less impressed, that was all. That was no one's fault but mine, of course, but this is something I regret, because these were the kinds of discussions that could change your life.

When I was growing up in Israel and studying in the Tel Aviv Academy, my first string quartet was with Nabeel Abboud-Ashkar from Nazareth, who later became my desk partner in the Divan. I had started going to the academy when I was fifteen years old, even before finishing school, because I was having more fun studying music than going to school.

I had started taking violin lessons with an old-school Russian teacher for youngsters; she was like a mother to her good students. In the beginning I used to go to her house after school and spend four or five hours there; she used to make me tea and cookies and I would practice in the other room while she taught. I would never have practiced at home. As time passed, it stopped being an after-school activity and started to be instead of school.

I told my mother that I wasn't studying anything at school. I was afraid to go to school because the kids were bigger than me, they were hitting each other, and I didn't like going and didn't learn anything from it. My mother said, "If you don't like it and you want to go to your teacher to practice, go to her to practice." She didn't see any problem with my dropping out if I said I wasn't studying anyway. What was the point?

My mother said, "Look, so you're not going to know a few things. When it will interest you and you have a will to know it, you'll open a book and you'll know it." And she was right.

I started going to the Tel Aviv Academy, where the director made a special arrangement for me to be able to take courses and get credit for them after I took my high school equivalency test. I was required to take a certain number of external, non-musical courses in order to get my degree in music, and one of my favorite non-musical courses was Dr. Unger's class, "Episodes in Western Civilization." I was very lucky to come across Dr. Unger; I admired and loved him beyond words. His course was about philosophy, but also much more than that; it included topics like the Industrial Revolution, or Shakespeare and Dante, or Galileo, representative ways of thinking in Western civilization. He had the power not so much to teach the material, but to make you feel, after leaving his class, that the most urgent thing was not to eat or drink but to quench your thirst for knowledge immediately.

In a way, my education should have led me to conclusions that I didn't come to. Before leaving Israel and spending time away from the country, I was unable to see how much I was indoctrinated myself, even though I didn't go through the normal experience of being an adolescent in Israel. It's not that I had so much education, but the kind of education I had should have told me to suspect that what I heard was only one side of the truth. The indoctrination was so strong, though, that I could not see it from within.

What I'm talking about is not something that I can even remember anyone saying to me. It goes a bit deeper than that. It's something that you observe and absorb from your surroundings, something that you hear in slogans, read in signs. It is like something out of Orwell: you've seen it a million times before, yet you can't remember a single situation in which someone actually tells you this. It's something that you just grow up with; it's truth that you cannot challenge.

I still remember the first time I heard Nabeel call himself a Palestinian. I was sitting next to him in an interview in the Divan workshop and someone asked him, "So you're also Israeli?" and he said, "I'm a Palestinian living in Israel." It suddenly hit me: that's not what I grew up believing about these people. It was a big shock that Nabeel saw himself as a part of the Palestinian people, not living in the occupied territories but on Israeli territory. In retrospect this is perfectly clear to me, but at the time it was something new, because I had met Nabeel under very different circumstances. I knew that he was an Arab—what we call an Israeli Arab. I would never have thought that he regarded himself as a Palestinian living in Israel; I thought they regarded themselves as Israelis of Arab origin. That was what I had always been told.

I had no interest in politics whatsoever when I was younger. In fact, I had no interest until very recently, only for the last year or so, long after my first Divan experience. This sounds really awful, but in a way I was on the right side of the conflict. I could afford not to be bothered with it.

Some of the experiences I had in the Divan awakened my current interest in the politics and history of my part of the world. The unforgettable concert we played with the orchestra on our trip to Ramallah in 2005 is one of them. It is also one of the things in my life I am most proud of having done. But the journey to Ramallah—or more precisely my decision to join the orchestra in going there—was neither brave nor easy.

After many speculations about security concerns and much discussion, Mr. Barenboim finally declared that we were indeed going to Ramallah. I must say that although I admired him for playing there and supported the idea of playing there wholeheartedly, his announcement did not fill me with joy. I am an abnormally timid person, and the prospect of crossing "enemy lines" and going into the occupied territories, protected only by Palestinian armed forces and by a Spanish diplomatic passport, did not appeal to me one bit. Images of the inhuman "Ramallah lynching" that I had seen on the television in 2000 haunted me. I was simply too scared. Mr. Barenboim had promised that if anyone felt unable or unwilling to go for any reason, he was free not to do so, and with that in mind, I decided not to go.

Mr. Barenboim insisted on speaking personally to every single member of the orchestra who had any doubts. He spent hours discussing these matters with Israelis who were worried about going into the occupied territories against the better judgment of their government, which prohibited Israeli citizens from entering them. He met with Syrians who were worried that by going to Ramallah they would in fact be crossing Israeli territory (an illegal act for Syrian and Lebanese citizens), and could get into trouble either there or upon their return to Syria. He even spoke with Spanish people who were worried for many other reasons, and so on and on. He gave each person as long as it took, answering, explaining, and reassuring with his characteristic passion and hot temper. I have never seen anyone believe in anything more than Mr. Barenboim believed in the importance of this orchestra's visit to Ramallah. Then came my turn.

When I told him that I didn't want to go, that I was scared, he asked me calmly, in a tired voice, whether I thought he would take his own son there (who was and still is the concertmaster of our orchestra) if he had any doubts as to the safety of the visit. When I persisted, he quickly lost his temper. He told me that from anyone else he would have accepted this, but not from me, and, shouting something about how I had more between my ears than between my legs, he stormed out of the room.

Since then I have often joked that I ended up in Ramallah because, at the end of the day, I was more afraid of Mr. Barenboim than I was of the Hamas. The truth is more complex than that, and has a lot to do with a phone conversation I had with my mother right after this traumatic argument. I was on a payphone outside the hotel in Wiesbaden, Germany, where the orchestra was staying at the time on our tour.

My mother is a truly miraculous woman. Like many Jewish mothers, she is overprotective of her youngest child to an almost insane degree. Full of fears and doubts, she is also full of contradictions. She listened to all I had to say and then asked me a simple question: "Do you think it is the right thing to do?" When I answered that I did, she said, "Then you need to do it."

I don't even know how to begin to explain what it meant for my mother to say this. Suffice it to say that her strength and support gave me the courage I was so lacking. I marched back into the hotel and saw Mr. Barenboim walking toward me. I said, "I just spoke to my mother and I am coming with you to Ramallah." He said not a word, but shook my hand with what I can only describe as an honest smile, and kept walking.

Ironically, I had a wonderful day on the trip itself, though I know this wasn't the purpose of the exercise. It wasn't all roses, but once we actually went I didn't feel afraid or unsafe in any way. The only part that made me feel unsafe was getting into the German bulletproof cars on the Israeli side. We had a private guard and armored cars with sirens and we were not allowed to leave the concert hall premises. Once I had made the resolution to go, it was actually easy. Very often in life you think that something is going to be very difficult and you spend too much energy worrying about it. In the end, when you do it, it's no big deal.

The 2005 tour had been difficult and long. We went to South America before the trip to Ramallah, and we had already been together for over a month. The Divan experience is very intense, and we had been together all the time, so after that, any time apart is a long time. The Arabs had to fly to Amman and enter the West Bank from the Jordanian side, and the Spanish musicians and we Israelis had to fly to Tel Aviv and stay in Israel. It wasn't like going to Ramallah on tour; we Israelis came back home and slept in our own beds and it was, in a way, like going back to being Israeli. Then we had to go from there to Ramallah. It was nothing that dramatic, but when you think about what it means not to go as a group of mixed nationalities but to actually split the group in two, it is a different story. We went through so much change during this period of separation. When you go to the Divan, there is a certain communal identity. There is certainly something different, not necessarily in how I think about the situation, but in how I feel about it when I actually lead my daily life in Israel. In that respect, it was a drastic change. Later, I was watching the documentary about the Divan (*Knowledge is the Beginning*) with my mother, and she saw us entering the hall in Ramallah, running to each other and hugging, with real joy. She asked me, "How long had you not seen each other?" I told her, "Two days."

The concert in Ramallah was the last one in a six-week tour, and when we said good-bye afterward we were parting with some people for two years, although we didn't know it yet. I found 2006 a very difficult year because of the Lebanon war. Even musically it was very difficult, because fifteen musicians were not there, and fifteen people make up a big part of the orchestra. People didn't come for so many reasons, but it was quite striking that so many of them didn't come. I remember feeling hurt that they didn't come. I've never actually mentioned this to them. As time passes, I see it a bit differently, because with time I've come to know more about what actually happened in Lebanon in 2006, and the state of things on the ground. I remember thinking, however: "It's wrong that we are here and they are not." I did not take this lightly at all, and I don't know if I would have come had I been in their place. Yet I did feel a bit betrayed when I got to Pilas and found out that so many of the Arabs hadn't turned up and that they felt that they couldn't come in this crucial moment. In that moment, I felt that they couldn't tolerate us while we, with all our resentment of the war and the violence, had still come to meet them.

I knew better than to think that they would equate us musicians with the actions of our government, and I refused to think that my friends would think of me as an aggressor. I certainly didn't think of them as aggressors. It was just that I had thought that what we did took precedence over the war, that the fact that we would come together during the war was more important than some of us making a statement that the war was wrong. I thought that, by staying in their countries, they made a much weaker point than if they had come and spent the time with us. But not actually having been there and gone through what they went through, I can't make that judgment. The 2006 workshop, in general, was very, very difficult. Part of the joy of making a communal effort was very much damaged by the fact that it wasn't very communal. The war also took a lot of our thinking and energy.

What sticks in my mind most about 2006 was the computer room. There were these two computers in Pilas, and people from all over the Middle East crammed into this room to see the news on the Internet. When you hear about something that happened—a missile falling in Haifa or a bomb in Beirut—in your room or surrounded by people of your own country, it's different from when you hear it and are in mixed company. That had a very strong effect on me, though I'm not sure I can really explain entirely what it was. I think shame and anger were part of it, but not all of it. I remember feeling that I didn't want to be a part of this, that I didn't want my friends to be looking at me through these events, as if they were looking through a screen. Maybe that's why I was so hurt that they didn't come to the Divan, that I felt that they were looking at me through the filter of these events, and I felt that, with all that we had done together, we had established a different kind of relationship.

I don't know if it's moral to put together such tragic and such comic events, but I remember arriving in Pilas for the Divan on July 24, 2006, and thinking about this wonderful *Fawlty Towers* sketch about the Germans, when they keep saying, "Don't mention the war!" I remember thinking, this is wrong that I am so sarcastic about these things. It's not that we were careful—we didn't even have to be careful not to mention the war. It was just so difficult to talk about the war that nobody did. I think it took about a week until people actually started to break open the wounds. It takes time to mention the unmentionable. It wasn't all sad and all bad, and I drew a lot of comfort from the fact that at least some of my friends from the Arab world did come; but on the whole, the summer of 2006 wasn't a pleasant experience.

One of the most difficult topics of discussion that year was the declaration against the war that was made in the name of the orchestra and printed in the programs of all the concerts we played while the war was still going on. Mr. Barenboim and Mariam Said wrote and proposed an anti-war declaration to the orchestra.

The objections people had to the declaration could be divided into three categories: cosmetic objections to wording or the emphasis in the declaration on the entities involved; ideological objections to its content or reading it as a betrayal of their country in a time of war; and principle-based objections that a non-political body, by definition, should refrain from making a political statement.

I was a part of the third group. Had this declaration been made by any political party in my country, I would have found it acceptable, even admirable. But, coming from a body of people that refers to itself time and again as non-political, it seemed to be overstepping the boundaries we had set for ourselves. At the end of a long and heated discussion, Mr. Barenboim, slightly losing patience with the amount of suggestions to alter the wording of the declaration, said that he had spent a lot of time and thought choosing the words very carefully, and would like to put forward a vote. He then asked if anyone objected to "the content of the declaration, not the wording of it," thus sidestepping our vote of approval for publishing such a statement in the first place.

Someone suggested that the declaration be published only under his and Mrs. Said's signatures, and he replied that it would have no value if the declaration did not come from each and every one of us. I was faced with the choice of either voting against a statement whose content I agreed with, or approving a statement I didn't want to make in that specific context. I chose to approve it. Thus, with a very small minority of objections, the declaration was approved. Though I did share the views put forward in the statement, I still think it was not in the spirit of the orchestra to make them.

I was very happy to see all of my friends from Syria and Lebanon again the following year. The summer of 2007 was musically very challenging, but also very rewarding. For the first time we played a work from the Second Viennese School, Schönberg's *Variations for Orchestra* Op. 31, and I thought people would complain more about it than they did. I heard a lot of people complaining before the summer. But I think once people actually got their parts, and once we started rehearsals with Mr. Barenboim, they were really liking it. Mr. Barenboim has an immense musical presence that brings this orchestra together. It's a sort of fiery energy melded with an extremely didactic approach and a lot of knowledge. That combination is the only one that could have worked for this orchestra. Inspiration alone would not have been enough. It takes an amazing amount of power, charisma, and personal strength to get this orchestra off the ground because of the diversity of its members. It can really be a glorious orchestra, but every summer is the beginning of a new musical struggle. We come from very different musical backgrounds and degrees of training. We have people like Nabil Shehata and Mor Biron who play in the Berlin Philharmonic, and then people who are playing in an orchestra for the first time. As for myself, I had quite decent musical training but never any good orchestral training. When I came to the Divan I had no idea how to play in an orchestra.

Mr. Barenboim has the unique ability to use his knowledge and patience to take any problem we might have, from intonation to phrasing, and narrow it down, break it down, and give us advice and guidance throughout the whole process. He patiently digs away to an abnormal degree, which made the first rehearsal of the Schönberg quite something. One would expect the conductor to say, well let's play the theme first; but he started with the introduction of the piece and then said, let's play the theme without the celli (who have the theme), and he proceeded to take every single chord and tune it. After that, we had the harmonic progression in our heads and we thought it through. So, unbelievably tortuous as it was, it gave us a sensation and a feel for where the harmony was drawing us. When he then put the theme on top of the harmonies, there was not much more explaining to be done.

I don't think any other orchestra could afford to have a three-and-a-half-hour rehearsal on the theme without a break. We got to know it in a way that I don't think any professional orchestra could ever do, for obvious reasons. Schönberg is not easy music, and this piece is not Schönberg lite: it's hard-core. It was a rough few days, but when it settled, it was actually incredibly fun, easy and enjoyable to play. It wasn't a struggle like I thought it would be. I was really fearing this piece, but in the end I felt that Brahms's First Symphony, which we had played the year before, was much harder for me to get through, musically and technically. I had always struggled with it. The orchestra's learning process was made very obvious with the Schönberg because it was a piece that very few of us would have naturally known how to handle. Mr. Barenboim must know that it will take a lot of patience, but it works because he gives us this inexplicable energy and inspiration in the concerts.

His attitude toward the Israeli–Palestinian conflict is also something that is slightly contagious, in a good way, because it has a lot of power behind it. Not just the power of his charisma, who he is, and what he stands for, but the power to help Israelis understand where they are living, and to help the Arabs to accept our existence in Israel as our right, and also as something that is not entirely bad. Mr. Barenboim looks at the conflict from the point of view of someone who knows an incredible amount and has a deep understanding of the facts; he has really thought it through with the most refined intellectual instruments. I don't think many Israelis agree with his political orientation, but I don't think anyone knows exactly what that is. He has not shared his political beliefs with us very often. He does share with us how he sees what is on the ground, how he sees the ignorance and the lack of interest in having contact with the Palestinians. I think a lot of us do agree with this.

The summer of 2007 was more significant than other summers: a lot changed for me then. I found that something settled in me that summer, like the pieces of a puzzle coming together. It was, in a good way, no longer unique to be in the Divan. Being in a room with three Syrians, two Lebanese people, and a Palestinian was nothing major. It was just normal. It was just being in a room with my friends. But this is *so* far from reality. That's sort of what got me into my current state. I don't know how to put this, but I've been going through a very strange time since then. I've been reading everything I can get my hands on about the conflict, and I've been very surprised at the availability (or unavailability) of books about the conflict in general, and in Hebrew in particular. There is a lot of rubbish written, but if you are looking for serious books or articles that are not obvious propaganda or silly conspiracy theories, if you want to know the history, what's going on, who stands where, what is this or that person's viewpoint, there is so little there. I'm sure there are more books than you can read in a lifetime, but what is on the shelves in bookshops in Tel Aviv at the moment is very disturbing. You can find tabloid-type memoirs of this or that politician, but in stores you cannot find books that have to do with the history of the region, the actual conflict, the agreements, and more serious research.

This is even more serious when it comes to literature from Palestine. Whether you want to make peace with these people or just stop fighting, they are still going to be your neighbors. One way or another, you are going to have some dealings with them. On one side, there's the sea, on the other, the Palestinians. You're stuck with them. It would stand to reason that there would be some curiosity about what the Palestinians are like. Not even about what they are thinking, how they think about the conflict, but simply who they are? What literature are they producing? What is their daily life like? And that is something that I had no interest in whatsoever while I was growing up. I only realized recently that every single conception and misconception I have and had about the conflict, I made by myself. I could also say I made them by myself and with what was told to me by people of my own country, who also probably had no dealings with the other side. If you go on the Internet and read the mainstream, normal stuff that is written on the Palestinian side, it's all more or less the same—they don't really know who we are. As I recently discovered, there are Hebrew translations of Palestinian books, mostly from the last five years. But you will not necessarily find a book, for example, by Raja Shehadeh in an Israeli bookstore. If you ask for it, they will order it for you, but they are not kept in stock. Things are available, but you have to know what you're looking for and ask for it. There isn't a Middle Eastern literature section anywhere to browse through. Even when you have the idea in your head to find this literature, you have to know the title of a specific book and its author in order to get it.

I came across a book by Shehadeh by accident one day while I was waiting in my cousin's house. She wasn't there yet. I had nothing to do; I found this book and started reading. I read the first ten pages and then I just couldn't put it down. I finished it in two days and it just amazed me. It was so powerfully honest.

I am ashamed of what I am about to say, and hope that Shehadeh will not be offended if he reads this someday. After reading his book I wrote to Nicole Foster, who worked for the Barenboim–Said Foundation for several years and always helped as an organizer with the Divan in the summer. I told her about this amazing book and wondered if she knew about it and whether it would be possible to bring him to the Divan. She said, "You must be either really stupid or really senile because he came to speak to you twice!" Having been told that now, I can remember the conversation, but I don't remember having taken a particular interest in it at the time, unfortunately. I am sure that today I could make much more out of meeting Raja Shehadeh, having read his books.

If you think about what it's like to stand right in front of a massive pointillist canvas and stare at it from a fifty-centimeter distance, then you can imagine how I experience the conflict when I'm in Israel. I see huge turmoil, lots of different emotions, a lot of resentment and a lot of anger toward my own government and toward our neighbors, and I can't really perceive it logically. The emotions are too strong. When I spend time away from Israel, it's a bit like taking a step back and actually being able to see the picture. I can see a process, I can see people's emotions, I can see people's reactions. I can bear to think about things without being too much in a rage. I can actually bear to think about things that make me too mad to think about when I am in Israel. After graduating from the Tel Aviv Academy and going to my first Divan workshop, I went to London to study, and those four years of study meant not being in contact with the latest news in Israel every single day. It meant not hearing every day that someone blew up in the middle of Tel Aviv, or that a scud missile fell on Ashkelon. It meant that for a few days I actually didn't hear anything about the conflict. But it actually did me a lot of good because then, when I came back into this madhouse, I thought, hang on, it's not every little event, horrible though it may be, that is fundamentally important; it's important to see a process, to see that retaliation is not the point here.

The people in charge on both sides actually think that retaliation is something morally justified and even useful. Being on the outside helped me see that we are asking the wrong questions. The question is not whether this, that or the other settlement has been evacuated: it is, rather, what is the actual process of building settlements in the occupied territories? What does all of this mean for our future, and for my children? When you're in Israel, it's all about keeping your head above water, about not drowning in the endless flow of information: three people getting murdered here, blown up there. It's all around you, this endless sea of people who are out to get you. It's always there.

The way I see these things never used to change my relationships. Recently I have felt that I am starting to pay a price. With my parents I have never had any problems; they are both incredibly open and incredibly tolerant people. They are not well versed in the conflict in any way; neither of them has an extraordinary amount of knowledge of the facts (I don't mean to suggest that I do either). In a way they're not political people, because politics is not the center of their lives. When it comes time to vote, they listen to what people have to say and vote as their conscience tells them, like many other people, but they are not staunch in any way. They have never taken an issue with me thinking this way or the other, and they have never tried to influence me to think this way or the other. Recently, though, they've become a bit worried, I think, because they've heard me say things about the way I think that have made them feel a bit threatened. To their credit, the thought of telling me what to think never entered their minds. They reacted differently. My mother said something like: "I don't know where you're coming from and I want you to explain it to me," and she actually asked me to give her some of the things I was reading. There was one time when she didn't quite lose her temper, but was very surprised. She said, "You speak like you are blaming your country for everything." I said, no, that couldn't be further from the truth, but we are talking about a certain kind of criticism that I have toward my country. I have many other criticisms toward our neighbors. That calmed her down a little, I think. But I do think she's worried.

My father has amazingly good common sense, and he said, "I don't mind you reading that stuff," referring to Avi Shlaim, an Israeli revisionist historian, and writers from Palestine, Lebanon, and Syria. He said, "I think that if you're going to have views, it's admirable that you know where these views come from. I only ask that you also read other stuff, not only these points of view."

Better paternal advice I can't really think of. Nevertheless, it's getting more and more difficult for me, because almost all of my relationships, be it in the family circle or with friends, have not had anything to do with the way that I think about the conflict, and I feel that, in some ways, this has become such a big part of me that that is beginning to change, and I think it will be more and more difficult for me as time goes by. So far I've been rather lucky.

I find that I don't really talk to people in Israel about the conflict. I can't really explain it. It's not that they wouldn't accept the fact that I'm friends with someone from Syria or Palestine, or even that they would think it was bad. I just don't think they would actually understand at all what I mean if I talked about my friendships. You can't really expect anything different, because most of these people that I'm talking about have never actually met anyone from Syria, or ever had a conversation with anyone from Ramallah, or Jordan or Egypt. So I think that if I have any hope for making things any better, it's not a hope for peace or anything as unrealistic as that—but I do hope that my children will have some contact with people from the countries along our borders. I'm not sure that they will find a solution between the Palestinians and the Israelis in the next generation. However, if that generation forms its opinions by actually knowing who is on the other side of the fence, it would at least be a start. It would at least be a more hopeful situation than it is today.

I cannot think of myself as anything but Israeli. At the same time, I can't think of Palestinians and other Arabs as a different people, because they are a part of my family. They are a part of my immediate, closest, most intimate circle of friends. So when I go back home, there is the issue of "them," of everybody else. And I don't have everybody else. I have only us. It sounds ludicrous, but that's the most honest way I can say it. I am crippled by not being able to think of Syrians as enemies or Palestinians as the "other people"; it's something everyone has such a natural gift for in Israel, and I am unable to do it. I know very few Syrians, and most of them are very good friends of mine; and I know even fewer Palestinians, and the few that I do know are some of the closest people that I have on this planet. Something is very obviously wrong for me when I go back to Israel and hear people in my government talking about "them." I think to myself, "Is it really possible that someone has managed to turn sixty, have an illustrious political career, get to a point where he represents me in my own government, and actually never have met a single person from the other side?" It's so absurd that I don't even know how to digest it.

I don't think we are ripe for a political solution yet. We are definitely ripe for military action, all too much so. But I don't think politics will do any good before some basic things change. I'm not talking about lambs sleeping among wolves, just about people needing to realize that there is more to know than they do know. I don't really think that any political solution is possible now: if I don't consider you a human being, how can I make a political agreement with you? And vice versa, of course. If I refer to you as "they," if you are a part of "they," then there is no discussion, no conversation. There would only be two simultaneous monologues. I feel very bad saying this because I know I didn't have this interest even after spending a few years in the Divan; it's something that has been awakened in me very recently.

It's really not very optimistic, if you think about it. The amount of contact I have had with people from "the other side" is probably about 100 times more than the average Israeli has had. I have actually met a person from Ramallah, without being in uniform. People who are born in Israel would not meet a person from an Arab country. They might if they went to Jordan, but they would never meet a Syrian unless it was in a military maneuver, which is not exactly a meeting. The amount of exposure I've had, not just to people in the street, but to the elite of thinking society, is quite a privilege. It took five years of having such extraordinary resources to get someone who basically does think one way about the conflict to think another way about the conflict. It's a big achievement, but if you think about actually changing something in the world, that's very sad. You might say, the workshop lasts only six weeks a year every year. I don't want to sound sentimental, but the summers always live with me throughout the year. The Divan doesn't just live on as a sweet memory, it's something that I really constantly and actively think about during the year. I feel like what I'm doing now, what I've been doing these past months with all this reading and thinking, is taking a look around my house. All these things I sort of knew about, but things are different from what they seem, somehow.

I have had the honor of being a part of the West-Eastern Divan Orchestra for five years and six tours. These people who I am proud to call my friends have become so meaningful to me that I find it difficult to explain in words. Some of the people I have met in this orchestra have become the closest and dearest people in my life. I find that, as a member of this strange and wonderful group, I am allowing myself to think about the conflict from a point of view that many people in Israel, Palestine, Jordan, Syria, Lebanon, Egypt or any of the other Arab countries will find difficult to comprehend. That is because of the simple fact that, although my country is Israel, my "people" includes all these nationalities.

INTERMEZZO

Daniel and Nabeel both come from the same country, have Israeli passports, and were at the Tel Aviv Academy together. Yet, as Daniel was so astonished to discover at the Divan workshop, Nabeel is and thinks of himself as a Palestinian. Nabeel is not one of the more outspoken members of the orchestra; he is not the type to seek confrontation. Nevertheless, his quiet, humble demeanor often reveals more about his philosophy than words ever could. Over the course of several days, we talked at length about music, his life in Israel, and the notion of a national identity. At some point during our conversations, we discovered that we had both attended the same Stephen Hawking lecture at the Aspen Institute in the early '90s. I had been in Aspen for the music festival and had gone to the lecture with an Israeli musician friend and her physicist father. Nabeel had accompanied his family to Aspen because his brother was having piano lessons there, but Nabeel himself was not taking part in the festival. If he had, we probably would have met then, but as it was, we met years later at the Divan workshop. It was a fitting coincidence, an appropriate beginning for a story about music, physics, and one's place in the world.

Nabeel Abboud-Ashkar

Nabeel was born on December 23 in the holy city of Nazareth, and grew up in a family that had been there for generations. During the War of Independence in 1948, the Israeli government made the decision not to take Nazareth by force. Consequently, the citizens of Nazareth neither resisted nor fled. Not knowing what would happen, Nabeel's grandparents left their house and went into hiding. When they returned, there was nothing left; the house had been ravaged. Even things of no commercial value had been taken, like the clothes Nabeel's mother had worn as a baby. Nazareth had become part of the new state of Israel, and Nabeel's grandparents had to learn Hebrew in order to survive in the new country, under the new government.

Nabeel never felt any particular attachment to his hometown, his country, or his "people." One of his friends once joked that if there were a prize for the smallest minority group, Nabeel would win it. In the Arab world outside of Israel he is seen as a Hebrew-speaking Israeli. In Israel he is seen as an Arab. He is a Christian, at least by birth, in a Jewish country. In Nazareth he is a classical musician, something strangely elite, foreign, and seemingly useless.

Nabeel's father Duaibis, an engineer in his first career, had always been deeply committed to the Palestinian community. A man of broad views, wide-ranging interests and considerable talent, he could have accepted numerous offers for work abroad. He rejected them all, however, because he believed in the importance of fostering culture in Palestinian society within Israel. At the time he was a member of the Communist Party, and he often spent his nights in Haifa after work, volunteering his services to repair the recalcitrant printing machines of the Party's newspaper. The Communist Party was the only party in Israel that had both Jewish and Arab supporters and that had also been in favor of the partition of Palestine.

Thanks to his father's great love for classical music, Nabeel grew up surrounded by it in a city where one hears mostly Arabian music, not much Western popular music, and almost no classical music. Duaibis's love of music began as an infant—his mother told him he used to cry when she sang sad songs to him—but was not consummated until he was seventeen years old and studying engineering at the Technion in Haifa. At that time, he discovered classical music by accident and rather prosaically, in a detective movie. The soundtrack included a beautiful piano concerto that drew him in more than the film itself. The next day, he went to a record store to find the music he had heard and was told that it was Tchaikovsky's First Piano Concerto.

Nabeel loved classical music, like the rest of his family, but had never considered a career as a performer. He was to study mathematics and physics and become an engineer like his father. After many years of working as an engineer, however, Nabeel's father retired in order to study history and philosophy at the Open University in Israel. Nabeel's parents then founded Orpheus, a non-profit cultural organization that would bring classical music to Nazareth. Duaibis and his wife began organizing a few concerts for Saleem, Nabeel's older brother, who was beginning to make a career as a concert pianist. They called up all their friends and all their friends' friends, collected mailing lists, and went knocking on people's doors to sell tickets. Soon the organization grew, and since then the Abboud-Ashkars have invited the Haifa Symphony, and even Zubin Mehta and the Israel Philharmonic, who performed to a sold-out basketball stadium in Nazareth.

While Nabeel was still studying physics at Tel Aviv University, one of Saleem's performances was broadcast on television while Edward Said happened to be watching. Said took great interest in the young Palestinian pianist and found sponsorship for him to study abroad. When Said co-founded the West-Eastern Divan Orchestra with Daniel Barenboim in 1999, he suggested that Nabeel audition for it. That was how Nabeel became a member of the orchestra, and that was when certain things in his life began to change.

Nabeel was used to the way things worked in Israel. When he began to study physics in Tel Aviv, he went looking for an apartment, like any other student. He saw one apartment after another, but when it came time to fill out the applications, there always seemed to be a problem. Suddenly the apartment was no longer available. Finally he resorted to sharing an apartment with a Jewish friend. When his flatmate filled out the forms, "forgetting" to mention that he had a roommate named Nabeel Abboud-Ashkar, an apartment finally became available.

Taxi rides could be adventurous, too. Like all Israeli Arabs, Nabeel spoke Hebrew fluently, but it was difficult to place his accent. It was not an Arab accent. One time a Tel Aviv taxi driver began to talk to Nabeel about the Arabs. "We should just drive our tanks right into the West Bank," he said. "We should drive straight into Ramallah and take everything down. I hate the f—ing Arabs, don't you? We should send them to hell!" There was some silence while Nabeel waited for the car to come closer to his destination. "Really?" said Nabeel. Another pause. "I'm an Arab," he said quietly. Suddenly Nabeel saw a bright look of fear in the taxi driver's eyes, visible in the rearview mirror. Nabeel paid and got out.

Another time, a large, muscular taxi driver who drove with one hand on the steering wheel and pumped a spring-loaded hand-strengthening device with the other, began a tirade whose essence was the virtue of throwing the Arabs into the sea. That time Nabeel kept quiet about his identity.

In the Divan things were different. According to Nabeel the physicist, it was a question of equilibrium. A gas in an enclosed space achieves a certain equilibrium. When you take the gas out of the enclosed space or introduce new elements, the gas must adjust until it finds a new equilibrium. If this principle of physics could be applied to people, then it stood to reason that Israelis would find a different equilibrium when they were only among themselves than when they were in a community that included Arabs from many different countries and, at the first workshop, Germans. At first, the Arabs from other countries seemed suspicious of Nabeel: this "Palestinian" was so friendly with the Israelis; he even spoke Hebrew with them all the time. It was noticeable, though, that people didn't speak or behave as they would at home. It was impossible. There was a certain way of thinking and expressing oneself that was only acceptable in homogeneous company. The society of the West-Eastern Divan was too diverse for such tactlessness.

One summer, Nabeel traveled together with a large group of his friends from Israel to the Divan workshop in Spain. They stood in line at the airport, talking and laughing. One by one, they proceeded through the preliminary security procedures before checking in. Passports were shown, and the line moved quickly. Nabeel was last in line, and the security personnel had seen him chatting to his friends all the time. When they saw his passport, they asked him if he knew all these other people. Yes, he said. And were they traveling together? Yes, he said. At that, the entire group was recalled for further questioning. Nabeel had to laugh a little, at least to himself. This was an opportunity for his Jewish Israeli friends to experience a very small part of what it meant to be a Palestinian living in Israel. For one thing, it meant that you had to be at the airport an hour and a half before everyone else.

Playing the violin had never come easily to Nabeel. It was not difficult for him to solve a complex mathematical equation, nor to understand complicated physics problems; but to play a single phrase of, say, a Mozart sonata, simply and beautifully, was a great challenge. After his first year in the Divan, he continued to study mathematics and physics in addition to music at the Tel Aviv Academy. As he went to the workshop year after year, his own equilibrium gradually began to adjust to the musical atmosphere there. Music grew more and more important to him, maybe because it put him on an equal basis with all the other young people from Israel, the Palestinian territories, and the surrounding Arab countries.

There was something in this process of listening, learning, understanding and expressing that became more tangible and more urgent to him than comprehending the physical laws of the universe. In the beginning, it was all rather slow for someone who was used to achieving great results at school and university with very little effort. His teacher and the coach of the first violin section of the Divan, Axel Wilczok, always placed him at the back of the section.

The easiest, most logical thing to do—the path of least resistance—would have been for him to become an engineer, perhaps go abroad to work, and make use of the kind of opportunity his father had always rejected in favor of doing something for his own people. As time went on, though, Nabeel began to think that he was learning something much more important for himself, and ultimately for life, in making music. After several summers of violin sectional rehearsals in the Divan with Mr. Wilczok, Nabeel decided to go to Rostock, Germany, to study with him at the conservatory there and get his second degree in music, not in science. That may have been the path of most resistance.

For Nabeel, there was great beauty in detail. He could read a book and become enraptured by a single sentence. He would read it over and over again, savoring its meaning, its implications, its rhythm, its perfect sense. It could engross him so entirely that he would be unable to read the rest of the book for fear of destroying the impression of this one sentence. When it came to learning a piece of music, he had the same problem. Mr. Wilczok used to tell Nabeel he was like an artist with a huge blank white canvas before him who would spend two weeks painting two square centimeters in one corner.

When Nabeel left Nazareth to study in Tel Aviv and then in Rostock, he was certain he would never return to live in his hometown. Nothing could have appealed to him less. Good riddance, he thought, to the insular mentality, the lack of any real cultural life, and the claustrophobic, closed society. As he continued to study music and attend Divan workshops nearly every summer, though, something began to change. He began to feel something like responsibility to the next generation of Palestinians growing up in Israel. Music began to seem the logical answer to the question of what form his responsibility should take. Music had provided opportunities for Nabeel to go abroad, to play with people from countries (and territories) he was not even allowed to enter, and to come to know himself better. The idea of going back to Nazareth to do something constructive slowly began to take shape.

In 1998, Nabeel had met Ramzi Aburedwan, a violist from Ramallah, at a program called the Apple Hill Chamber Music Center in New Hampshire. At seventeen, Ramzi was just beginning to play the viola, but a few years later he had started his own music school in Ramallah, Al Kamandjati. The Barenboim–Said Foundation, led by Barenboim's conducting assistant Julien Salemkour, began to work with Ramzi and Nabeel to organize workshops for a Palestinian children's orchestra.

In December 2005, Ramzi brought some of his students to Nazareth for an orchestra workshop. Being underage, his students were legally allowed to leave the West Bank; for Ramzi it was a different story. As an adult resident of the occupied territories, it was much more difficult for him to enter Israel.

In April 2006, the workshop was repeated in Ramallah, and Barenboim came personally to conduct the small orchestra. Nabeel traveled to the workshop with children from Nazareth, taking a risk; as an Israeli citizen he was not allowed to enter Palestinian territory. He was becoming more and more convinced of the necessity of opening a full-fledged music school in his hometown. After Barenboim worked with the children from Nazareth, he saw and heard the potential that was waiting to be developed. Orpheus had already begun to develop this potential, creating the infrastructure necessary for a new conservatory to succeed. Orpheus not only organized concerts, it also cooperated with several schools to offer music lessons to children. The organization's philosophy was not simply to teach music, but to attempt to educate society through music. This included having constant contact with their students' parents. Every year they presented a memorial concert on the anniversary of Edward Said's death, and on these occasions they also read some of Said's writings on music. Nabeel discussed the next step to be taken in Nazareth with Barenboim and Mariam Said, and together they planted the seed for another music school.

Later that year, in June, Nabeel sought and found sponsorship to bring a piano trio—three of the most talented children from Nazareth—to the conservatory in Rostock to receive chamber music lessons for several days. The professors were very supportive of the children and of the idea of an educational exchange program.

On the day he arrived with the children in Rostock, he received a phone call at 11PM from Mr. Barenboim's personal assistant, Tabaré Perlas, who informed him that Mr. Barenboim wanted Nabeel to present a proposal for a music school in Nazareth, including a detailed budget, by 8 o'clock the next morning. During the course of the long night that followed, Nabeel wrote the first budget proposal he had ever written in his life. He spoke to his parents on the phone and emailed his brother Saleem the proposal so that he could check it for mistakes or oversights. At 7AM, Nabeel e-mailed the proposal to Mr. Perlas and then went to bed.

Two weeks later, another phone call came from Mr. Perlas, who wanted to put Nabeel through to Mr. Barenboim in Chicago.

Something was wrong with the telephone lines that day, and it took many attempts over several hours to establish a connection. When they finally succeeded, Nabeel heard that he was going to be the director of the new Barenboim–Said Conservatory in Nazareth.

The school year started in September; that meant that Nabeel had two months to move back to Nazareth, hire teachers, and look for students to study there. Of those two months, six weeks were already taken up by the Divan workshop. He had not yet even completed his studies in Rostock; but the decision had been made, and it was for the best. While Nabeel was still on tour with the Divan orchestra, Orpheus contacted the municipality of Nazareth and the administration of an elementary school to secure the use of some of the school's classrooms in the afternoon. This solved the problem of finding a building for the Conservatory. Nabeel moved back to Nazareth immediately after the workshop was over and set about looking for teachers.

Rather than settling for the convenience of having teachers who lived nearby and would always be available, he opted for the more complicated but ultimately more rewarding idea of hiring young musicians from Tel Aviv who had their own performing careers. It meant that the children had to be a bit more flexible; they might have their lesson on Tuesday one week and on Wednesday the following week, according to their teachers' concert schedules. It also meant that they would have very good teachers.

At the beginning of the school year, Nabeel visited all the elementary schools in Nazareth, looking for students. He was going to be teaching beginners, so he created some easy musical games to test their ability to hear different pitches, to reproduce a rhythm by clapping, and so on. Teaching, and teaching beginners in particular, became a subject of passionate research for Nabeel. He read volumes about different pedagogical schools of thought and the process of learning.

With his scientific background, he developed his own theory that the process of learning to practice the violin was analogous to the evolutionary development of the human being. The first two steps in learning were imitation and recall; primates were also capable of these steps. The third step was the ability to use complex acquired knowledge creatively; only human beings were capable of this step.

Nabeel was very much interested in producing creative human beings. Creativity in general, and musical excellence in particular, might help these children to find their way as members of a minority in Israeli society. There was an unspoken preconception that classical music could not be understood or performed by Arabs in general—if at all, then perhaps by Christian Arabs, but not by Muslims. When he put together the roster of his students, however, he was pleased to see that he had discovered equal musical talent in Christian and Muslim families.

After so many years of having no particularly patriotic feelings toward any place at all, Nabeel was beginning to feel something for Nazareth, the city he had never wanted to live in again. He brought as much of Europe and the rest of the world back to Nazareth with him as he could, and was continually looking for ways to develop international connections and initiate exchange programs for the children in his school. He took them to Rostock and Osnabrück, and to the Divan workshops in Pilas and Salzburg.

At the end of 2007, Nabeel invited me to help him lead a ten-day chamber music workshop which began at the YMCA in Tiberias, situated directly at the Sea of Galilee, and continued in Nazareth.

The children were mostly between the ages of seven and fifteen. I had taught some of them already the summer before in Salzburg, when they came to the rehearsal session of the Divan workshop. The workshop in Tiberias was the first time that some of the younger children had been away from home and their parents. It was a mere forty-minute drive from Nazareth, but it was a new dimension of freedom for the youngest ones.

The YMCA's director insisted on sponsoring room and board for the entire group, including all the teachers. While we were there, every available bedroom was occupied from morning to night with children practicing or having lessons. All day for four days, the children's time was completely occupied with music, except for a half an hour or so after lunch, when they would go down to the lake to throw rocks into the water. Sometimes Nabeel would get out his fishing gear after lunch and stand chest-deep in the cold water while the children stood on land, watching. After several days spent amassing a collection of wet T-shirts, he lost his bet against the children that he would be able to fish up some dinner.

When the children were not occupied in a lesson or rehearsal, they would go and listen to the lesson or rehearsal of other children, or they would practice together in groups in their bedrooms, or outside in the gardens overlooking the lake. Nabeel gave each of his beginning students two hours of lessons every day for four days, although they were used to having two lessons a week at home.

Nights in the YMCA were devoid of any dull moments, or any peace and quiet for that matter. The "older" children, the ten- to twelve-year-olds, were especially appreciative of their freedom to stay up making noise most of the night. One evening at 9 o'clock, following a sleepless night and a very long day of rehearsals and lessons, I was coaching three children who were playing a Mozart piano trio. Their eyelids were beginning to droop, so I asked them whether they would like to stop for the day, or just take a break and go on. Feras, the violinist, said, "Let's take a short-short break and go on!" and the others were in agreement. They all got up, and there was some screaming and running and frolicking for a few minutes, after which they sat down again to play with deep seriousness and concentration.

The children behaved like normal kids among themselves, but with their teachers, and with Nabeel in particular, they knew the rules and respected them. They knew they could spend their lunch-break fencing with him using empty plastic cola bottles or zipping each other up in nylon cello cases, but the moment they knew they had crossed the line in any way, they would look up in fearful silence before Nabeel could even open his mouth.

During the workshop, some of the older children would come to my lessons to help translate for the younger children who didn't understand English. Others would go to fetch pencils, stands, or chairs when they were needed. They were pleased with themselves when they mastered something on their instruments, and that feeling was supported by the achievements of the other children around them, who were learning from each other as much as from the teachers. The beginners watched the older and more proficient children, and were motivated to practice.

Daniel Cohen came to visit from his hometown Netanya, about two hours' drive away, to spend an afternoon with the children. Daniel had studied conducting in London after finishing his degree in music in Tel Aviv. He was already spending much of his time conducting his own ensemble, apart from summers with the Divan, where he played the violin. He spent several hours rehearsing a Corelli Concerto Grosso and a movement from Grieg's *Peer Gynt* Suite with the children's ensemble. He was not very good with children, he said; but then, he felt a special warmth toward these particular children. He could rehearse with them the same way he could rehearse with adults. Daniel was in awe of what Nabeel was doing with his conservatory and his students.

As I left Nazareth, Nabeel was about to move into the new house he was preparing for himself and his fiancée. His new house was, in fact, the old house his grandmother had built sixty years ago, upon which his parents' apartment was built. It was a common thing to build an extra floor on top of an existing structure in Nazareth; there was not much room to spread out sideways.

The renovation of the old house seemed a fitting analogy for the life-path Nabeel had chosen for himself. During the excavation work, he had found many beautiful things: an unexpected and perfectly preserved stone wall beneath a layer of crumbling plaster, an enormous antique wooden radio. He also discovered a few unpleasant truths: one of the many walls whose corners did not quite meet at right angles proved to be made entirely of mud and gravel. You could reach in and scoop away part of the wall that was supposed to be supporting the structure above it.

There was much about Nazareth that Nabeel knew he would find irritating or frustrating. He had never expected to make his home there, but now that he was doing so, he set about righting obtuse angles, pouring concrete to replace the mud walls, installing German shower fixtures and German windows that sealed properly. Having lived in Germany for several years, he had become accustomed to the quality of materials and appliances there, just as he had come to appreciate the tradition and importance of music in German culture.

One of the things that made him happiest about founding the conservatory was that it gave him the opportunity to surround himself with some of the people he had met in the Divan workshop and through his studies who had become very important to him: Daniel Cohen, Ramzi Aburedwan, and his teacher, Axel Wilczok.

It was not easy to come back to the place he had once been eager to leave, nor was it always easy to master all the aspects of being responsible for the education of so many young children, whose needs were naturally not limited to musical education. His tasks sometimes resembled social work more than musical training—but then, that was part of the project: a project that began with twenty-five children and has since grown to seventy-five.

For Nabeel, the miracle of the world that Daniel Barenboim and Edward Said created—the world of the Divan—lay in the opportunity for individuals to meet outside of their environments to find their new equilibrium, perhaps even a new identity that went beyond their national identities. If Nabeel could give his own students even a faint echo of these possibilities through exchange programs and contact with the musical world of Europe, it was time well spent.

Nabeel dreams of eventually going back to university to get his doctorate in education in order to continue to elevate the position of Palestinians in Israeli society. In the meantime, step by step, he is bringing to Nazareth everything that he has found most valuable in the West-Eastern Divan Orchestra, in Germany, and in his knowledge of human nature. Slowly but methodically, he is building a new foundation for his city's cultural life.

INTERMEZZO

The musical mentors from the Staatskapelle Berlin, invisible to audiences who hear only the result of their work, spend two weeks of their summer vacation every year preparing and teaching the young musicians of the Divan. Many of the orchestra members have developed lasting personal and professional relationships with their summer teachers, and the creation of the Barenboim–Said Foundation in 2003 made it much easier, by awarding scholarships, for many musicians to study with their teachers during the year. The story of the Divan would not be complete without the story of its musical "parents."

Axel Wilczok, concertmaster, and Matthias Glander, principal clarinetist, were my colleagues in the Staatskapelle Berlin before I joined the Divan. In 2006, when I began to teach at the Academia de Estudios Orquestales in Seville, I got to know them as teachers as well. They are adored and revered by their students, both as teachers and as human beings. Axel and Matthias are both outstanding members of the Staatskapelle, and I often had the pleasure of playing next to Axel during symphony concerts (Barenboim's preferred seating arrangement for the strings has both violin sections on either side of the conductor's podium, with the violas next to the second violins and the celli next to the first violins). Axel's musical spirit was always an inspiration to me during my years in the orchestra.

Both Matthias and Axel radiate a sense of fulfillment and pride when they speak about their work with the Divan. Being a member of an excellent professional orchestra is by no means a guarantee of fulfillment for a musician. It is very easy to descend into a routine of soulless, mechanical rehearsal and performance, in the process losing the passion, energy and idealism required to achieve such a position in the first place. The discipline required to put the music above all else day after day and year after year is akin to the strength of religious belief, and probably equally powerful. Music lovers who have never been on the inside of a professional orchestra might imagine it as a utopian institution whose members are united by their dedication to music. In fact, it can be just like any other workplace; orchestra musicians are not immune to intrigues, conspiracies, and petty rivalries.

Perhaps for these reasons, I was never able to force myself to stay in any one orchestra for more than three years; my own lack of constancy fills me with even more respect for the discipline and spirit exemplified by Axel, Matthias, and many others in the Staatskapelle. I received the distinct impression from both of them that a substantial part of their sense of musical fulfillment came from their years with the Divan, years of witnessing and contributing to the transformation of an unpredictable social experiment into a wonderful orchestra.

Backstage

The first orchestra concert of the summer is the end of a long story that begins in April every year. Since 2003, Matthias Glander, Axel Wilczok, and Tabaré Perlas have been traveling to the Middle East and Spain once a year in April to choose the musicians who will participate in the summer workshop.

Until 2003, there was no standard audition procedure. They accepted recordings for a time, but soon they realized that a recording could not possibly demonstrate all the aspects of musical talent they were looking for: above all, an individual's potential to develop and learn.

Axel and Matthias had been coaching the young musicians of the orchestra since the first workshop in 1999, when no one knew what to expect. No one knew what level of musical proficiency would be awaiting them; no one knew how and if such a society would function. The only thing they knew beforehand was how many musicians there would be in the orchestra.

In the spring of 1999, Daniel Barenboim asked Axel if he would be interested in coaching the violin section of a youth orchestra made up of Israeli and Palestinian musicians, among others. "Yes, why, not?" he said. Matthias also agreed to coach the entire woodwind section; it was not a very large orchestra, and one teacher would be sufficient for the flutes, oboes, clarinets, and bassoons. Axel had never worked with a youth orchestra before, and knew of the Israeli–Palestinian conflict only from the television. As far as he was concerned, any collaboration with Maestro Barenboim would, by its nature, be artistically enriching.

Axel and Matthias were both members of the Staatskapelle before the fall of the Berlin Wall and the former German Democratic Republic in 1989. Israel was not a common topic of discussion at home, at school, or in the news in East Germany, as it was in West Germany. There were no diplomatic relations between former East Germany and Israel; there was, however, East German support for the Palestinians and Yasser Arafat.

The first time Axel found himself confronted with the topic of anti-Semitism was at a boarding school in Moscow where he was studying music in 1972. There was a great uproar one day in the dormitory; people were running through the halls shouting, and the students were told to come to the boys' toilets. A message had been pasted together from letters cut out of the newspaper onto the door of one of the lavatories. Axel got out his dictionary and translated: "No space for Jews here." He was astonished and confused; a friend had to explain to him what it was all about. Until that point the entire subject of anti-Semitism had been taboo; it had not existed in his world.

In 1999, all that changed for good. The Middle East was no longer a disheartening report on the television lasting only a few minutes a day; it became a personal and immensely important part of his life, thanks to the West-Eastern Divan Orchestra.

From the beginning, it was clear that this was not going to be a casual "summer music camp" for young people to meet and mingle in a relaxed atmosphere. It was going to be about making music. The young musicians would be encouraged to have fun only through the seriousness, precision, intensity, and commitment of music-making according to Barenboim. Axel, Matthias, and the other coaches from the Staatskapelle were there to contribute to the process of creating a musically homogeneous orchestra out of eighty-odd musicians from mutually hostile countries and territories.

The technical proficiency of the musicians varied greatly; some had been very well trained, others were just beginning or had not had good teachers at all. The workshop began with sectional rehearsals: each string section (first violins, second violins, violas, celli, basses), and the wind and brass sections rehearsed their parts for Beethoven's Seventh Symphony separately with their teachers, like any ordinary youth orchestra. Soon, though, things began to happen which did not generally happen in an ordinary youth orchestra.

There was the young man in the first violins, for example, who had been stationed at the Lebanese border as a soldier in the army until the workshop started. Because the objective of the workshop was to bring musicians from different sides into direct contact with each other, he was sharing a music stand with a girl from Lebanon. After a few days he seemed terribly sad and depressed and began to cry. Axel asked him what was wrong.

"One month ago," he said, "who knows? I was standing at the border and, who knows, if something had gone wrong, if this girl had been there and made a wrong move, I might have shot at her. And now I'm sitting here next to her and we are playing Beethoven with Barenboim; I just don't understand . . ."

He had completely lost his bearings; the thoughtless logic of violence which had made sense only a month before had been shattered.

As taxing as it was to be personally faced with the "enemy" though, there was no lenience for the musicians when it came to musical challenges. On the contrary, Barenboim and his team of teachers demanded as much of them as of a professional orchestra. Axel still remembers the first time Barenboim rehearsed Beethoven's *Leonore* Overture no. 3 with the orchestra. There is a notoriously difficult passage in the first violin part near the end of the piece; Axel had heard wonderful professional orchestras play it badly before.

Barenboim rehearsed the eight-bar section endlessly with the first violins while the rest of the orchestra sat waiting. He took three notes at a time, then another three, and another; he explained the structure patiently in its every detail; he dissected it until each and every violinist from the first to the last stand understood the architecture of the passage. He explained to them what to do physically to realize the right articulation and phrasing: in which part of the bow and with how much bow to play, and how each musician fit into the whole to make it work. The violinists were sitting on the edges of their chairs, concentrating to the utmost; even those who were not playing (including Axel) felt their patience wearing thin. It was a test of everyone's nerves.

After one and a half hours of this kind of work, they played the whole passage through: it was phenomenal. Axel had never heard it played so well in all his life. During the badly needed break that followed, Axel walked to the teachers' lounge with the Maestro, who fell into an armchair, lit a fat cylinder of a cigar, and said, "So, Professor Wilczok?"

"It was sensational," he said.

"Look, Mr. Wilczok, in case you ever think of committing suicide . . ."

"Suicide? Excuse me?"

"Well, just in case you do, you never know—please let me know beforehand, because then I would arrange for you to be able to lead a rehearsal like the one I just led, but with the first violin section of the Staatskapelle Berlin, including all the concertmasters. After ten minutes at the very most, I promise you, one of them would kill you."

With his black humor, the Maestro was making a good point: to do this kind of work and to accomplish these results, musical talent and technical skill were not enough: the musicians also had to be humble before the music. One could hope that humility, regardless of the context, might become the first step toward acceptance of the other's, the "enemy's" point of view. The idea of making music at the highest level possible was in fact at one with the humanitarian ideals of the project. Commitment, humility, self-control, acceptance, and generosity were all virtues that had to be learned in order to make music with the passionate attitude that Barenboim demanded.

In order to make music at such a high level, some very basic work needed to be done. Matthias was in charge of the whole woodwind section, so the two Egyptian beauties playing the flute the first year were also under his supervision. It took Matthias some time to realize that they were neither stubborn nor untalented; they had simply not been taught properly. Although they knew when they were playing too sharp or too flat, no one had ever explained to them how to control their intonation on the instrument. Matthias demonstrated the principle of intonation control on the mouth of a half-empty cola bottle; what he wanted to explain could not be demonstrated on a clarinet, and Matthias had never played the flute. He tipped the bottle toward his chin and blew into it: "When you turn the flute toward you the pitch goes down." Then he turned it away from him and blew into it again: "And when you turn it away from you the pitch goes up."

Matthias could not help grinning while the two beautiful girls—"daughters of Cleopatra," as he called them—dutifully wrote his instructions into their music in Arabic. After that, they made progress much more easily.

Of course, no one expected that social and musical interaction between the young people in the workshop would be without its hazards; no one imagined that Israeli, Palestinian, Syrian, Lebanese, Egyptian, and Jordanian musicians would sit around being picturesquely harmonious and peaceful.

On the first day of the first workshop, no hierarchy had yet been established. In the string sections ranking was not terribly important, because everyone played the same part, but in the wind section there were solo parts to be meted out. Matthias noticed immediately that the Israelis, more than the Arabs, were coming to him to ask if they could play the first part. One particular

Israeli wind player repeatedly demanded to play the first part, and let Matthias know that his father had a very important position in the Israeli music world, and that this fact should be taken into consideration. Needless to say, Matthias did not let himself be bullied, but he did find a diplomatic solution: he allowed the musicians to rotate, sometimes playing first and sometimes playing second. This would become impossible in later years, when the prestigious concert venues and difficult programs demanded world-class soloists on all the first parts.

In the early years of the workshop, Axel had coached a group that was playing Mendelssohn's Octet. One of the violists was an Israeli boy—a brusque, macho type—and the fourth violinist was a certain Nabeel Abboud-Ashkar. At some point in the piece, Nabeel had to turn the page; he then had exactly three quarter-note rests before he had to play again. Axel watched while Nabeel turned the page, smoothed his hair, settled the violin into place, sought his inner calm, and began to play, by which time the passage in question was long over. Instead of fitting into the counterpoint, his entrance caused a train wreck.

The Israeli violist became very impatient, and began to criticize Nabeel rather aggressively. They tried the same passage again with the same cacophonous result. This time the violist's criticism was more personal. At that point Axel stepped in and gave him a piece of his mind. "I would appreciate it if you would behave like a normal human being," he said to the violist, "and I want you to help him. It doesn't do anyone any good if you yell at him and push him down. You're playing together; if you want this section of the piece to work, take it apart, help him, go and practice with him, support him. But don't harass him!"

After that there was a truce, at least for a time. Axel could only hope the boy would learn that each part is mutually dependent upon all the other parts in chamber music, and that the violist might someday apply the same lesson to a situation outside of rehearsal, in a non-musical context.

All of this took place before Nabeel began to study with Axel in Rostock. Nabeel would come to the orchestra and sit at the back of the section, and Axel would do his best to pound the notes into his highly intelligent but musically undisciplined head. That was, after all, Axel's job in the orchestra. In the Divan, he would start by rehearsing with the whole first violin section and then work with smaller groups of two stands each, working through the whole group this way to develop a more direct connection with each player. Then, if necessary, he would take individual students at the end of a ten- or eleven-hour day and help them with their orchestra parts. Nabeel was one such student.

After some time in the orchestra, and after Nabeel had already finished his degree in physics, his brother approached Axel to talk about Nabeel's future in music. Having grown up in East Germany and studied in Moscow, Axel's best second language was Russian, not English. He had always struggled with English; in rehearsals with the kids, he got by with musical terms, demonstrations, and body language. Nabeel's question was too complicated for sign language, so he brought his brother Saleem, who spoke to Axel in German.

Saleem began, "Could you imagine, perhaps, that Nabeel might study with you?"

Axel reflected. "I can imagine many things; I have a good imagination. But what is he thinking? What's his intention? What does he hope to accomplish by studying with me? He has a good profession, he's a very intelligent boy. He can play the violin for the rest of his life for fun."

Nabeel explained through Saleem that he wanted to know what it would be like to really study the violin, to practice every day for two or three years. Saleem had told Axel earlier about Nabeel's musical history: when Nabeel was younger, he would have his violin lesson on Monday afternoon, and from the end of the lesson until the following Monday, the violin would remain in the case. But now Nabeel said he was ready to work, and he only wanted to know whether it would still make sense to try at his age, having already finished one degree.

Axel relented. "All right," he said. "There's nothing wrong with you as far as I can see—both ears are in the right place. If you practice hard, someday it has to work!"

Axel consented to help Nabeel prepare for his entrance examination at the conservatory in Rostock where he taught. They chose the program together, they worked on the repertoire together, and Nabeel was accepted. When the semester began, Axel said to him, "Come to me every day for a lesson. That way, at least you'll have taken your violin out of the case once a day." The idea was that he would make the most of his studies in Rostock and then go back to Nazareth to start something of his own. "Well," thought Axel, "wait and see."

Slowly, Axel began to be convinced of Nabeel's willpower. He watched while an astonishing transformation took place. Nabeel was the only one of Axel's Divan students to rent an apartment in Rostock and not in the nearby, far more diverting capital city of Berlin, where most of his classmates lived. He learned German. He went to all of his courses at the conservatory. Nabeel explored the surrounding area and told his teacher about places Axel had never known about himself, although he had been teaching there for years. Nabeel even found sponsors in *Rostock* (of all places!), to bring children there from Nazareth for music lessons. Rostock was certainly not the first place one would think of when looking for sponsors.

This was it, thought Axel; this was the whole idea of the Divan.

Recently, on the latest audition tour, Axel went to visit his former student in Nazareth and met his "grandstudents," Nabeel's own students. It was not the first time he had met some of them. In the summer of 2006, at the end of the rehearsal period of the workshop, the Palestinian children from Nazareth and Ramallah had played a short concert in Seville for the members of the Divan. Feras, the then ten-year-old concertmaster of the small ensemble, came out on stage and handed his violin to Nabeel, who sat behind him, to tune it. Feras then sat down and played, leading like a real concertmaster. Two years later, at the age of twelve, he was invited by Barenboim to play in the "big" orchestra. The programs for the summer tour were daunting for even the more experienced members of the orchestra: Brahms's Fourth Symphony, Schönberg's Variations for Orchestra Op. 31, and the first act of Wagner's *Die Walküre*. Feras was perfectly prepared and intensely interested in learning all the new pieces. After only nine years of the workshop, the next generation of Divan violinists had emerged.

The ritual of the annual audition tour began in 2003, when Barenboim decided to send two of his most trusted "disciples" on a Middle Eastern journey for which they would need an extra passport: one for going to Israel and one for Syria and Lebanon. An Israeli stamp in their passports was not an obstacle when traveling to Jordan and Egypt, but it would prevent them from entering Syria and Lebanon.

The beginning of the audition tour was the real beginning of the Divan each year—the first stage in a journey that culminated in the first note of the first concert. It was a journey fraught with responsibility, adventure, and sometimes temporary discomfort.

Their responsibility was to find musicians who would become integral members of an already existing, by now quite virtuosic ensemble: musicians who would individually rise to the demands of the "boss" while blending into the unique and unified collective sound of the orchestra. It was a sound, in fact, that had taken on many aspects of the "Staatskapelle sound": the ideals of *legato*, sustaining the sound, clarity of articulation, and certain expressive fingerings in the string section. Matthias and Axel went forth every year in search of musicians who would contribute something of their own while fitting into this mould.

Adventure was unavoidable on nearly every trip. The first time, in 2003, when they didn't know any better, they took a taxi in

Cairo. Egypt was a long way from Germany: land of regulations, automobile inspections and certified taxi drivers. They found themselves sitting on the backseat of a vehicle that looked to be the construction of an amateur welder. Shortly after the wild ride began, a pedestrian leaped over the hood of the car in order to avoid being run over. Axel and Matthias started, gripping the battered upholstery.

"No problem," said the taxi driver. "We have 20 million more of them."

Axel took a deep breath, and thought: "Okay, relax. Maybe this is the way things are supposed to be."

The ride continued. Like a zombie, the driver went the wrong way down a one-way street. Other cars were coming toward them, honking and braking suddenly, but the driver was immune to their exclamations. It was faster this way, he explained. Otherwise they would have to take a much longer route.

Sometimes adventure went hand-in-hand with temporary discomfort. Tabaré Perlas always planned the trip meticulously from beginning to end, including flights, hotels and visas; but there were always things he couldn't plan for. He would not have planned to spend four and a half hours at the Syrian–Lebanese border, for example.

Axel, Matthias, and Tabaré were on their way from auditions in Damascus to auditions in Beirut. Tabaré had inquired in all the appropriate embassies in Berlin about visas. They had secured visas for Syria in Germany, and were told that they would have to buy a Lebanese visa at the border. They approached the border police; first Matthias and then Axel bought their visas. It was all going smoothly. Then Tabaré presented his Uruguayan passport—the only one he had.

"Sorry," the official told him, "you can't get a visa here. You'll have to go back to Syria."

Going back to Syria was out of the question. The audition tour had to go on. They began to argue.

"Where do you live?" asked the official.

"In Berlin," said Tabaré.

"Then you'll have to get a visa from the embassy in Berlin."

"But they told me there that I would have to get the visa here."

And so it went, back and forth, with Axel and Matthias refusing to enter Lebanon without Tabaré, and Tabaré refusing to return to Syria. After further argument, during which Matthias told the border police about their friend in Beirut who was waiting for them, the police said, "Okay. If you know people in Beirut, tell them to fax a letter of recommendation to the number above the door outside." Axel and Matthias stepped outside, looked up at the sign and saw Arabic numbers, those graceful arabesque cousins of Hindu-Arabic numerals that seemed deceptively familiar but were not what you thought they were.

Matthias called his friend, a German woman married to the Lebanese director of the government hospital in Beirut, and did his best to decipher the numbers. Axel paced back and forth, smoking. Luckily he still smoked and had brought enough cigarettes with him. The toilets were locked; that left only the forest. They could hear the muezzin calling, from which country they didn't know. For the time being, they were in a no-man's-land in between countries, with no passports—they had been confiscated—and no one to translate. Mariam Said, who would be joining them in Beirut, would have been a help at that moment.

Finally, four and a half hours later, when it was dark and Axel had smoked his last cigarette, the fax miraculously arrived, Tabaré was allowed to purchase a visa, and at midnight they were in Beirut, trying to forget everything.

Egypt was one of the few Arab countries to come to an official peace agreement with Israel, but the Egyptians had become more reluctant to cooperate with the Divan over the years. One year it suddenly became impossible to hold auditions for the Divan in the Cairo conservatory where they had always been held. When Tabaré contacted the director of the conservatory, she said she would have to see, there were difficulties, it was unpredictable. Eventually they sought another location and other advertising methods. Mariam Said called up an old friend of her late husband who had a large apartment in Cairo with a grand piano, and asked him if he would be willing to hold the auditions in his home. He consented, and Tabaré and his team announced the Divan auditions in Cairo by e-mail, SMS, and word of mouth.

Matthias's first direct experience of Damascus contradicted all his expectations. He had heard so much talk of the "axis of evil" to which Syria supposedly belonged. The first time they arrived at the airport in Damascus, the very courteous former director of the conservatory was there in an elegant pinstriped suit waiting for them. He drove them personally into Damascus, a clean, pleasant, very well-organized city. Matthias was particularly impressed by the opera house with its three halls for chamber music, theater, and opera, and the adjoining conservatory. During their stay, the conservatory director took care of their every need and always picked them up personally.

Over the years, the audition process had become an efficient machine run by the "infernal trio," as Matthias called himself, Axel, and Tabaré. Matthias and Axel sat at the table on either side of Tabaré, who typed vigorously on his laptop while Axel made his notes and immediately covered them with another piece of paper so that Tabaré and Matthias would not be able to see what he had written. At the end of the day, they compared notes and often discovered that they had come to the same conclusions. It was often difficult to remember one person among the hundreds who auditioned over the course of their tour, so they took pictures of the applicants to add to their notes.

One good-looking young man came to the auditions in Damascus: a real character with his hair slicked back, his collar turned up, and polished white shoes. He ceremoniously lifted the violin into position, a somewhat wrong and crooked position. When he began to play, Axel thought, "This guy has something."

It was all wrong in a way, but there was something impressive about him.

His posture was all macho confidence, but after his audition, when Axel asked him carefully if he might tell him a few things, the violinist was extremely polite and receptive. Axel worked with him, showed him what he might do differently, and the young man was quite grateful. He took everything in that was said to him, and Axel and Matthias decided to take him into the Divan, where he proved himself a worthwhile experiment.

Then there was the chubby boy with the fat fingers in Amman, who had obviously not reached a sufficient technical mastery of the violin to be able to play Tchaikovsky's Violin Concerto, but was doing it anyway, and making a rather convincing case for it. Axel took him aside, too, and gave him a little lesson. The boy reacted and adjusted immediately, and Axel saw how intelligent he was. He and Matthias decided they had another member of the Divan.

Axel knew that the young boy was not really quite ready to play Tchaikovsky's Fifth Symphony, which was on the program that year, but he also sensed that he was intelligent and eager enough to get through it without causing any disruptions. Axel worked with the boy individually that summer, showing him how to get from the beginning to the end of a difficult run without getting stuck in the middle. The important thing was to have the right finger in the right place on the string at the beginning of the run, and the right finger in the right place on the string at the end of the run, and to start and end with everybody else. "The rest," said Axel, "will be between you and almighty God and Maestro Barenboim, who sees everything too."

He placed him in the second stand, close to the Maestro, and told him he wanted him to memorize the violin part of the entire symphony. "Every time I look at you," Axel told the boy, "I want your eyes to be glued to the Maestro."

And they were. The boy learned the piece well enough to look up at the conductor all the time, and the next year, it was easier for him. He grew taller and slimmer, his fingers were a little less fat and a little more agile, and he now knew how to play in an orchestra.

That was the point of the audition tours, the sectional rehearsals, and the lessons: to find talented young musicians and teach them how to play in an orchestra.

Barenboim tells the story of how he fell in love with the Staatskapelle Berlin: when he first heard them play in the late 1980s, before the collapse of Communism, he recognized the sound he had grown up with in Israel, the rich sound of the Israel Philharmonic of the 1950s, which was the sound of the old German school of playing. The East German Opera Orchestra had been insulated from the outside world for decades and had maintained the old German orchestral traditions: the dark string sound, the smooth connections from one note to the next, the mellow sound of the German clarinet and trumpet. All these qualities gave the orchestra a distinct identity, distinguishing it from the sound of orchestras in America, France, or any other country.

Axel remembers the first Barenboim LP he ever bought, a recording of the *Moonlight* Sonata. He was studying in Moscow at the time and had heard that there were new records from EMI, and everyone had hurried over to the store to buy them before they were gone. The record is still in his house in Berlin; it has been played so often there are hardly any grooves left on it.

After the Berlin Wall fell, there were rumors that Barenboim was going to become the next music director of the Staatsoper. When he came to conduct a rehearsal one day, Axel was certain the Maestro would change his mind. "We played badly," he thought, "We were lousy. He'll come to his senses." Matthias the optimist saw things differently. In his opinion there was a lot of work to be done, but he thought it could be done with the Staatskapelle.

As always, the Maestro knew what he wanted, and he wanted to be the music director of the Staatsoper: an enormous, unexpected blessing for many in the orchestra, including Axel. Everything

Axel had learned in Moscow about sound, about *legato* playing, articulation, and phrasing, was being reinstated and honed in the Staatskapelle, thanks to this Israeli musician from Argentina.

Now, after nearly twenty years of playing under Barenboim with the Staatskapelle, Matthias, Axel, and their colleagues from the orchestra who have spent many summers teaching the young musicians of the West-Eastern Divan Orchestra have seen the story of this sound come full circle. The sound that had stayed in Barenboim's ears from his childhood in Israel, the sound whose potential he recognized and cultivated in the Staatskapelle, is now on its way back to the Middle East. Against all odds, and with the help of musicians who themselves lived through the collapse of a wall that divided a country, this historical sound is being reincarnated by the Israelis, the Palestinians, and all their neighbors.

INTERMEZZO

I was extremely pleased to discover an utter lack of hierarchy in the West-Eastern Divan Orchestra. In any professional orchestra, there is an unquestioned hierarchy. It would be taboo for someone at the back of the second violins to say anything directly to the conductor during a rehearsal, no matter how important or banal. In the Divan, of course, there were musicians playing solo parts and others playing less prominent parts, but this was a musical hierarchy, not a social one. The expression of curiosity was not a privilege restricted to the front desks of the string sections or the solo parts of the wind, brass, and percussion sections.

The first person I ever saw stand up and confront Maestro Barenboim about an issue that bothered her was the Israeli violinist Sharon Cohen. After that, I saw many others stand up during a discussion to contradict or argue with the Maestro, and each time this happened, my respect for the orchestra grew. I admired the fact that they expected Barenboim to listen to their concerns just as they listened to his musical advice. In discussion they made no secret of their opinions when they differed from his, and in rehearsal they did not hesitate to ask whether they could repeat a musical passage they hadn't understood, no matter where they sat. In professional orchestras, many musicians assumed that a strict code of behavior went hand-in-hand with a homogeneous orchestral sound. In the Divan, there was no such confusion between musical and social homogeneity.

In 2006, after the rehearsal of *Tristan und Isolde* with Waltraud Meier in Pilas, there was a discussion about the proposed anti-war declaration. Sharon then stood up at the back of the second violin section and explained to Barenboim what she felt was wrong with the declaration. I have never forgotten the impression this left.

It is one thing to have a discussion with a person of authority when you are sitting together at a table, in a circle, or even in a large group. It is an entirely different thing, however, to speak from the back of the second violin section, a position of low visibility and still less influence, and confront a great conductor who is standing on a podium above the orchestra, calling the shots. There was neither chutzpah nor timidity in her posture or attitude. What struck me about their exchange of words was that they spoke to each other without taking their status into consideration. Barenboim had the last word, of course; but Sharon characteristically made the most out of the penultimate one.

Sharon Cohen

Last year, Sharon was living near the New England Conservatory in Boston, where she was studying. Between her apartment and the school there was a little supermarket called Symphony Market. She knew the owners of the store were Arabs because she had heard them speaking Arabic before. One day she went there to buy something and found a white container in the refrigerated section that was labeled only in Arabic. She took it to one of the people from the store and asked what it was.

"It's *labbeneh*," he said. *Labbeneh* was a kind of Middle Eastern yogurt cheese.

She said, "Wow, where is this from?"

He looked over at the store owner and said, "It's from his country."

Sharon went over to the owner and said, "Thank you for having this; it's making me feel very much at home. Where are you from?"

"I'm from Palestine," he said.

"Oh!" she said, excited. "I'm from Israel!"

He looked at her.

"Palestine," he said.

An awkward silence followed and she found a way to leave without saying anything else. The next day she walked in for something—she couldn't remember why she went in the next day—and the store owner was there again.

He saw her and said, "Are you the girl from Israel?"

"Yes," she said.

He took out a piece of chocolate from behind the counter and gave it to her: an apology, she thought. They became friends after that and started to talk about his family and his life in Boston, and she also became friendly with some of the other people who worked there. There was one guy in particular who always worked the night shift, and they saw each other every few days when she went in on her way home from school. The first time she noticed him was when he greeted her in Hebrew.

"*Ma nishma*? [How are you?]" he said.

"*Beseder* [Fine]," she said. Then she asked him in English, "Where are you from?"

"Jordan," he said.

"How did you know I spoke Hebrew? Did you hear me speaking to my friends?" He had. They went on talking. He was a student, just like her, and he had left his country to study just like she had. He was working in the store to make some money and finance his education. She told him about her orchestra and her friends from Palestine and Jordan and Egypt and Syria, and after a while he said, "Um, I'm actually from Bethlehem."

"How interesting," she thought. "He was afraid to tell me where he was from."

They saw each other often because of his hours in the store and her nocturnal schedule. She invited him to her school orchestra concerts because they were right across the street at the conservatory. One time she decided to invite him to her solo recital, which was a kind of final exam before getting her degree. He said he would come; they exchanged e-mail addresses so that she could send him the details.

One day, after she had already invited him, she suddenly realized that, if she were in Israel, she would never have invited a Palestinian to her recital to sit in a room full of Israelis. She thought to herself, "All the Israelis I know in Boston are going to be in that room, and I'm bringing a Palestinian guy that I met in a supermarket."

They had been e-mailing back and forth, and he had written to her last, but she didn't answer him for a few days. Finally, she wrote back:

> Look, I'm sorry. I got scared suddenly. I don't know you and it's not an easy thing for me to invite a Palestinian person to my recital when all my Israeli friends will be there. I want to trust you but I feel it's difficult for me. The situation is difficult.

He wrote back that maybe they should talk about it beforehand. They did. They talked a lot. He was very curious: he had never been to a concert or heard classical music before. He wanted to know what he should wear and how much the tickets cost. That made her laugh.

"This is my school concert," she said. "And, well, you should wear whatever you want, and it's a free concert."

After they had talked, they both felt more secure about it, and he came with all his Palestinian friends who had also never heard classical music before. He loved it, and he wanted to come to the next concert too. They stayed in touch over the summer while she was with the Divan, and they are still friends now, just two people leading their lives in a foreign country.

This episode may have been very tiny, but it was very big for Sharon. She would never have started talking to, let alone become friends with, a Palestinian before the Divan. Her experiences and friendships in the orchestra had taught her to trust; she knew now that Palestinians were just people, whereas before she had been afraid.

Sharon knew all about the Divan before she was accepted to play in the orchestra because she had heard about it in detail from friends who had been going since 1999. She auditioned three years in a row before being accepted and added to the reserve list in 2003. That year they had some cancellations and started calling people from the reserve list, including her. When she finally got there, she recognized all the people from her friends' pictures. It didn't seem strange, for some reason, to be sitting and playing music with people from all these different countries that she only knew about through their wars. Her friends had told her all their stories about the orchestra, and when she went, she didn't think of the novelty of playing together with Arabs. She only thought about playing in an orchestra where all her friends played.

Going to the Divan that particular year was also an opportunity for her to finish her army duty a month and a half early. She was twenty years old and nearly at the end of her one-year-and-nine-month compulsory service. She was an army musician, which meant that she had certain privileges. She never had to stay at the base too many nights in a row, and was allowed to leave for special musical activities like festivals or master classes or the Divan workshop. The workshop started just before the end of her service, so she was allowed to leave the army early.

Both her parents had served in the Israeli army. Her mother had been an air traffic controller in Sinai for two years, and her father had been seriously injured in the Yom Kippur War when his tank was bombed. He looked fine, and you couldn't tell that he was injured, but he had been severely burned.

Sharon had had a lot of friends who didn't go into the army (a lot of musicians didn't) but it was important to her to go. The army was so much a part of her country's culture. Only a few years ago did they make it illegal for an employer to ask job applicants whether they had served their army duty. There had been too much discrimination; it was almost as if you weren't a real citizen unless you had done your army duty. Teenagers listened to the army radio station; it was the most popular station among the kids. Military language even made its way into everyday speech. It was sometimes difficult to notice, because the army was such a big part of normal life that you couldn't really separate it from civilian language. In the army you might say something like, "Twenty seconds, you've delivered the mail to so-and-so and you're back," and they sometimes spoke like that outside of the army too. It was like belonging to a club and sharing a fraternity language. She felt that she would be able to understand her culture better by going into the army.

Even though she was a musician in the army, she had had to do basic training like everybody else, and learn how to fire a gun and clean it. It was so simple: all you had to do to be a soldier was wear a uniform and have a certificate saying that you could fire a gun. She never needed to fire a gun, but she felt that the ability to use a gun changed her somehow, even if she would never, never, never do it. While she was learning to do it, it hadn't seemed strange; it was like learning a group sport with a bunch of friends, just like at school. Later, living in the States, she would hear people talk about guns and the right to bear arms and think: "I can actually do that: how strange."

Looking back, she realizes that she was pretty ignorant about a lot of things while she was in the army. She hadn't thought about what the army looked like to people outside of Israel.

The first thing she talked about in the Divan was being in the army, and it was the first time she felt uncomfortable about it. She had always been really proud of it, and suddenly she was really not proud of it. It made her feel uncomfortable with her friends in the orchestra, because the army was hurting those friends. There had been that one discussion in particular in 2004, when the whole orchestra watched a documentary film called *Route 181* that was difficult to watch. It seemed so one-sided to Sharon and her friends that they felt they were being attacked. People felt very emotional about it and were crying, and some felt the need to leave the room during the film.

There was an annoying scene at a checkpoint where the Israeli director was asked to show his identification and he got very upset with the soldier on duty. The director started yelling at the soldier to speak to him nicely and treat him like a human being. The soldier replied, "I have my orders." The Israeli director said, "Orders? Is there a brain under that helmet?"

After the film was over everyone started to talk about it. All the people who had been in the Israeli army wanted people to understand how you could get into a situation where you could say: "These are the orders." They explained the whole process of going through basic training—how they erased your own thought processes and taught you how to obey without thinking. That was the whole point of basic training, and when you reached that point, it didn't seem irrational. It seemed normal. It seemed very right at the moment. It came with a good explanation, too, because in a war situation, you didn't want to stop and think: "Is this really what I want to do?" You wanted a military structure that functioned quickly and well.

Sharon and her friends tried to explain that this Israeli director was presenting points of view that did not represent the way most people in Israel felt. They also tried to explain the difficulties of life in their country and the feeling of being in danger all the time. When she had been in the army herself, she had constantly felt like a target even though she was only a musician. She still had to wear a uniform all the time, and people were afraid of her violin case when she sat next to them on the bus.

While they were talking about the film, the arguments became more personal and defensive. Each group wanted to defend its position, and the Israelis felt their position was being attacked. Each group assumed it had to struggle in order to be heard by the other. The Arabs kept saying: "You don't understand about the checkpoints and the humiliation," and the Israelis kept saying, "You don't understand about being in the army." Finally one of the Arabs stood up and said, "Well, explain it to us, because we want to understand. We're here to listen." This seemed to be a turning point, not just of this particular discussion, but of the entire workshop. Suddenly the quality of the explaining and listening was different. These words created the space people needed, the space to express rather than defend their feelings.

That was the way things were in the Divan. You would stick it out: you would play all day, hang out all night, play all day; you would always be together, even when truly difficult things happened. The difficulties, the personal conflicts, the bigger Middle Eastern conflict, and then the willingness to get through the difficulties and the smaller conflicts: these things brought you closer together. Sharon couldn't recall one difficult situation she had been in that she couldn't find her way out of through friendship.

During that process of talking and thinking about the army, it occurred to Sharon that it was very hard for people who were or had been in the army even to consider that maybe what they were doing might be wrong. It was very hard, in the army or in Israel, to feel that you might have made a wrong decision when Israel had lost a lot of lives and suffered a lot over it. It was very hard to come to a point when you might say: "Actually, this was a bad decision. Actually, this wasn't worth it."

She didn't feel she had come to that point, but she felt more open to the possibility than she had been before. She had always admired her father very much for the fact that, although he was injured in the war, he was keenly aware of what was happening in the occupied territories. He read about human rights in the occupied territories in a newspaper called *B'tselem* to hear the other side of the story, and he even went to the West Bank once to see for himself what was going on there. Now that she had started going to the Divan and questioning things, it was nice to have that at home, to realize that even her dad, who had lost almost all his friends in the war, still questioned the way things were.

When Sharon came to the Divan for the first time, she already knew that a lot of people at home saw the orchestra as very pro-Palestinian and felt it didn't represent Israel enough. She knew people in the orchestra who struggled with this too, who felt that the Divan was only about supporting Arab views, not Israeli views. She had sympathy for them, but it became harder as the years went by for her to understand how they could still think this way. Seeking equality was not easy; she wasn't sure it was possible to think about the Middle Eastern conflict in equal terms. It had become even more difficult in the orchestra since Edward Said had passed away. Something he once said about suffering in the Middle Eastern conflict had stayed with her always: "Suffering, in my opinion, is the monopoly of no one." Sharon didn't know who was suffering more, but both sides were suffering and one side had more power.

Before going to the Divan, Sharon had really not thought of Syrians as human beings. She had only ever heard them spoken of as killers. The only thing she knew about Syrians was that they were sitting on the Golan Heights and shooting Israelis. That seemed like a very evil thing to do, so she thought they must be evil people. If she had spent time thinking of them as people, she would probably have come to different conclusions.

When Sharon spoke to Israelis about her orchestra, "Syrian" was always the key word, more than Egyptian, Lebanese, Jordanian, or any other Arab nationality. Many Israelis have been to Egypt or Jordan, but never to Syria. Sharon's mother's family had nothing against her playing in the Divan, but many of them couldn't resist saying, "So, you're playing with *Syrians*, huh?" whenever the opportunity arose. It just wasn't something they could take seriously.

Many people in Israel were shocked that there were even classical musicians in Syria. This was not the most astonishing fact for Sharon; to her, it was much more of a surprise to discover that they could have so much in common, and even become friends. Their cultural differences were still there, of course, and differences created distance. It was more of an effort to make friends with someone who had different ideas about having fun or going out.

Getting to know people in the orchestra could be determined by something as simple as who you went out with at night. The Muslims in the orchestra didn't drink, which meant that Sharon wouldn't go out to drink with them, and then she would know them less. People from the same country tended to stay in their own group. It was more comfortable for them; often they were all simply friends from home who liked to speak their language and be together, just like Sharon's friends, who had all gone to high school and the army and studied together. They knew each other so well, and maybe the musicians from other countries knew each other just as well, and that made their groups closer-knit and further apart from each other.

Sharon didn't mind sitting at a table in the cafeteria where people were speaking a different language; she had made some wonderful friends in the orchestra who didn't speak her language. She could sit at a table with people she loved and not understand what they were talking about. It didn't matter to her because she was close to them and knew that they felt the same way. She could learn a little bit of their language and their culture.

This was not to say that everyone understood everyone else in the Divan. During one of the orchestra's group discussions in the summer of 2007, a musician from Ramallah spoke about a girl he had played with in a certain European youth orchestra for peace. Then he said that he had later seen her in Ramallah, with a gun. He mentioned her name, and Sharon realized that it was her best friend from high school. Her friend had been in training in the air force during a very tense period when they recruited a lot of reservists to go to Ramallah or to checkpoints in the West Bank. Two of Sharon's girlfriends had gone there for a week, and the other girl had told her that she had had to fire her gun. Both of them were musicians who went to Sharon's arts high school. It had been an awful, traumatic thing to hear her friends talk about this.

When her colleague from the Divan told them this story, Sharon felt that he had told it to hurt them, the Israelis. It was as if he were saying: "I saw someone like you with a gun in my city."

She told him, "If you want me to understand you, you don't have to accomplish it by making me feel like shit. You can accomplish it in other ways."

He said to her, "I don't want to make you feel bad; I just want you to understand me."

She replied, "I want to understand you too, but it doesn't mean you have to hurt me on the way."

There were many different ways to express the same thing and to make your point. Of course there was a lot of pain to be expressed at the workshop, because the Middle Eastern conflict was a painful thing. Still, it was sometimes difficult for Sharon not to imagine that stories like this were told at least partly to make people feel uncomfortable.

People who came to the Divan for the first time couldn't imagine how accepting the community could be, and often they came passionately charged, urgently wanting to present their point of view. They didn't know at first that they didn't have to fight to be understood. That was why it was comforting to Sharon that the orchestra was more or less the same group of people every year, with a handful of new people each time. They had a common history now, which made it easier to communicate, especially with the people who had been at that film discussion in 2004 and really wanted to understand each other.

The Spanish musicians came into the picture when the orchestra moved to Andalusia in 2002. Without them, social life in the orchestra would never have been so smooth; a third party took the edge away. With the Spaniards it was possible to sometimes focus on something other than politics without feeling they were avoiding the obvious. If it had been an orchestra of only Israelis and Arabs, it might have taken longer to break the ice and develop real friendships. It was very easy for the Israelis to connect to the Spanish people. They were culturally close, especially in Sharon's case: half of her family was Sephardic. Her mother's family even spoke Ladino (a Jewish dialect of Spanish), which was very similar to Andalusian Spanish: the consonants were smoothed out in both dialects.

One summer, the administration tried to come up with a way to account for everyone quickly whenever the orchestra had to go anywhere by bus. One of the staff members decided to make bus seating lists by nationality: one bus for the Arabs, one for the Israelis, and one for the Spaniards. Sharon and her friend Meirav Kadichevski, an oboist, were infuriated. Bus rides were essential for getting to know different people in the orchestra. They decided to lead a rebellion: if the seating lists were really necessary, then they could at least be used to mix nationalities, not segregate them. Sharon and Meirav reorganized the lists themselves, distributing the citizens of each country among the three buses, and handed out the new lists on one of the flights. Of course, some people thought the two girls were doing this for personal reasons in order to sit with their friends, and they rejected the new lists. Maybe there were some personal interests involved, but that wasn't the point! Separating people by nationality went against the whole idea of the orchestra.

Eventually the issue made it to the ultimate authority: Maestro Barenboim. Sharon and Meirav explained to him how they felt it was wrong to segregate the buses. He had not been aware that this was happening. He asked them what the purpose of the lists was, and what they wanted to do about it. Sharon explained that the staff were afraid of losing people, and said, "I want to be able to get on a bus when I see one without thinking about where I come from!" Barenboim agreed and told the staff to do away with the lists and simply make sure that everyone got on the buses when it was time to leave.

There was never a dull moment in the Divan; every summer there was a new huge issue you had to deal with. In 2004 they had discussed whether to go to Ramallah or not, and Sharon was very glad in the end that they didn't go (they voted in favor of going, but it was impossible that year). Then they had another year to think about it, and the following summer she knew from the beginning that if it were possible go to Ramallah, she wanted to go. The first year she had been extremely scared when they talked about it. They all trusted Barenboim very much, especially when he said he wouldn't take his own son there if he thought there might be a security risk. At the same time, though, she wasn't sure she felt strongly enough about the orchestra to risk her life for it. She wasn't sure that if something bad were to happen, they would feel that it had been worth it. Of course it would be worth it to go and play, but Sharon just didn't know if the orchestra's performance would change the lives of Palestinians so much that it was worth taking such a personal risk. After she'd had a year to think about it, she decided that it was worth it after all. By the time it was possible to go there with the orchestra, she was emotionally prepared for the trip.

During Sharon's army duty, her quartet had gone to play at a base in the West Bank near Ramallah. They were taken there in an Israeli army car with escorts and they had been very scared, but at the time she hadn't hesitated because she had felt the importance of what she was doing. The next time she crossed the same border with the Divan, she was uncertain. She wasn't sure what the Palestinians would make of it. She wanted it to be more of a big deal for them to hear the orchestra than it was for the orchestra to go there. She didn't want them to think that the orchestra was going there to say that Israel was in the wrong. Sharon felt very patriotic and supported her country, and didn't want it to seem like they were going there to apologize for Israel's behavior. That was why music was so important; it was not specific about what you felt politically. It wasn't necessary to agree on other things in order to play well together.

After it was over, Sharon didn't know whether it had been a big deal or not for the audience in Ramallah. When the orchestra played in Europe and she could see tears in people's eyes, she always felt it was worth it. In Ramallah she only felt that a symphony orchestra concert was something foreign for them. Then again, maybe the people there were no different from audiences in Tel Aviv; it was all so subjective.

There was something a bit forced about playing classical music for Middle Eastern people, even her own family; she loved inviting her family to her concerts, but she knew that some of them would always come just to make her happy without really enjoying it. They didn't really understand the expression of the music. She didn't know if that was how the Palestinian people were feeling, but it was definitely a different kind of audience than what they were used to. The real excitement she felt was for her friend Tyme, her closest Palestinian friend and one of her closest friends in general. Tyme was at home, the orchestra was in her city, and all of her friends were there. Her mother was helping to organize the concert, and she was radiantly happy. She was very moved and Sharon was very happy for her. So it was worth it for that.

Sharon would be just as ecstatic as Tyme was in Ramallah, if the orchestra could play in Israel one day. The only time the Divan was ever in the papers in Israel was when they played Wagner or went to the West Bank. The press made it look like the orchestra was just trying to do everything that was forbidden. It irritated Sharon; the press never presented the whole picture, and the reports never came with an explanation of why these were positive things to do. Some people saw the orchestra's performance in Ramallah as offensive to Israel. The journalists never explained why it might be good for Israel to have this orchestra.

Sharon felt that if the orchestra could play in Israel, people would understand why it was good for the country. The message of their togetherness came across so strongly when they performed, and people would have no choice but to see it. As it was, she would always defend the orchestra in Israel, trying to explain things to critical friends. She would try to change people's image of Barenboim, because they thought he was against Israel, and that if you played with him you must be against Israel too. When he accepted the Wolf Prize in the Knesset (the Israeli legislature), many people read or heard his speech and saw it as an attack. Sharon didn't see it that way at all. When he conducted Wagner with the Staatskapelle Berlin in Jerusalem, very many people felt strongly against it, also perceiving it as an attack, but all the people Sharon knew in the audience felt differently.

The father of the cellist from Sharon's army quartet had been at that concert, and it might have been the first time he had ever heard Wagner live. He was in his fifties and his parents were Holocaust survivors. He grew up not buying any German products or having anything to do with Germany, let alone Wagner. This boycott was very common. His father had published a book about his Holocaust experience, and it was a big part of their family life. He had listened to the long discussion between Barenboim and the audience members after the concert, when Barenboim suggested that they play the Prelude and *Liebestod* from *Tristan und Isolde* as an encore. The cellist's father had stayed to listen and had been extremely moved. He was an amateur musician himself and admired Barenboim immensely as a musician, and when he heard the Staatskapelle playing Wagner in his country, he felt that they were trying to give him something. He felt it was important to these German musicians to play this music in Israel, and he appreciated it deeply and loved the music. The summer after that concert, his daughter played in the Divan for the first time, and he decided to buy tickets for the whole family to go to the orchestra's performance in Germany. It was the first time he had ever been to Germany.

Many of the people who stayed in the concert hall in Jerusalem to hear the Staatskapelle play Wagner appreciated it and were moved. Many people left, of course, but it seemed ironic that other people all over the country were terribly upset by it—people who hadn't been there and hadn't heard the music. At the time Sharon was studying at the Jerusalem Academy, and they didn't study Wagner there. It was a big hole in their education: they just pretended that Wagner didn't exist. After the Staatskapelle concert, one of Sharon's teachers at the Academy spent an entire class talking about how provocative it was for Barenboim to play Wagner in Israel. Sharon didn't understand the fuss. Most of the people in Israel who thought playing Wagner's music was a bad thing didn't know how many other composers were anti-Semitic, or that it had been played by Jewish musicians in Israel before the Holocaust. There was this stubbornness: "This is something you just don't do."

Sharon had nothing against playing Wagner with the Divan and was eager to learn the music, but the decision came the same year that they discussed going to Ramallah. It seemed like there were more issues dividing the orchestra than uniting it. They didn't need any added tension or any more conflicts than there were already. Wagner was such a sensitive issue for the Israelis, especially for people who came from families of Holocaust survivors. They were also concerned about playing Wagner in places where there were large Jewish communities, possibly with Holocaust survivors; they didn't want to offend anyone.

Sometimes there were discussions in the orchestra that threatened to get out of hand. Emotions and patriotic feelings could become strong enough to test friendships. Sharon herself sometimes didn't realize what was happening to her in a moment of heated discussion; it seemed very reasonable in her head to become so passionate.

The discussion about Barenboim's and Mrs. Said's anti-war declaration in 2006 was one such example. There was one sentence in it that disturbed the Israelis:

> Israel's destruction of life-giving infrastructure in Lebanon and Gaza, uprooting a million people and inflicting heavy casualties on civilians, and Hezbollah's indiscriminate shelling of civilians in northern Israel are in total opposition to what we believe in.

They wanted it to say that, in this war, everybody was suffering. "You can't weigh suffering," Sharon thought, and then, a moment later: "Or can you? Maybe you can."

In any case she didn't think it was important to say that this many people on this side were killed and this many on the other side. She thought it was important to say that everyone felt their lives were in danger. She felt that, the way this sentence was written, it was trying to make the Israelis feel bad and apologize. The Arabs did not identify with Hezbollah, a terrorist organization, but "Israel" included all of the country's citizens. She felt that Barenboim and Mrs. Said were trying to be sensitive with the Arab population and forgot that Israel was also at war. Yes, it was awful what their army did. They all agreed on this. But it wasn't so black and white, she felt; Israel had been attacked and had to fight back, that was the Israeli point of view. When you sympathized with other people all the time, it didn't mean that you lost faith in your own point of view. Sharon and her friends wanted to come up with a phrase that didn't make it sound like they were trying to apologize for Israel's behavior.

Barenboim had told them after reading the text that if anyone had a fundamental problem with the declaration, they should think about it, bring him suggestions, and he would make changes. Because of the printing deadline, any desired changes would have to be presented by the following morning. It was difficult to communicate with everyone for a while after that, because quite a few people from both sides were very upset. They talked about it all night and all day and it only created more tension. Some of Sharon's Arab friends said they felt uncomfortable that the Israelis were uncomfortable; they identified with the Israelis so strongly. But some of the other Arabs were upset about it and thought the Israelis were trying to make the war sound like a nice thing. The next day, after they had talked about it among themselves all night, they suggested three possible changes to the declaration. Barenboim eventually agreed to change "Israel" to "the Israeli government," which did not appease many people.

She could have decided to go home because she didn't agree with what was being said in her name, but she didn't want to go;

it wasn't part of what the orchestra had been doing. Word of the declaration spread to Israel and negative articles about the orchestra appeared. Some of Sharon's friends from Israel called her, asking, "What's happening? Why are you playing in this orchestra that is against Israel?"

The distance between the Israelis and the Arabs was tangible during that period, not so much because of the war as because of the declaration and the resulting discussions. Everyone was on edge during the war, and the declaration certainly didn't help make things any easier.

After the war had started and before the workshop began, Sharon didn't even know if there would be a Divan that summer. She and her friends were scared; they were calling and asking each other if they would come. It was crazy, she thought: their countries were at war with each other and they were e-mailing each other, asking, "How do you feel about this war?"

The hardest thing about going to the Divan in 2006 for Sharon was to leave her family at that time. There was a war going on, and she left the country to have her fun playing in the orchestra, and it felt very wrong. She was somewhat angry with herself, and worried about her family at the same time. One day they e-mailed her that they would be leaving in an hour for her grandmother's birthday party, and the next hour Sharon heard that there had been a bombing in the city where her grandmother lived. It was very scary not to be home at that time.

A few months later, in December 2006, the orchestra went on a short tour to the States, and all the people who had been missing during the summer came along then. When they came, everyone told them, "We really missed you," and they said, "We really wished we had been there."

It didn't matter what they thought during the war, or whether they felt it was right or wrong; the main thing was that they felt they were a missing part of the orchestra, and the orchestra felt it was missing a part of itself. Sharon almost couldn't even remember now that they had been missing, because they had always been there before and after.

The thing about the Divan that had changed Sharon's life the most was being on stage with a hundred people she loved who all wanted to do the same thing; all of them were learning from the same person and striving in the same direction. She felt a deep commitment to her friends in the Divan: it was a different kind of loving with them, almost like a family. Sharon knew that every friend of hers from the orchestra would do anything for her.

The Divan was so many things all at once for Sharon: an unparalleled musical experience, a social laboratory, a family, an open environment where you could ask all your questions. She thought of Barenboim as her teacher; the musical knowledge she gained from him accompanied her every day of the year. The Divan was also a place to learn about life: not necessarily about the answers to your questions, but about how to ask the questions and be open to more than one truth.

Maybe these were small things, like Sharon's friendship with the Palestinian student from Symphony Market, but this was her way to contribute to the world, she thought: talking to friends, family, and strangers; helping them to understand that not all the Arabs in the world wanted to kill them.

She wanted people at home to know just one simple thing: that some people on the "other side" think exactly the same way you do.

INTERMEZZO

One day at the Divan workshop in 2008, Georges Yammine took me aside and said, "I never told you my story of the Divan. *Ich habe eine schöne Geschichte für Dich!* [I have a nice story for you!]" He didn't want to impose, he said, but this was really a nice story. We walked over to a bench facing one of the lawns of the Lantana guest house. Switching back and forth between English and German, with the occasional French or Arabic word in between, he told me how the Divan had changed his life. His big eyes grew even bigger behind his black rectangular glasses when he came to one of the climaxes in his story, emphasizing his surprise or delight. He fixed his gaze on me with such deep concentration that he was nearly comical in his seriousness. With broad gestures of his arms he illustrated his ideas in the sweltering Andalusian air.

No one in Georges's family had any background whatsoever in classical music. When he was twelve years old, he wanted to learn to play the violin so that he could play Arabian music, but the Civil War in Lebanon was still going on, and he had to wait another two years before he could start taking lessons.

When he applied to the conservatory to study the violin, he was told that he would have to study classical music. "Classical music?!" he exclaimed, his voice jumping an octave. "What is this classical music? I don't know classical music. I see the violin all the time in Oriental music, I want to play Oriental music!"

Classical music was what you saw on television at the funeral of a president or a prime minister. It was not what you listened to at home with your family or at parties. Nevertheless, they told him at the conservatory, "If you want to play the violin, you have to study classical music." He reluctantly gave in. At the time, there was not much live classical music in Lebanon. There was no symphony orchestra yet; there were no foreign teachers, and consequently no great tradition of string playing. For the first two years of his violin studies, he was also neglected by his teacher: "Who takes you seriously if you start to play the violin at fourteen? He gave me ten-minute lessons!"

Then, during one school holiday when he was sixteen, everything changed. He was at home for two weeks and had found the music for an Accolay violin concerto, which was much too difficult for him at his stage of development. When he went to his first lesson after the break, he told his teacher, "I learned this concerto and I would like to play it for you." He proceeded to play the first part of it, which he had somehow managed to learn by himself.

His teacher was shocked. "Now I believe that you can actually play the violin," he said. "Now we have to change everything." Until that day his teacher had not taken Georges seriously. From then on, he began to give him two lessons a week.

Four years later, at twenty, Georges had learned everything he could learn from his teacher. There was no one else in Lebanon who could help him develop further musically. Fortunately, that was the year of the first Divan workshop, where he met Mathis Fischer, a violinist in the Staatskapelle Berlin and coach for the Divan's second violin section.

After the first sectional rehearsal with Mathis, Georges stayed in the room after everyone else had left. Playing in an orchestra for the first time was an immense challenge for Georges, and he asked Mathis if he could have a private lesson with him; Mathis obliged. The first time Georges played for Mathis he could hardly keep the hair of the bow on the violin strings; his right arm was so tense that he produced more noise than tone. Nevertheless, Mathis noticed Georges's eagerness to learn and started to ask him every day, "So, what do you want to play for me today?" Georges would bring him solo repertoire in addition to the Beethoven symphony they were playing, and Mathis was very generous with his time for Georges.

At the end of the summer Georges wanted to go on learning, but he didn't know where to turn for help. He knew that he was not yet advanced enough to pass the entrance examination of a German *Musikhochschule*, and yet he knew he wanted to study in Germany. He had never thought of studying in Germany before going to Weimar; he didn't speak the language and didn't know anyone else from Lebanon who had studied in Germany.

Then there was the problem of finances; Georges and his family did not have the money to finance his studies abroad. Tuition fees were not high in Germany, but he had very little to spend on food and housing. He would only need a simple room in the student dormitory, which would cost 200 Deutschmarks a month, but this exceeded his budget. The Barenboim–Said Foundation, which would later award scholarships to many Divan musicians, had not yet been created. Georges spoke to Karin Davison, who had helped organize the first Divan workshop, about his desire to study in Germany. Miraculously, she found an unorthodox solution to his housing problem.

She introduced him to the general manager of the Dorint Hotel in Weimar, Kai Petry. He was unable to grant Georges a scholarship, but he offered to let him live in the hotel for free if he were to study in Weimar.

At this point in his tale, Georges smiled, raised his thick, dark eyebrows, and said, "Is it a good story?" He laughed. "No one was willing to finance a small student room for me, but here was someone who gave me a room in a five-star hotel for a year. Sometimes you think you are living in a bad world, but you become very happy when you see that there are still very good people in it.

I always thought that this kind of story only happens in books or films; I couldn't understand how this became my reality!"

He would have preferred to live in the dormitory, of course. He didn't want the other students to think he was getting preferential treatment because he was somehow better. He knew that what he deserved was to live in a simple student home, not in a five-star hotel, and maybe this pushed him to work even harder to deserve such an absurdly generous gift.

Nevertheless, the problem of getting into the Hochschule remained. Georges would have to learn more in order to be accepted to the Hochschule, where he would be able to learn even more. This time it was Mathis who came to the rescue. He told Georges that if he came to Berlin, Mathis would help him prepare for his entrance examination in Weimar. Georges took him up on his offer and spent four months in Berlin, having at least two lessons a week with Mathis. Sometimes the lessons lasted two hours, and Mathis never demanded a penny in return. Four months later, Georges auditioned for the Hochschule in Weimar and was accepted. He studied there for four years, and Petry let him live in the Dorint the whole time.

In a way, Georges opened the door to Germany for other young Lebanese musicians. There was always a tendency for young people to study where their older classmates had gone to study, and Georges's presence in Weimar made it easier for other Lebanese musicians to decide to go there rather than France, an easier choice for many because of the language.

During his time in Weimar, where some of his classmates mistook him for an Arabian prince because of his address, Georges traveled to Berlin regularly to take lessons with Axel Wilczok or Mathis. Even after completing his studies in Weimar, Georges continued to visit Berlin from Paris, where he was officially enrolled in the conservatory. His relationship with Mathis became very friendly; Georges would often stay at his house for two days, conversing and taking lessons.

After six years of studying abroad, Georges returned to Lebanon to play in the National Symphony and teach. After a year, he wanted to go back to Germany to get his doctoral degree in music; he needed another intellectual challenge. He applied to several universities in Germany, and his proposal was accepted by some. Once again Mathis intervened, changing Georges's destiny. "You would spend a whole year writing your thesis," he said. "Why not spend a year practicing and then audition for a few orchestras? You can do it." Georges considered his options. A doctorate would not change his life as much as a position in a good orchestra. If Mathis thought he could do it, then Georges would give it a try. He spent a year practicing repertoire for orchestral auditions, and early in 2008 he won a position in the newly formed Qatar Symphony Orchestra.

"Now I have a second step in my life, a new life is waiting for me," he said to me with wonder and amazement, gesticulating toward the lawn, indicating his future. "These are the things that have touched me in the workshop: how I came to it, how I could find this person to sponsor me so long, and these teachers teaching me for free."

Mathis had once had to start from scratch teaching Georges how to play the violin, and now he treated him like a colleague. They could discuss musical questions as equals. For Georges, it was a great privilege to be taken seriously by such wonderful musicians as Axel Wilczok and Mathis Fischer.

"*Ich bin im Divan wiedergeboren und in Weimar, groß geworden*," he said with a grin, enjoying the double-entendre. "I was reborn in the Divan and I grew up (or became great) in Weimar."

When I first met the Lebanese cellist Nassib Al Ahmadieh in the summer of 2007 in Salzburg, I was convinced that we already knew each other. I greeted him as if we were old acquaintances; only after he responded with a confused but friendly smile did I realize that I had seen him in the documentary about the orchestra,

Knowledge is the Beginning. He had such a direct and involving way of telling a story that his appearance in the film had left a lasting impression of familiarity on me.

By birth, Nassib is a member of the Druze religion, which was founded in the eleventh century. The Druzes attempted to reform and eventually broke away from Islam. Its followers were persecuted, and fled to the mountains of Syria and Lebanon in order to practice their religion freely. Tradition forbids them to marry outside of their religion even today; they generally do not even do business outside of the Druze community. Nassib is a great exception, both in his community and his country: in Lebanon it is so unusual to move from one area to another that people who move are often referred to for decades, if not generations, according to their place of origin rather than their family name.

I visited Nassib in December 2007 in his student apartment in Weimar. I was glad of the opportunity to visit the site of the first Divan workshop, the setting for Georges's story. Weimar is a very pleasant university town full of parks and innumerable landmarks and monuments to the many artists and philosophers who have lived there. I spent the entire day with Nassib, asking questions and listening to his fascinating stories. I had never spoken to anyone at such length about Lebanese society before, and was grateful for a glimpse into its complex structures and divisions.

Nassib seemed very much at home in Weimar. His German was as fluent as his English, and everywhere we went people greeted him on the street and in cafés. When Nassib spoke, his vowels sounded as if he were smiling, and he often was, even when talking about something unpleasant or painful. Behind the smile, though, there was an immense reserve of patience, persistence, and motivation, which has probably developed both thanks to and in spite of his life story.

Nassib Al Ahmadieh

The invasion of Kuwait began at about 3AM on August 2, 1990. I was thirteen years old and living there with my family, where my father had a job as a construction worker. My family and I got in the car, taking what we could with us and leaving everything else behind. By 8AM everyone's bank accounts were frozen. We were lucky we had a house to go back to in Lebanon. Many people had nothing to go back to, and Kuwait does not grant citizenship to foreigners: that meant that anything left behind was forfeited property. My siblings and I were born in Kuwait, but our parents come from Sharoun, a small Druze village not far from Beirut in the mountains in central Lebanon. During the years that my father worked in Kuwait, my parents gradually built their own house in Lebanon, ten minutes away from the village where they were born.

My parents are simple people who grew up in the Druze community. They barely learned to read and write, since their own parents could not spare their help as farm workers after only four years of elementary school. My parents may not have had an education, but their pride drove them to want to know things, and to push us children to learn as much as possible and to get our university degrees, which we all did.

Kuwait was a relatively new country that was full of mixed foreigners—people from India, Vietnam, Sri Lanka, China, Lebanon, Egypt, Syria, Jordan, and Palestine. There was no sense of community, though, and no cultural exchange. People were there to work, that was all. It was just desert and oil. Our parents encouraged us to have hobbies at home in order to keep us off the streets in our neighborhood, which may not have been dangerous but was not especially desirable either. They reasoned that they were too poor to live anywhere else, but could at least afford to keep their children at home and educate them as they wished. My father always said we didn't have the money for a video recorder, computer games, or a proper television: we had only a very small old one for watching the news. On the other hand, in order to keep us occupied at home, he bought us books, puzzles, musical instruments: we had a whole band of instruments at home, with accordions and organs that must have cost five times as much as a television and a VCR. In any case, it worked. We didn't get bored at home and we didn't watch television.

We had very little contact with other cultures in Kuwait, and certainly no background in classical music. My parents barely knew that Western classical music existed, and the only music we heard at home was Arabic, mostly Egyptian music from the '50s and '60s. At school we had only one hour of general music lessons every week. I first heard classical music when I was thirteen, in Lebanon. I saw a symphony orchestra concert broadcast on a French television station, and I was so impressed by this huge ensemble and all these men in tails. I had never seen more than five musicians together on stage before. I was absolutely blown away by this classical music, and I wanted to learn to play a classical instrument; but this was 1990, and the Lebanese Civil War had just ended. Beirut was devastated and the conservatory was still closed. I had to wait a while for things to settle down.

Around this time I started to play the oud (the Middle Eastern predecessor of the lute), which my older brother already played. We were both very inspired by the Rahbani brothers, who orchestrated and harmonized Arabic music, combining classical Arabic melodies with Western counterpoint. We also listened to Marcel Khalife, who sang nationalistic revolutionary songs and wrote a lot of pieces for two ouds and small ensemble. My brother and I started to listen to classical music and try to play it on the ouds. We made arrangements of pieces like the *Nutcracker* Suite for two ouds. We were very active and motivated then, when I was fourteen and my brother twenty. I have the feeling that I was more talented and creative then than I am now! We took dictation of all these pieces, and I wrote so quickly I could notate almost as fast as the music played. These days, whenever I have a dictation exam at the conservatory in Weimar, I seem to miss everything.

We had much more freedom in Lebanon than we had had in Kuwait. Our parents were not afraid to let us go out, and we started to perform our arrangements in little places in our region. We started to meet other musicians, and soon I was impatient to learn another instrument. I thought I might like to play the violin, because that was a classical instrument and it was also used in a lot of Arabic music. I thought I could play the violin together with my brother on the oud. I never thought of making a career as a classical musician, so I never would have considered learning an instrument that was only used in classical music. I thought the violin would be a good compromise, so I bought a violin and started to try to play some scales and a few little pieces by ear. I would try to play the beginnings of some Mozart symphonies, but when it got too complicated I would stop. I figured that that was what they would teach me when I finally started having lessons.

In 1995, I finished high school and applied for the music conservatory in Beirut, which had recently been reopened. They didn't have such high standards at the time and were accepting a lot of beginners, because they wanted to attract as many students as possible in order to rebuild the school. When I told them I wanted to play the violin, they said that they already had far too many violin applicants. They had almost no applicants for cello, though. The violin teachers looked at me and my hands and tried to convince me that I was made to play the cello because of my physique and the length of my fingers. I was so disappointed. The cello was not very much in demand in Arabic music, and it was not an instrument you even noticed in the orchestra, or at least not as much as you noticed the violins. I told them I would think about it for a few days. After I thought about it for a while, I decided: "What the hell, it's better than nothing." This is how it happened that I had my first cello lesson in September 1995, when I was eighteen years old.

I started much later than most classical musicians, and yet I had a well-developed left hand from playing the oud, which requires a similar hand position, and I had a feeling for the way the bow works from my experiments with the violin. I took cello lessons in the conservatory, but there was no orchestra, because there were not enough students. I first heard about the West-Eastern Divan Orchestra in 1999 through the conservatory, but that year I had to begin my army duty. It was mandatory to do twelve months of army duty, although it was clear that the Lebanese army would never have a chance against the Israeli army. Together with all the people doing their mandatory service, the army numbered only 75,000 badly equipped soldiers. It was a waste of good resources. Nevertheless, at the time of its creation, mandatory service was a good idea; after the Civil War the army was intended to unify the nation under one flag and get everyone involved in the issue of internal security. There were very many ex-militia fighters who were left without an occupation, and the army gave them a purpose.

The Lebanese army had had no history of aggressive actions or scandalous behavior, except for the Civil War, when there was no actual unified army anyway. There was no ideological reason for me to refuse to go to the army; I never thought I would be in a situation where I would have to compromise my principles. The army takes its orders from the government, though, and while I was in the army my unit was sent to monitor an uprising in a Palestinian refugee camp. I didn't think the situation would be too dangerous. The Lebanese army has a reputation for commanding respect upon appearance. People stop fighting without obliging the army to take action. In that moment, though, the situation was very hot and our presence alone was not enough. The officer warned the refugees that if they didn't stop, there would be orders to take action. The Palestinian refugees have an agreement with the Lebanese government that they are allowed to keep weapons inside the camps, but not carry them outside. At the time the Palestinians were only demonstrating, not shooting, but they were carrying guns outside the area of the refugee camp.

You find yourself standing there, thinking you don't want to open fire, but in that moment you can no longer choose what to do with your gun. If it comes to the point of self-defense, you are forced to kill rather than be killed. Fortunately the situation resolved itself and we didn't have to take action, but right then I thought to myself, this is as close as you can get. I finished my army duty in the summer of 2000 and went from carrying a gun to playing in the Divan with Daniel Barenboim—the first time I had ever played in an orchestra. We played Brahms's First Symphony that year.

If I were to audition for the Divan now, playing the way I did in 2000, I don't think I would be accepted. The musical level of the orchestra has improved so drastically. Back then, they accepted motivated musicians who were not necessarily very advanced technically. I had real difficulties in the orchestra at first. It was the first time I was able to listen to an oboe live, for example, and I was really distracted. I remember telling Steven Balderston, the cellist who came from the Chicago Symphony to coach the section: "I really have problems because I am so overwhelmed, sitting in the orchestra listening to the harmonies going through me—I get sometimes so overwhelmed from pleasure that I cannot play anymore!" When you have only been playing for five years, and have only had contact with classical music for seven, and then you meet Daniel Barenboim and all these musicians who come from the Chicago Symphony and the Staatskapelle Berlin to teach and lead sectional rehearsals and you soak up the whole atmosphere, it just boosts your motivation like crazy.

There were a few musicians from the conservatory in Beirut who had gone to the first session of the Divan in 1999, and from them I knew that there would be discussions and that you could make personal contacts and express your views. I was particularly interested in the discussions, since I have always been interested in politics, even though I have never had any ambition to become a politician or even an active member of any political party. Everyday life in Lebanon depends on politics; your family name establishes your identity in society. You have to fight all the time for the recognition of your individual personality. You get used to talking about politics to avoid being pigeonholed. Sometimes you have to exaggerate your reaction to prove that you are not religious, that you don't belong to any particular political party, that you will not always take the side people expect you to take. You have to do this to gain the respect of the whole community. In Lebanon there are at least eighteen different religions, and each one is associated with a certain region of the country, a certain political party and a certain way of thinking. When I tell people my name is Nassib Al Ahmadieh, they automatically assume from the etymology of my last name that I come from this part of the country, I practice this religion, I vote for these politicians, and my people are responsible for these events in the Civil War. This is too restrictive for a young man searching for his own ideology.

By the time I went to the Divan I was already used to detaching myself from Lebanese society and establishing my own personality. I think I was the only Druze musician in the Beirut conservatory. After the Civil War it was a big deal to be suddenly sitting in one place with all these different people. Your teacher may have been on the other side in the war, and even if he personally didn't take part in the war, he probably got lots of bombs from your side. Whenever you walked into a room, this was in the air. Musicians tend to be more open than most people, but you still had to show you didn't belong to the mainstream, you didn't agree with it. It helped that I had been exposed to different ways of thinking at home while my brother was studying theater at the American University in Beirut. He was reading a lot of philosophy and came home with a lot of new ideas and books: Plato, George Bernard Shaw, Nietzsche. I was still only fourteen, and these ideas really impressed me.

I was very interested in presenting my views to the other side. We Arabs think that the whole world, including the media, is pro-Israeli, and that we have been portrayed as fools. Whenever we have a chance to express our opinions and frustrations, we are very happy. This is why you see all these Arab politicians screaming on television; they think the wrong story is being told to the world, which is partially true. Over the years I have grown to believe that this is an exaggeration. It's not that the world is so against us, but that we are against ourselves in many ways. Our political leaders use this conflict to stay in power, and to work against us. It's like any totalitarian regime: if you don't like me, it means you're cooperating with the enemy. There is some truth in this too, of course. You are not supposed to think otherwise in your own country; it's a kind of tradition. "Our nation is in danger, and this is where the danger comes from." If you say "I don't think so, I'm not sure about that," or you point your finger to another danger that you believe is coming from within the country, you are almost seen as a traitor, or at least as a collaborator.

My first interaction with Israelis in the Divan was really interesting. Lebanese people are not supposed to have contact with Israelis. For example, if Miss Lebanon is photographed standing too close to Miss Israel, she is attacked by the press and forced to relinquish her position. It was sometimes very difficult and challenging for me to be at the Divan workshop in 2000. In the first few moments I was absolutely skeptical about talking to Israelis. You have to talk to each other because you play together, sometimes even in small groups, and you have to discuss a lot of things musically. It was very unsettling at first to sit in the same room with an Israeli. You are raised to hate them, to think of them as bad people, or at least as people taking part in a bad movement. They represent your enemy.

The atmosphere in 2000 was much tenser than it is now, partly because we know each other better today. A big part of the orchestra is used to these discussions, so the process of integration is easier. If another Arab comes and sees I am getting along with the Israelis, it motivates him or her to do the same. In the beginning, though, people would express their opinions in an aggressive way. Edward Said couldn't come that year because of his illness, and they invited other thinkers who may not have been the right people. They were all highly intellectual, but not necessarily sensitive enough to deal with the tension between us. In one discussion the Egyptian members of the orchestra left the room and threatened to leave the workshop because of one of these thinkers. In Arabic, we say: "My brother and I are against my cousin, but my cousin and I are against any foreigner." These were the emotional traditions we had on our side, and the same was true of the Israelis. They have their own internal problems with immigrants and different political or religious movements, but when confronted, they stand together as Israelis.

In the beginning these reactions were extreme. Whenever anyone criticized anything from the other side, it was very personal. I always respect these patriotic feelings and the obligations to defend your country's position, even if you have a lot of criticisms of your own country. It is a stupid human reaction, though, not to accept criticism from certain people because you feel they have no right to criticize you, as if truth were dependent on the person speaking it. This kind of behavior is not necessarily gone now, but it has become much milder. People listen until the end and then think: "Okay, I don't like the fact that it's coming from him, but he's right."

I made some very close friends at the first Divan workshop I attended, and some of them were Israelis. The first two summers,

1999 and 2000, the workshops were held in Weimar, and there were some German musicians in the orchestra. It was part of Daniel Barenboim and Edward Said's philosophy to include students from the host country, which in this case was so deeply involved with the history of the creation of Israel. That first year I was quite shocked to realize that I had more in common with the Israelis than with the Germans! The way we Arabs react to something, our body language and responses, is much more similar to the Israelis' than to the Germans'. It shows that we belong to one region. Even though most of the Israelis' family names come from Europe, they have a Middle Eastern temperament. There really *is* something in common.

I didn't always keep in touch with my Israeli friends, especially in the early years. In the beginning I was quite skeptical about exchanging e-mail addresses because you never know what will happen with e-mail. We had no contact during the year between summer workshops, but that didn't make it more difficult to pick up where we left off the year before.

When I came back to Lebanon after my first Divan workshop in 2000, I was so motivated; but at the same time I was crying, thinking, "What am I doing here? I have to get out of here, do something else." The Divan opened my eyes to so many things, and not just about the political situation. I came back with a whole new idea of what was possible for myself in music. I had never realized that I could just play, say, the Dvorak Cello Concerto as an ordinary person. I had always thought of solo repertoire and chamber music as something highly specialized for very virtuosic players, but in the Divan I saw normally talented people, students, practicing a concerto just to study it, and enjoying it. That summer I also played my first chamber music, the Mendelssohn Octet, which we played very often in later years with different members.

I was immediately motivated to start some chamber music in Lebanon, but at first my friends and I faced big problems finding music, since the library had burned down during the Civil War. In

1998 the Lebanese National Symphony Orchestra was founded, and we hoped that we would be able to find chamber music in their library, but they had spent all their money buying orchestral music. Fortunately, though, musicians had come from other countries to play in the orchestra, and they brought a lot of music with them. The former principal cellist of the Bucharest Opera came to be a part of the new orchestra in Beirut, and he became my cello teacher. He listened to one of my exams in the conservatory and said to me, "You play very well. I am very moved by how you play, but you do everything wrong. You have a strong will to play, but you cannot keep playing if you go on like this. You have bad habits in your bow arm and in your left arm." He offered to teach me, and he worked with me three or four times a week without charging me anything. He had a contract to play one rehearsal a day and one concert every two weeks or so with the symphony, and I guess he was bored. He wanted to do something. He enjoyed teaching me, and I think it was also a pleasure for him. He tried every possible stupid trick with me, like putting champagne corks between the fingers of the left hand. He would even sit and listen to me practice my trill or my vibrato, things that try any teacher's patience. He was an extremely big help to me.

When I went to the Divan workshop again in 2001, Steven Balderston noticed that I had made a big leap in my progress, and he was very happy. Since then I have been rapidly improving. I have been so lucky to be able to play with Barenboim not just once or twice, but eight years in a row. He even selected me along with a handful of other musicians from the Divan to represent the orchestra on a tour with the Gustav Mahler Youth Orchestra. When Barenboim's friend James Wolfensohn, former president of the World Bank and an amateur cellist, wanted to have a big birthday celebration, he rented Carnegie Hall and invited some of his musician friends to play with him—Yo-Yo Ma, Pinchas Zukerman, Vladimir Ashkenazy, and Itzhak Perlman, to name a few—and some of us Divan musicians, including me. We played the Mendelssohn Octet with twenty-four string players; each individual part was played by one star musician and two students. It was a fantastic opportunity for us.

All the same, now the time has come to make sure that these experiences don't just turn into good memories from the distant past. Now I want to get a good job in an orchestra. I have been studying in Weimar since 2004, and it's been quite a journey, when I think about the fact that I spent my childhood and early teenage years playing football in the desert in Kuwait, and that I now play regularly as a substitute in the Deutsches Nationaltheater in Weimar. It's kind of frustrating, though, when you know that you could do this, you could be a really good musician, but you have much less time to do it than everyone else. You regret that you still have to work on things at thirty that you should have taken care of when you were eight.

Through the Divan I began to understand the conflict more objectively, as neither victor nor victim. In every conflict, one side's heroes are the other side's bad guys or oppressors. The history of Israel obliges its citizens to be paranoid. History has shown that this is a hostile region; the Holocaust and anti-Semitism in Europe have made it difficult for Israel to accept the idea that it can live in peace with its neighbors. Israelis have their own right to be skeptical about this. On the other hand, their own development has suffered because of this conflict.

My contact with Israelis gave me the opportunity to learn about this. I learned that they were scared, and for good reason. I hope that they also learned from our contact that the people on the other side are not against them. The most ridiculous thing is that the Middle Eastern conflict is being turned into the Muslims against the Jews. Jews have been in our countries since the dawn of time; there were Jews in Lebanon until 1948. No one kicked them out either; there are still Jewish-owned properties there that no one can buy or sell. Jews were never considered foreigners in

Lebanon. My mother grew up with Jewish neighbors in southern Lebanon (Sidon) in the '50s and '60s, the children played together, the parents drank coffee together. The Jews in Israel think they are being persecuted, but the conflict is about land and identity, not about being Jewish. There is no Jewish–Muslim conflict. Between the twelfth century and the creation of the state of Israel, no one ever even spoke about the "Arab world." In the twentieth century people began to search for an Arab identity while they were liberating themselves from colonial powers, and then the creation of Israel brought about solidarity among the Arab countries, but this Muslim—Jewish problem does not exist. The problem concerns land and rights. Egypt and Jordan signed peace treaties with Israel as soon as their land was returned or liberated. We are allowing fanatics to abuse this conflict, using their religious motives to obscure the underlying political plots.

I have learned so much from my experiences in the Divan, but as the years go by I start to wonder: What are we aiming for? Do we want to change people's minds? Do we want to educate them, or do we just want to make personal contact? And why are we inviting these politicians to the workshop? Why do we discuss politics when even the experts are going crazy dealing with it? There are so many aspects to this conflict. In Lebanon, for example, religious/ethnic groups have always been related to larger powers. The Muslims were supported by the Ottoman Empire while it lasted; later on, the Catholics were allied with France, the Protestants with the United States, the Shiites with Iran, the Sunnis with Saudi Arabia and Syria, and the Druze with Great Britain. All of these relationships play a role in the Palestinian–Israeli conflict. It's just too complicated. It goes on and on. Everyone knows that Hezbollah is funded by Iran through Syria, and it is very probable that the 2006 Lebanon war was about much more than two kidnapped soldiers and Israel's attack in self-defense. If we want to discuss politics with any real understanding of the situation, then we have to be full-time politicians.

I think that, rather than talking about politics, we orchestra members should be discussing a way for our generation to make a statement that we are radically against war. Whatever is happening in politics, we are being killed, no matter who is responsible. The wars in 1967 and 1973 were nationalistic wars; they were necessary for our existence, but what are we trying to accomplish now? In the past, Israel fought to establish itself and the Arabs fought to regain Palestine—but now? Now there is simply a chaos of motivations. What are we fighting for? The 1967 borders are internationally accepted as the borders of Israel and the future Palestine. The West Bank and Gaza are under occupation and must be liberated, of course, but there is no longer any justification for violence.

When we discuss politics in the orchestra, are we discussing politics in order to change people's minds? Or is the object of the workshop to gather as many new members as possible each year, to repeat the same experiment of mixing new people? I know that some Arab members come for the first time and listen to, say, Joschka Fischer speak, and yet they are not even really prepared to speak to Israelis. I know how some of them talk in the background—they still think the way I did the first time I came. I feel comfortable discussing politics with my Israeli friends that I have known for years already, because we have developed mutual trust in each other; we respect each other's views. This is impossible for the new people. It seems like the workshop no longer tries to make and build personal connections, or at least not enough.

We have had discussions with Mustafa Barghouti, whom I love, but who has become a Palestinian politician, which makes his unanimous acceptance in the workshop very difficult. One year he came to show us how the wall was being built in the West Bank, and it caused a real upheaval for the Israelis. With all due respect, this was too much for me in this setting, even though I am interested in politics. In fact, the year after Barghouti's presentation, Avi Shlaim, the Israeli historian, came and said the same things, and they were accepted. I think these discussions should start with training on how to become objective. The human potential in the Divan is far greater than what we make of it. When Said was alive, he was also like a conductor. He didn't represent any side in particular; he was highly intellectual. He concentrated on achieving something with us the way Barenboim does with the music. There is always a concrete musical goal now, but no longer any concrete, non-musical goal.

I believe that the workshop is a way of saying that there can be a non-political approach to all of this. Barenboim and the late Edward Said always said that there is no military solution. We don't have to wait for a political solution in order to have a cultural exchange. The trust required on both sides for a better future will not be attained by military action.

Despite my belief in the workshop and its importance, I didn't feel able to participate in 2006, during the war. I know that Mr Barenboim was very disappointed with me for not coming that year. I even read an article in the German weekly newspaper *Die Zeit* in which he specifically mentioned a Lebanese cellist who had a scholarship from the Barenboim–Said Foundation and didn't come to the workshop in 2006. Looking back now, I don't think I established anything by not going; I don't think anyone appreciated my not having taken part in the Divan. For me, though, it was a moral question on many sides. I didn't feel like going on tour playing Beethoven's Ninth Symphony—*O Freude*—at a time when 1.5 million people were dislocated in Lebanon and a hundred people were dying every day for a month. My parents were also in danger. They were fortunately not in one of the hottest areas of bombardment, but they live next to one of highest and longest bridges in the Middle East, which connected the coast to the Bekaa valley. Over the course of three or four days it was bombarded until the whole two-kilometer section of the bridge was destroyed. During the first attack, some of the windows in my parents' house were shattered. My brother's apartment in Beirut was also affected by the bombing; his children went crazy, and he took them to my parents' house for a while to live. This was not a situation in which I could go on tour, no matter with whom or for what purpose. I was not psychologically prepared for it.

The other Lebanese musicians couldn't go to the workshop because they were trapped in Lebanon at the start of the war. Physically and practically, I could have gone, since I was in Germany at the time, but I didn't want to take advantage of that fact to be able to go to the Divan without taking the other factors into consideration. In the first few hours of the war they bombarded the airport and the checkpoints, and Syria closed its borders. People were trapped. All the ports were bombarded, and a few days after the war started, foreign embassies started repatriating their citizens. Nevertheless, I spent the whole week between the start of the war and the beginning of the workshop writing e-mails to Arab and Israeli members of the orchestra, encouraging them all to go. I wanted the Divan to make an announcement against the war. The Arabs said that this was a time to stay home; it was a time for mourning and not for negotiations. Mr. Barenboim called me personally from Seville to ask me why I wouldn't come; I told him it was my psychological situation that prevented me from coming. He told me he thought this should not have been a nationalistic movement within the orchestra, and I told him that I hadn't wanted it to be.

I hadn't expected to find out that (with a few exceptions) the Jordanians who did have permission to travel decided to act in solidarity with the Lebanese people who couldn't go. I told them not to do this, that it was not necessary. For me it was a personal decision not to go, as well as a security issue. I also got the feeling from phone calls and e-mails with my Israeli friends that if I went to Pilas, I would be going through very hot discussions and would not be able to control myself, because I was really burning under psychological pressure. I got so irritated by some opinions I heard from good friends of mine from Israel on the phone or in emails that I thought, if I were to go to Pilas, I would make some enemies. If I had gone, I would have talked about the war.

I was shocked that people on the Israeli side didn't dare to question whether the Israeli army was exaggerating its actions, and this created a big question mark for me in the purpose of the Divan workshop. Obviously the workshop should not necessarily change people's mentalities, but if you have seen so many films and gone through so many discussions with honest people who are just sharing their innermost feelings, how can you still react this way? As soon as crisis strikes, people on all sides react as if they had never been exposed to other ideas.

I stayed in Weimar throughout the war, and when the orchestra came there to play on August 28, after the war was over, I went to the concert and to the orchestra's hotel afterward to talk to them. They stayed for three days and I was always in discussion with them, but they told me it was a pity I hadn't been there to discuss things during the war. Before the war, friends of mine had told me that all Lebanese people were guilty of not stopping Hezbollah, and this was why they were being punished. You might as well say that you could also hold all the Israelis guilty for a "mistake" one soldier made by dropping a rocket on a refugee shelter. I still call these people friends because I know they didn't mean to direct this against me personally—they were just in a state of psychological terror because of the media in their country. While they were in Weimar I tried to convince my friends of the truth, and they apologized and said they hadn't seen the magnitude of the destruction until two or three weeks after the war began. Then they began to think that Israel may have reacted in an excessive manner.

I cannot expect our Divaners to influence the Israeli government or army any more than they can expect me to stop Hezbollah. We must understand that these military actions serve only the interests of larger powers that we cannot influence. All we can do is to say that we don't want violence. Our generation can say that, even if

Hezbollah or the Israeli army has the right to attack in their defense, this is the wrong way to do it. The experts say that bombardment only weakens a country's infrastructure and accomplishes nothing politically.

All we Divaners can do is to present an example in our own countries. Maybe I can soften the fear and hate, maybe I can help to put these emotions in a rational perspective. What is definite is that we can present an example of how we have developed in these particular ways after having had contact with each other all these years. For me, the obligation to participate in the development of Lebanese society is always in my mind, but the society there is so restricted. If I want to teach music in southern Lebanon, they might see it as a Druze initiative from a political leader who wants to diminish the influence of another political leader, and so on and so forth. I am exaggerating, of course, but not very much. There is no point in my going back before I can achieve something in Europe that would change my status and earn professional respect for me in Lebanon. If I have proved myself on the international scene, then people will listen to me more. Without that, my effect would be very limited, as a member of the orchestra or a teacher in the conservatory. This would be better than nothing, but I already had a job in the Lebanese National Orchestra for four years before going to study in Weimar. In the orchestra, you have the feeling that you are the entire musical life of the country. You play in the orchestra, you make recordings of Arabic music and recordings for television, and after a while it's boring. That is why I am working on earning my recognition to go back, so that they will be happy that I have come back to contribute something and not think, "Oh no, another person who needs a job."

It will take decades to change the structure of the government in Lebanon. Everything is connected to religious and social identity—all government positions are distributed according to quotas. The president must be a Christian Marronite, the prime minister a Muslim Sunni, the head of parliament a Muslim Shiite, and so on. Employment in Lebanon also follows a certain code of religion. For example, if there are too many cellists from the X religion in the orchestra or the conservatory, and you are the best in the world but happen to be of the X religion as well, you will not be accepted. This may not be the case in the music world, but in other fields and for bigger jobs it definitely is. This makes it very complicated to be liberal. If you want a job you have to belong to a religion or a political party. There are competitions, exams, interviews, and so on, but the person with the best connections and most sought-after religion will get the job. This happens everywhere, of course, but in Lebanon it is extreme.

The political situation forces you to belong to a group in order to get a job, which traps the young generation in a vicious cycle. It is very difficult to attain intellectual, social, and religious independence. Intellectual life is something that exists almost exclusively in Beirut, and outside Beirut the mentality is almost the same as it was two hundred years ago. People from northern Lebanon would emigrate to Australia before thinking of looking for a job in southern Lebanon. People inherit political ideas from their families without understanding anything, without reading one book on the subject. People do not choose their religions, and some want to leave their religion but are afraid. They don't see a way out because the economic situation does not allow them to be independent. Young people cannot afford to live alone. In many cases, people don't leave home until they marry; and even then, after they marry, often they build another floor above their parents' house to live in. Of course the economic situation cannot improve as long as there is so much violence in the region. You can't change your parents, but you also can't live against their will while you are living with them.

From the day I began to play in 1995, until today, the cello has taken me to a lot of places. It has taken me all over Europe. When we were on tour with the Divan in 2005, I thought that Buenos

Aires and São Paolo were the farthest places I could go with my cello. In Buenos Aires we played Schönberg's *Verklärte Nacht* for 3,500 people. In moments like this I always have to stop and think about where I started. These are like dreams for me; I never expected any of this. The moment we made the decision to go to Ramallah, though, I thought to myself: "My cello just took me one step farther. I crossed an uncrossable border." It was such a moment of confusion, standing at the checkpoint holding a Spanish diplomatic passport, exchanging words with an Israeli soldier, and then going beyond the checkpoint and getting on another bus. It was absurd, absolutely.

The audience gave us a standing ovation with ten minutes of applause before we even played one note. It's too much to explain. But then you have to concentrate on playing, and you forget about everything the moment you start. But when you finish and you look at the audience and you see the poster of Edward Said, and the Israelis have to be rushed out as soon as the concert is over, then you realize this is really a war business.

These are feelings you cannot talk about. I grew up with my Arab national heritage and the feeling of trying to fight against a conspiracy to separate the Arab countries in the Middle East. Going through this transformation and becoming non-religious, moderate, trying to understand Israeli suffering with the background I have, it's like schizophrenia in your head. Your inner feelings and your bad memories fight against your rational thoughts. But then, going into a land that you think of as Palestine through an Israeli checkpoint to meet other Israelis to make music together with them for the freedom of Palestine—it's simply too much to take in all at once. You cannot dream in your wildest dreams to have these emotional and intellectual ups and downs. And then you are behind the forbidden border with Israelis.

The Maestro at Work

In early July 2008, the Divan was invited to play a single concert in Marseille's Palais du Pharo to celebrate the beginning of France's European Union presidency and the founding of the Mediterranean Union. It was unusual for the orchestra to get together before the summer tour, which began in late July; this single concert was an exception in the history of the orchestra. It was a one-hour, all-Beethoven program: the *Leonore* Overture no. 3 and the Fifth Symphony. The orchestra had not played the symphony since the famous Ramallah concert in 2005, and there were some new members who had never played it at all.

Most youth orchestra conductors would play through the piece several times to make sure the orchestra knew it and felt secure. When I played in youth orchestras as a kid, we played through pieces so often that I always memorized my parts and spent rehearsals making silly faces at my friends while we played through a piece for the two-hundredth time. There was nothing else to concentrate on; the cello parts of the Haydn or early Mozart symphonies that we used to play were usually not very challenging.

Barenboim is of course not a youth orchestra conductor. He has never treated the West-Eastern Divan Orchestra like a youth orchestra. On the morning of the concert he rehearsed the Beethoven symphony for three hours in detail, with no run-throughs. He rehearsed as if the concert were two weeks away. He went to the root of every ensemble problem, rather than patching it up superficially.

If the first violins were faster than the second violins in a certain passage, Barenboim took every aspect of musical expression into consideration while analyzing the problem. How much bow was each section using? Did they start with the bow on the string or above it? Did they understand where the summit of the phrase was? Did they understand where the harmony changed, altering the course of the progression? Did they make the crescendo in the right place and at the same rate as the rest of the orchestra? Did they know which voice was the most important during this passage? In many orchestras, professional or not, these questions were never asked. If at all, they came up at the first rehearsal, not the last. Throughout the dress rehearsal, he made us all listen to the music with his ears.

Playing in an orchestra for the first time, or even the second or third, can be disorienting because all the voices that are clearly and separately audible from a distance are crowded into a small space: the stage. String players usually cannot hear what they are playing individually; they only hear the sound of their section, which plays the same part in unison. Wind players, on the other hand, hear themselves and the other wind players much louder than they hear the strings. This sometimes makes it difficult to know how loud or soft they should play. A good conductor balances the volume of different voices to maintain the transparency of the ensemble, so that the important voices come through while countermelodies can still be heard. A great conductor teaches the orchestra musicians to balance themselves based on what they hear and their knowledge of the score. This is what Barenboim did on the morning of the concert in Marseille: he continued teaching the orchestra how to listen, as he always does.

The third movement of the Beethoven symphony opens with the celli playing the theme in C Minor. First Barenboim made us play this phrase. Then he made us play the same theme when it returns after the first entrance of the second theme. There the first theme begins in B-flat minor and continues to modulate. With this simple comparison he was showing all of us how to listen with his ears. The difference in expression between the same theme in C minor and B-flat minor, before and after the entrance of the second theme, was now obvious to all the musicians in the orchestra, and they knew it from hearing as well as playing it.

Later, he tuned chords in the woodwinds and brass, making sure each musician knew which part of the chord he or she was playing, and how important that note was in relation to the others. This was Barenboim the teacher, the mentor, the orchestra's schooling and inspiration. In rehearsal, he taught the orchestra not only what to listen for but with which attitude to listen: neither as a dispassionate musicologist nor as an instrumentalist guided solely by feeling and intuition, but with exactly the right combination of intellectual analysis, emotion, and awe. In rehearsal, I felt everyone around me soaking up his words of wisdom, and in performance everything he had explained was audible. The orchestra absorbed his lessons and made his principles their own, not with academic obedience but with passion.

There was, however, a dark side to the Maestro's attention to detail: once a principle had been demonstrated and established, it was practically a personal affront to him not to uphold it constantly. This could bring forth the evil cousin of Barenboim the patient pedagogue: Barenboim the ominous ogre.

"Noooooo!!!" the kids were fond of yelling in imitation of their Maestro. "Here! Here! With me!" they would implore, while pointing to the end of an imaginary baton. If a musician transgressed during a concert, there was of course no yelling; there was only the "evil eye," which could be even more frightening. This could last for several bars, or until the inattentive victim had seen the error of his ways and glued his eyes to the baton. If the transgressor sat in the first stand of the string section, the effect of the evil eye might in the worst case be reinforced by rhythmic beating of the Maestro's baton on top of the metal stand. Almost worse than the evil eye was the sour-milk face, a wrinkling of the nose and turning down of the corners of the mouth, sometimes accompanied by shaking of the head or an upward-turned palm that asked: "Why?? Why are you doing this to the music?" Anyone on the receiving end of this expression knew that his or her transgression was so unforgivable that the Maestro could cope with it only by spitting it out like last month's unpasteurized milk.

After the concert, forgiveness was granted to all who had the courage to approach and apologize. Sometimes the sin had long been forgotten, except by the sinner. With the Maestro, punishment was usually doled out immediately so that the error could be promptly forgiven and forgotten. Since music was subject to the progression of time, the damage had to be left behind as soon as it was done. Thinking about a botched phrase while playing the next one meant focusing on the past rather than the fleeting present phrase.

When something happened, it was the musical offense itself, not the musician, which angered Barenboim. The Divan musicians seemed to grasp this distinction better than any other orchestra. I had seen adults, professionals, break down in tears because of Barenboim's relentless demands, and I always had the feeling that it was the result of an absurd misunderstanding. In a way, it was an error in translation. During rehearsal, Barenboim was concerned with nothing other than the language of music, and he had no patience for formalities and pleasantries that distracted from the power of his concentration. Most of the time, the musicians interpreted his outbursts of impatience in terms of everyday conversation rather than on his terms—in the minimalist, unadorned, efficient language he spoke to rehearse music.

The first rehearsal I ever played with the Staatskapelle Berlin after my appointment as temporary principal cellist was a dress rehearsal for a new production of *Parsifal*. At the end of the first act, the technical staff played the recorded bell soundtrack too soon, and at a deafening volume. After we had finished playing through the act, Barenboim scrambled up out of the orchestra pit, first climbing up onto his conductor's stool and then leaping over the railing into the house with fierce agility. Taking the microphone in his hand, he bellowed into it: "*Who* is responsible for this technical mess? Who is there backstage who can promise me that this *damned* technology will work in the premiere?! Give me a name, I want to know who is responsible!" A disembodied, resigned voice stated his name over the loudspeakers and promised Barenboim that he would personally see to it that everything worked properly for the premiere.

At that, Barenboim jumped back into the pit and continued rehearsing a few spots from the first act before dismissing the orchestra for a break. He carried on as if nothing had happened; he had let out the necessary steam, dealt with the problem, and everything was now back to normal. I looked around to see whether anyone else was suppressing giggles as I was, but most of the faces around me were professionally earnest.

This was not so in the Divan. There, humor was the salve that could be applied to almost any wound. It was always better to laugh than to cry. There were a handful of specialists in the orchestra who could imitate the Maestro to perfection in any situation, whether it was rage or rapture. When he was in good spirits, after a concert or on a flight, some of the musicians had no reservations about imitating the Maestro to the Maestro. One Egyptian violinist who conducted his own chamber orchestra in the United States was once allowed to lead the Divan through the entire *Leonore* Overture no. 3 because Barenboim wanted to go into the house to hear the balance of the instruments in the orchestra. The violinist had obviously been taking note of Barenboim's every gesture, facial expression, playful dance move, and stylistic nuance of baton technique; the impersonation was so complete that the winds and brass could hardly play for laughter. When Barenboim had heard enough from the house, he came back on stage and took a seat at the back of the orchestra, enjoying the parody and laughing with everyone else.

Unless he had important reasons to be elsewhere, Barenboim stayed in the same hotels with the Divan on tour, even when they were not very luxurious. Sometimes they were very luxurious, but that only guaranteed another threat to the nocturnal peace and quiet of the other guests: the all-night room party, better known as the "kimono party" (the "kimono" was in this case actually the hotel bathrobe.)

Barenboim traveled with the musicians throughout the tour and had dinner with them after concerts. Sometimes, arriving late to dinner, he would walk around the dining room with upturned palms and a look of consternation (not quite the sour-milk face), and ask: "Why are you all sitting like this? All the Spaniards together, all the Israelis together, all the Egyptians together, all the Jordanians and Palestinians together, all the Syrians and Lebanese together, and then the three Iranians! Why?"

Observing the dynamic between conductor and orchestra in the Divan, I have begun to suspect that Barenboim has finally found a worthy opponent and partner in the orchestra, and vice versa. In rehearsal, the musicians are absolutely obedient and respectful of the most minor musical detail; outside of rehearsal and performance, they are irreverent. Perhaps it is just conjecture, but it seems to me that this is one of the things Barenboim loves most about the orchestra: the Divan musicians carry out his every musical wish to the letter *and* have enough chutzpah to poke fun at anything, including the Maestro himself.

INTERMEZZO

Each section of an orchestra has its own personality, and the brass players are often regarded as the "football team" of the orchestra: they are often predominantly male, if not macho. They practice together, talk a lot about physical endurance, and look at the girls from their vantage point on risers behind the orchestra. This is the stereotype, which of course falls short of the truth in the Divan. It is not entirely inaccurate either, though.

Bassam Mussad, Boris Kertsman, and Yuval Shapiro made up the trumpet section from 2004 to 2007, and they were a motley team, if not the sort you would meet on a football field. They were often seen as a threesome on tour, at meals, and of course in the orchestra. Bassam is from Egypt; Boris and Yuval are from Israel. Thanks to his American passport, Bassam is one of the few Arab members of the orchestra, if not the only one, able to visit Israel as well as all the Arab countries, and he has made use of his advantage. Boris was his roommate for a time in Berlin, where they both played in the orchestral academy of the Staatskapelle Berlin, and he once invited Bassam to his family's house in Israel. The last I heard, Bassam was also planning a trip to Syria.

Bassam is a good-natured, even-tempered young man who finds it easy to remain level-headed in the midst of turbulent arguments. Yuval, on the other hand, is quite a different character. Easily provoked, he would often lose his temper during political discussions.

While the orchestra was on tour in 2006 in Cologne, a discussion was organized after dinner on a free day. It was one of the first discussions of the summer, because it had seemed impossible to talk about the war while it was going on, and a discussion about anything else would have been artificial. Barenboim and Mariam Said led the discussion, and Waltraud Meier was also there; she took the opportunity to express her admiration for the courage of all the musicians there, and her joy and surprise at being able to sing Wagner with an orchestra of Israelis and Arabs. During the discussion, Yuval stood up and started talking about the progression of his ideas over the years of his participation in the orchestra. He started out by saying, "I know you all think I'm obnoxious and a loudmouth." No one in the room protested or tried to reassure him that this was not the case. In fact, he was often the loudest one on the bus, in the hallways at night, or at the back of the orchestra: Barenboim always had to tell him to shut up and stop talking during rehearsal. But then Yuval explained that he had had a problem with his ears as a child, and that he had lost some of his hearing because of it. He wasn't always aware of the volume of his speaking voice, and he apologized for his behavior. Then he started to talk about his views.

> I admit that I first came to the Divan only because I wanted to play with Daniel Barenboim and because the repertoire was Mahler's First Symphony, which is great for trumpet. I was determined not to change any of my opinions and I wasn't interested in the discussion part of the orchestra at all. But then I started to realize after a while that some of my beliefs came from what I was taught in school, and I found out that I was taught some things that were not true.

He went on this way, and it turned out that he had been reading all the books that were available to the orchestra, books by the Israeli and Palestinian authors who had come to speak to them. He had begun a process of autodidactic re-education, and was on his way to a personal transformation. I spoke to him and Bassam on separate occasions about the same topics, and without knowing it they constructed a lively dialogue.

From the Trumpet Section: Yuval Shapiro and Bassam Mussad

Yuval

When I met Mr. Barenboim, I told him the story of how my father became a musician: on his first day of school in Tel Aviv, the principal showed the kids around the classrooms and then said, "Now Danny from the fifth grade will play something for you on the piano." My father went home and wanted to play the piano too, but his family couldn't afford one, so he started playing the accordion. When he got older, he made a career out of it and accompanied every big-name singer in Israel. Then, at twenty-four, he changed to percussion, and three or four years later he got into the Israel Philharmonic as a percussionist. When Barenboim came to conduct the opera *Wozzeck* in 1991, my father was playing the accordion in the stage band, and Barenboim asked him, "How come a percussionist can play the accordion?"

He said, "Because of you." Daniel Barenboim was Danny from the fifth grade. He was the reason my father became a musician.

My father has quite right-wing opinions, but my mother's brother was a novelist and journalist who was very active in the left-wing scene in Tel Aviv, although he was not a politician. He had a big Internet site starting in 1995, and he used to write a blog (before there even was such a thing) about everything that was happening in Israel regarding the Middle Eastern conflict. He wrote in English very well; he was a Harvard graduate. I remember hearing these discussions all the time at home, at Friday night Shabbat dinners—they were always very heated.

My own opinion about the conflict until after I finished high school was definitely: "Well, we're here and we're not moving." Before I went to the Divan in 2005 my dad said to me, "Look, they're going to brainwash you," and I said, "No they're not. Anyway, I have my opinion, it's me. I'm not under any pressure to change."

I came to the Divan thinking I just wanted to play Mahler with Daniel Barenboim and go on this great tour to Argentina and all over the place. To be honest, practically everybody who comes to the Divan for the first time says this. I don't know if it's only an Israeli thing, or a big ego thing, but I hear it all the time. When I hear new people coming and saying, "Yeah, well I'm not gonna go to the discussions and listen, it's a waste of time because I need to practice; I'm not gonna get involved, I don't care," I just laugh and think, "Yeah, right. That's a big phoney baloney because you cannot ignore it. You'll see."

In my first week I was just being myself with all the Israeli guys I knew from before, and I was busy doing new things like playing the German trumpet for the first time and having lessons with Konradin Groth from the Berlin Philharmonic. Then, slowly, I couldn't avoid getting involved. I had to listen to what people were saying. We saw some movies and heard some discussions, and I saw that these were normal people on the other side. I didn't expect them to be animals, of course—never had I ever thought so—but they were just regular people.

Bassam

I was studying at the Manhattan School of Music when I heard about the Divan for the first time. In the cafeteria I met Maria, a

Syrian violinist from the Divan who was studying at the Manhattan School too, and we started talking. She told me about this orchestra and said I should apply. I didn't know her—I didn't really have any contact with her apart from this one time, but I sent a CD to apply for the orchestra and I got in.

I was born in Sudan, where my parents were working as Evangelical Protestant missionaries. They met while they were working there, but they are both Egyptian. We used to spend a few months a year in Egypt, but I lived and went to school in Sudan until I was nine years old.

That was when we moved to Pasadena, California, where my father went to get his doctorate in Islamic studies. It was around then that I started to play the trumpet. It was funny how I started playing; at school you could sign up for a band instrument, and I wanted to play the saxophone. My English was okay, but I confused the names of the instruments: I signed up for a trumpet but I was expecting to get a saxophone. When I opened the case I said, "Wait a minute, there must be a mistake, this is a saxophone." They said, "No, it's a trumpet." Then, when they finally convinced me I had the names wrong, I asked for a saxophone but they said they didn't have any more, so I was stuck with the trumpet. I kept playing, and in my senior year of high school I decided I wanted to study music.

I had very little to do with the Middle Eastern conflict and really didn't know much about it before coming to the Divan. I was very interested in everything, though, so I would just go and listen. The summer before my first Divan workshop, I went to a bookstore and by chance picked up a book by Edward Said, *The Politics of Dispossession*, and started reading it. Later, when I got my acceptance letter from the Divan, I saw that it had been co-founded by him, which I hadn't known before. I was very sad because I had wanted to meet him that summer, and I found out that he had just passed away a few months earlier. His book was my first insight into the whole thing.

Yuval

In the beginning, I didn't know anybody from the other side; I didn't understand. When I was in the army band, sometimes they would just send me and a drummer to play fanfares at these military ceremonies. I had been to bases in Gush Etzion (in the occupied territories) and all around, so I'd driven through these places and seen how life was there, but I still didn't really know. We never got stopped at any checkpoint in an army vehicle, of course. My opinion about the situation was that they were trying to attack us all the time for no reason and we would retaliate. I had no idea that they were retaliating against the way we were forcing their lives to be.

Mustafa Barghouti came to give a talk about the wall my first year and the Israelis were so offended that it turned into a long discussion. Everyone would stand up and say, "First of all, I want to say I'm against the wall, *but* . . ." and everybody was going on like this. Finally I stood up and said, "Well, I'm not so much against the wall, and I don't think it's *so* bad because if you look statistically, there are fewer terrorist attacks in Israel now." I think everybody was completely shocked at what I said. Then at some point Bassam stood up and said, "I don't get it, why are you all so self-defensive about the Israeli government's actions? If the American government does something, not everybody protects the president; it's not like a national thing: 'Oh my God, America has done something bad, we must defend its name though it was bad.'" For some reason Israelis automatically feel this way, it's like a collective responsibility.

All these discussions went on into the night and got really intense. I remember speaking to a Syrian violinist and another Palestinian girl from Lebanon who never came back to the Divan. It was just Bassam and me and these two girls, and we were speaking for hours and could not understand the basics of each other's arguments. I finally realized that these basic things, these little triggers made each of us react instinctively but *so* differently, at least when we talked about the wall. If we talked about food or something, I don't think our reactions would be so different.

It was so sad; I felt it was just terrible that we couldn't see eye to eye. And from that point on I thought, "Okay, I can't just be a musician here."

Bassam

My family doesn't hate Jews or Israelis; they're very liberal people who never had any direct contact with the Middle Eastern conflict. My first impression of the Divan workshop was: "Wow, look at these people, they really get inflamed when they talk about politics," especially the Israelis. We saw this documentary, *Route 181*, and all the Israelis just walked out. I thought they all had something else to do; I didn't realize what was going on, only afterward I found out that they were all really upset. I was shocked. If somebody showed a movie about the bad things the United States did, American teenagers would not get upset.

I listened to all their discussions without knowing much about the background, but I've learned a lot through this orchestra, and now I have a much more personal connection to the political situation there than I ever thought I would. In Berlin, where I'm studying in the academy of the Staatskapelle, I live with an Israeli, Boris, who is my other trumpet colleague in the Divan. I have lots of Israeli friends, and I even went to Ramallah for a month to teach.

I like to let people go at it in the Divan. That's how I learn. I've often watched Yuval going at it with other people. When he first came to the Divan, he was very defensive about any sort of political issues. Not only was he very defensive, he could articulate what he believed—he's a good debater. Since then he's changed a lot in many ways and learned many things. He knew a lot when he first came to the Divan, but what he knew was only from an Israeli perspective.

Yuval is a special person; he knows what he wants and does what he wants. He doesn't care much about what people think or say, so we're a bit different that way. It's been interesting to see him develop over these last three years. He's learned many things about the Arabs, how they think, their mentality. One time he was absolutely shocked that Nabeel Abboud-Ashkar from Nazareth would call himself a Palestinian. He said, "You have an Israeli passport, you're an Israeli Arab!"

Yuval was shocked, and he doesn't hide his shock—he doesn't pretend like he knows something he doesn't. When he learns something, he really learns it. He likes to speak to people and engage people in conversation. He doesn't like to talk about nonsense. He likes to hear what people have to say. He wants to know what you think about something, and he'll tell you what he thinks.

Many Israelis actually feel the same way Yuval does, but they don't say it. At least he says it; they should respect him for that. In fact, some people in the orchestra are much more conservative than he is. I think it's not his fault if someone doesn't like him because of his political views. It's just that he expresses himself very openly and directly.

Yuval

The year of the war in Lebanon was really terrible. I left for Germany to audition for the Musikhochschule in Karlsruhe the day before those two Israeli soldiers in the north were kidnapped. I was sitting in the Internet café in Karlsruhe reading the news and thinking, *uh-oh*. My mom wrote me an e-mail: "I think we should call and ask if the Divan is still going to happen." I said I didn't think it would be cancelled, but it would definitely be very, very strange. I told her it's not some kindergarten camp where you have to call the teacher and ask, "Is it still happening?"

It did happen, but when we got there it was so depressing. There were no Lebanese and too few Arabs in general, and way too many

Israelis. It felt like there were just too many of us. Every time Barenboim said, "This is not an Arab orchestra with some Israeli members in it or an Israeli orchestra with some Arab members in it," I thought, *Yes it is!* Then there was that stupid declaration against the war. That was one of the stupidest things I encountered in the last three years in the Divan.

It was a stupid thing to do because it made a political statement. We're not idiots, all of us know this is a political place; no other youth orchestra holds press conferences with dozens of cameras and reporters; no other youth orchestra gets interviewed all the time or has two secretaries who follow them around to handle the media. They say it's not political but that's bullshit—it is political and we all know it, and we don't care. It's part of what it is and it's great, so we do it. I personally have answered questions at press conferences a few times, but I have this problem that my words get stuck, so I'm not used as often as Daniel Cohen, for example. However, I have spoken sometimes and I don't mind. Then Barenboim came up with this declaration that he claimed was not political; he claimed it was humane or general. I sat up until 5:30 in the morning trying to rewrite this unbalanced sentence in it about the uprooting and the infrastructure. I sat with a pianist from Nazareth and some other people, and we could not understand the point of it.

That year, an Egyptian musician and I got to talking about what we learned in school, and we sat down and went through the histories of our countries as we were taught them, starting from the beginning of the Zionist movement. I'm not a big historian; a lot of times I didn't pay attention in class or didn't care much, so I had to use every bit of memory I had to tell the story of what I knew. It was so crazy to hear the exact opposite story about the same event from the Egyptian point of view! A few other people, Israelis and Jordanians, were there too, pitching in a little bit here and there, but it was basically my Egyptian friend and me saying what we knew. It was actually very emotional; both of us were crying at some stage because we could not believe what the other was saying.

Half-jokingly, I said, "Well, obviously the '67 borders aren't enough for you guys, we should go back to '49," and he said, "Not '49, *'47*." He wasn't joking, he was serious.

One of the hardest things to deal with in that conversation was the fact that he and the other Arabs felt the need to compare things to the Holocaust. They said, "Well, the life in the refugee camps is practically like life in the ghetto." I just cannot hear this, I still cannot believe this. No matter how many pictures Ramzi brings to show us or how many stories people tell, I don't believe it. People were forced to live this way in the ghetto, they had no other way. Some of these refugee camps in the West Bank date to 1949—they're not like camps anymore, they're like cities. They have sewer systems, running water, electricity.

We kept going on and on, but by the time we got to the 1973 war and the peace treaty in 1978 between Begin and Sadat, it was the middle of the night and we stopped; it was just too much.

Another time I told my Egyptian friend how I had spent a week in Sinai for the first time in April, a few months before the Divan. A lot of Israelis do this, but before I went to the Divan I had always said there was no way I would ever go to Egypt. Then we went to Ramallah with the Divan in my first year, and after that I said, "I think I want to go to Sinai."

My parents were hysterical about my going there, and while I was in Sinai there was a suicide bombing in Israel. My parents called me and said, "There was a bombing. You have to come back."

I asked, "Where was the bombing?"

"In Tel Aviv," they said.

"I'm in the desert and there was a bombing where *you* live, and I should come back to where *you* live?"

"Never mind that, you have to come back."

"I'm coming back in two days, leave me alone," I said.

It was the craziest moment. Anyway, I showed my Egyptian friend from the orchestra the Egyptian stamp in my passport and he said, "That's very nice. I wish I could go to Israel for vacation and come back without losing my job and possibly being held at the border for ten hours."

I think he didn't come to Ramallah with us because he was too scared of the consequences. Before we went, he asked, "What if the Egyptians see that I got a stamp when I left Europe? Then I go back to Egypt four days later but I don't have a stamp that shows where I was those four days because I used the Spanish diplomatic passport. What if they ask me where I was for those four days? What will I say?"

We asked, "Are they so fanatic?"

He said, "Yes they are, and if they see I was there, there will be such shit."

Egypt has been at peace with Israel for thirty years! I said, "I've been to Egypt. Why can't you come to Israel?"

This is when we stopped talking about the subject because it was really, really terrible.

Bassam

I don't like conflict when it involves me, but when it involves two other people I'm happy to watch. I think it's important for people to deal with conflict; that's what this workshop is all about. They may be a little aggressive while they're having the conversation, but later, when they're a bit calmer, they start to think about the things the other person said. That's just the nature of this kind of conversation. They get all fired up and you feel that one person's not listening to the other person. I've seen people change, so I know they think about these things later. Or I hope so, at least. I know that it's true in Yuval's case.

When I'm in the orchestra, I try to spend time with people from different places. I speak English and Arabic and a bit of

Spanish too, and because I live with an Israeli, I learn little bits of Hebrew just for fun. When things start to flare up politically in the region, I get into discussions with my friends in Berlin, too. With the Israelis I always try to speak for the Palestinians and vice versa. I don't think it's an even conflict, or that both sides are equally to blame, but I think there are faults on both sides, naturally. It's important for people to recognize that their own people have faults, so that's what I try to do when I speak with them. But I want to sympathize with them too. I can understand why they feel the way they do.

While I was teaching in Ramallah, I heard a lot about people's situations first-hand. People would just start telling me what things were like. They were curious, because after I would say two words, they could tell I was Egyptian from my accent. They don't see many Egyptians, so they wanted to tell me about what's happening. I learned a lot about how people feel there just by going out and buying a *shawarma* (an Arabic roasted meat sandwich) or talking to taxi drivers.

People in Ramallah said things like, "You see what the Jews are doing to us!" This was all very surprising to me. The people there are basically very upset. There were very negative sentiments. It was basically everyone who felt this way. I never met anyone who said, "Oh, it's not so bad." Maybe they just want to pity themselves, or maybe they really do feel that way, but everybody was angry. Everybody had a story about it.

They live their lives, and they're actually happy people, surprisingly. It's encouraging and inspiring that they do the things they do when they're actually living in a cage. I understand how they can be upset. Since people knew I was coming from the outside, they liked to let me know that they were not happy with what was going on.

I went out with the older kids I taught in Ramallah, who were about seventeen or eighteen. I learned a lot about how they live. Most of the kids in Ramallah have everything that other teenagers in Europe have: televisions, computer games, and other distractions. They have everything, except the freedom to come and go as they please. At the end of my time there, we had a youth orchestra concert, which was such a rewarding experience. One kid came up to me afterward and said to me in English (it was the first time he spoke to me in English), "When we were standing up there and all the people were clapping, I felt like it was something really glorious," and he was standing up really proud for at least an hour.

In Nablus, a smaller city in the West Bank, kids have fewer distractions; I went there three times to teach. We always traveled in a group with the other teachers from the Barenboim–Said Foundation. Going to Nablus is very difficult. It's not very far away from Ramallah but it takes a very long time to get there. The checkpoint there is a walk-through checkpoint; cars can't go through. You take a taxi to the checkpoint and then walk through and take another taxi on the other side.

When I went to Ramallah I saw posters of young men with guns along the streets. I asked someone, "Who are all these people?" and they said, "They're martyrs."

This was a bit scary for me, but in Nablus there were so many more posters. In Ramallah there were maybe ten or eleven posters around the city, but in Nablus there were so, so many, all over the walls—huge posters that say "in memory of." I didn't really like it much; it makes a big impression on young kids who see all these people who are glorified for this.

After I was told what these people were, I said, "Oh, so these people are militants?"

"No," they said, "they're martyrs."

On the one hand, it's just terrible that militants are glorified like that. On the other hand, you can understand how somebody coming from Nablus has nothing to lose, and would do something they thought might have an effect. Seeing the settlements is really eye-opening, too. Going from Ramallah to Nablus, you go through all these settlements that are like huge cities on mountaintops with walls and security, right next to Arab villages. The settlements have red roofs, so you can tell a settlement very easily from an Arab village. The settlers are totally safe; what are the Arabs going to do? They're not allowed to build anything on the land they own, and here's a settlement right next to them. The only thing they can do is to throw stones across the wall. The settlements are very well guarded by the Israeli army. To hear about this in the news is one thing, but to see a settlement right next to a village is another.

One time, one of my students from Ramallah showed me a picture on his cell phone of him holding a gun. He said he had seen some guy on the street with this gun and asked him if he could take a picture with it. I said, "Listen, I'd prefer to see pictures of you with your instrument than of you with a gun."

He said, "Yeah, yeah."

Yuval

I think that part of the Palestinian problem is that they have to start feeling responsible for themselves, they have to say, "We were responsible for not helping ourselves or for feeling bad for ourselves for the last sixty years and not trying to do something." You can't always blame the lack of leadership; it comes from within, I think. It's easy for me to say, I guess; I was born in a democratic country, I always lived in a house and had a car and never lacked anything.

There are many successful, rich Arabs who live abroad. Do you mean to tell me they can't support the Palestinian people? Why, for the last sixty years, has no one said, "Enough of this, let's try to help ourselves"? The Palestinians are always waiting for somebody to recognize their pain. I just don't get it. I could understand it if somebody told me now that Israel has been butchering the Palestinians the whole time and they had no way to help themselves because there was no chance Israel would let them. But it's not true. People say that from 1967 until the '80s the Palestinians were happy. Okay, I'm sure this is a myth—I'm sure they were not thrilled to be occupied by the Israelis, but they worked in Israel and they were sending home loads of cash, much more than when they were under Jordan. Until the First Intifada, they had a lot more opportunities to help themselves.

When Joschka Fischer came to talk to us in Berlin in 2006 while we were on tour with the Divan, I asked him, "Just hypothetically, what if Jordan decided that all these refugee camps along the river would now become Palestine?" He replied, "No, no, you don't want to go there. You already have peace with Jordan. You don't want to bring up the subject of the Palestinians and Jordan again. It's none of your business." So everybody moved on and nobody paid attention to the question.

I read *One Country* by the Palestinian author Ali Abunimah, who came to speak to us in 2007; it's about how two countries for two peoples won't work. It should be one country for two peoples. I got really scared reading it. I agreed with many things he had to say but I really freaked out about it, too. The Jews really wanted Israel, and we Israelis made so many mistakes. Now some people are saying we should make one nation, and it's insane. Two states for two nations is almost the mainstream concept now; even on the extreme right, there's always someone who wants to give the Palestinians a country.

My biggest question which is still unanswered is: What if Israel decided to have two states and gave the Palestinians the exact amount of land they had according to the 1967 borders? I wonder how many of the Israeli Palestinians would want to go there and give up their Israeli passports and all the rights and privileges they have there to become Palestinian citizens. You can't ask that, though, because you'll be attacked. One thing I did learn from the Divan is that you have to filter your questions.

I've spoken to Ramzi a few times about the Palestinian situation, and it was really interesting. I really like Ramzi. I can't believe this guy was actually throwing rocks in '86—it's crazy. When I was a very young kid in pre-school, every Friday you would hear that there were some disturbances around the Temple Mount, and I never really understood what it meant. Growing up in Tel Aviv I had no idea what Jerusalem looked like, and they always talked about these kids throwing rocks. I said, "What? Why are these kids throwing rocks all the time? I'm not throwing rocks!" And when Ramzi showed these pictures of him as a kid throwing rocks, I couldn't believe it. He was on that side. It was so strange for me. It was obvious why he was doing it, everyone was doing it. I guess that was when they started to try to help themselves, but they chose the wrong way for the Palestinian nation.

I asked him many things about what it was like in Ramallah. He gave me a map showing how Palestine became smaller and smaller over the last forty years with each successive peace plan. First there was 1947, and then 1967, and then Camp David, when Barak made an offer and Arafat said no. You can see why he said no; we always thought Barak was insane because he was giving the Palestinians way too much, and people in Israel would never agree to such a big concession, but it wasn't like that. There was a big map of where the wall goes. It showed how they separated one Palestinian town from another in order to make a little passageway for Israelis to get to the settlements. To get from a town on one side of the settlements to a town on the other side, you have to drive for four hours. I actually studied these maps very carefully, and reading them was very upsetting.

The maps changed my opinion about the wall, and I think it should just take a different route. They talk about how a bunch of settlements make a *gush*, a block, and about trying to get people to live in blocks so they won't be so scattered and there will be less suffering for the Palestinians. Some of these settlements are just two trailers and a generator, and I don't know the exact numbers of how many people live in settlements. The question is, what should we do? You cannot argue with the fact that terror has been dramatically reduced since the wall was built. If I said this to some guy from the Divan he would freak out. I said this once to a Palestinian musician from Jordan, and he said, "It's not terrorism, it's resistance." Then it turned into a big fight and Bassam was with me; he's always the peacemaker, the neutral one, with the American way. He said, "Wait a minute—terrorist acts and suicide bombers cannot be a legitimate means of resistance."

The worst part about the Divan is when you go home after the workshop and people there hear little bits about the things we did: this letter we signed, and how we went to Ramallah. They say, "How could you have done that?" I say, "You've been misinformed, you didn't hear the whole story, you don't understand." They say, "You've been brainwashed."

It happens on the other side, too. People go home, and their friends say, "You played with Israelis? Are you crazy?"

Bassam

There is some truth to what Yuval says about self-pity in Palestine, but it's not entirely true. The Palestinians do have an infrastructure. Ramallah is a working city; it's amazing that it does work in a cage. The other thing is that, since Hamas has been in power, the United States and Europe have cut all aid to Palestine, so it's very difficult to continue building an infrastructure.

The Jews are experts at building things up; it's amazing that a country like Israel could be built in sixty years in the middle of the Arab world. This is my contention: instead of just giving the Palestinians money (Israel does give them money), Israel should really take the lead in developing infrastructure and educational projects in Palestine. These are the things that are really going to get people to be less radical. Just giving them money is not enough. When people have the things they need for life—and I do not mean luxuries: when their electricity is not being cut off, when they have jobs and the things they need in order to support families—then they will be much less likely to be radical. I think this is also the problem with Iraq: America thinks it has to kill all the terrorists first and then start building infrastructure, but it should be the other way around.

I'm not saying Israel should completely open the borders, but something has to start happening slowly. It's easy to sit here and say it; it's very difficult to actually do it.

Yuval

Before I came to the Divan in 2005, I was driving with an Israeli trombone player, and we were listening to Wagner overtures. I said, "It would be so nice to play Wagner in the Divan," and he said, "You know, that's a good idea—we should ask Barenboim about it."

So he and an Israeli horn player went to Barenboim as soon as they got there and asked him about it. He said, "What a good idea! I never thought of that." So he decided we would play the Prelude and *Liebestod* from *Tristan und Isolde*. They got the music from Berlin and then it happened. It was great, but of course all the discussions about it were really intense.

I remember our first Wagner rehearsal very well. The trumpet section decided I would play first trumpet. It's not a big deal; it's only about four bars. There were video cameras there in Pilas— it was a big thing; and I think Sharon Cohen and another girl left crying, and the cameras swooped around and followed them out. I thought it was so ridiculous. I was very proactive for the idea of playing Wagner only for historical reasons. It was so important; how could you not play this music? I thought this would be the best opportunity *ever* for Israelis to play Wagner unless they got into a German orchestra someday. I thought the people who were feeling bad about it had no reason to feel so bad.

One of my high school music teachers was a retired trombone player from the Israel Philharmonic. He played the second trombone there from 1955 until the '80s, and he was a very good teacher. He had stayed in Europe until the Second World War began, and then he had to escape. He lived in the woods for six years and then came to Israel in 1947 or '48. He had very strong feelings about Wagner. When Zubin Mehta wanted to play Wagner with the orchestra, my teacher stood up and said, "Not as long as I'm alive." He was also a member of the orchestra committee, so the orchestra decided that they would continue the ban until after that generation retired.

The Israel Philharmonic was founded as the Palestine Symphony Orchestra in 1936, and they played Wagner regularly in the first two years. After Kristallnacht in 1938, they decided to ban Wagner from their repertoire; his music became taboo in Israel. I think it's stupid, it's terrible. We have German trains, we have BMWs and Volkswagens, we have AEG and Bosch power tools; everything is okay except this composer who died in 1883. Most people in Israel only know Wagner from Bugs Bunny cartoons: you know, when Elmer Fudd sings "Kill the wabbit" to the melody of the "Ride of the Valkyries."

One girl said, "My grandfather was in the death camps," and I said, "Do you think you're honoring his memory if you decide never to play Wagner?"

I have this idea about how you should have an experience and not overdo it, and I think three years in one place is enough. First of all, why shouldn't other people, other trumpet players, go to the Divan also? I think this experience should be a global one. I would sacrifice my chair for another young trumpet player.

It's also stressful to go through the discussions. People already know I have a short temper, and they expect me to get emotional and loud and opinionated and go wild. I don't want people to have these expectations about me; that's not what I'm about, I hope.

This orchestra will not last forever; we have to be realistic and see that. The orchestra will not work without Daniel Barenboim. If he decides he's tired of it, it will stop, and I want other people to go through what I went through while it still exists. My friends from the Divan say, "But we like you there and you like it there and it won't be the same without you."

I tell them, "Look, the cemeteries are filled with people you cannot live without."

The orchestra will go on without me and without most people, except for Barenboim, so I think other people should experience this as well. I'd love to never stop coming, I'd love for it to be a permanent orchestra, but come on, we have to be realistic.

In a way, the workshop is like a great way to take a vacation: you play with this great conductor in fantastic halls and stay in nice hotels. The only thing is that there's this stress that you have to discuss things. I guess if we weren't forced to, we wouldn't do it. If they didn't tell us, "Okay, now we're going to sit down and discuss," we wouldn't. People don't like to dig in their own sores; it's a painful thing, you don't want to do it.

I think the main purpose of the orchestra is to teach us about music and how to play in an orchestra. The fact that we're not a professional orchestra makes it all the more amazing that Barenboim can take us to such a high musical level. It's fascinating to listen to him talk, too.

Secondly, I think it's a big deal to try to get the musicians to realize that, when the music starts, you might think differently about everything else in the world, but you have to play together. When we play, we really play together and it's a great thing. In the trumpet section, I learn a lot from Bassam and I think he learns a lot from me. We want to sound great as a section and I hope we do.

This orchestra is so symbolic. Why do all these newspapers care about us? It's too much of a big deal; it's a youth orchestra and we make DVDs and CDs and win prizes and have all this publicity. I don't know if it's necessarily a good thing. I like how Barenboim says that the Divan is a democratic society; it's just too bad it's such a small one. I hope this will continue for many, many years, and I hope a lot of people get to be part of it. I think many more people should be exposed to this personally and not through story-telling in the media.

INTERMEZZO

A member of the Divan since 2001, flutist Guy Eshed grew up right in the middle of Tel Aviv, the happiest city he could think of. It was not a happy city in the normal sense; it was a city in a bubble. There was no feeling of conflict, no sense that this city was in the middle of a country at war. It was a hedonistic place, a seaside "non-stop city" where you could go for pizza or buy shampoo in the middle of the night. It was an ugly city according to people from Jerusalem. There was Bauhaus architecture in old Tel Aviv, but apart from that there was nothing to see, really. It was a place to enjoy food, the beach, and a liberal cultural life.

Guy was always conscious of the Middle Eastern conflict. His parents were very liberal, and Guy himself became a member of the peace organization Shalom Akshav (Peace Now) at fifteen. He often joined their political demonstrations in the city. His awareness was exceptional for the Tel Aviv mentality, however. People read and saw all the same news in Tel Aviv as in the rest of the country, but the news was not part of conversation in Tel Aviv. It didn't belong to the city's atmosphere.

It felt extremely safe to be in Tel Aviv, just a few kilometers away from the checkpoints and occupied territories. It was almost as if the city's special energy could protect its residents from the conflict outside. Guy thought Tel Aviv's hedonism might be an unconscious escape from the violent reality in the rest of the country. It was a place where you could live the way you might be able to in Paris,

London, or New York. Those were the cities Tel Aviv still looked up to and tried to imitate. There was a lot of humor in Tel Aviv about the tense political situation, but to Guy, this was the humor of a people without a nation. There was an undeniable connection between humor and escape, which was sometimes positive; Jewish humor had helped some Holocaust survivors to mentally escape their suffering. This Jewish sarcasm had not changed in sixty years, even though the status of the Jews had changed dramatically: they had gone from being persecuted to being in power. The Jews now had their own state and responsibilities. Guy sometimes wished that Jewish humor would update itself.

In 2005 Guy went to Ramallah with the Divan orchestra, but he did not see anything outside the hall until the following year, when he performed there with Barenboim and a small group from the Jerusalem International Chamber Music Festival. During his first visit he had been given a Spanish diplomatic passport and, like all the other Israelis in the orchestra, he was not allowed leave the yard of the Cultural Palace in Ramallah for security reasons. The next time he went to Ramallah, he showed his German passport when they crossed the checkpoint (Guy's maternal grandparents were born in Hamburg, which entitled him to German citizenship). They went to Al Kamandjati, Ramzi Aburedwan's music school in Ramallah's old city, where Guy performed a solo piece for flute. Barenboim performed Schubert's *Trout Quintet* with his son Michael, among others, and Michael played a violin sonata with his father.

After it was over, they were invited to Ramzi's family home in a refugee camp that adjoined Ramallah. Guy was not afraid to be there, even if their small group attracted a lot of attention in the neighborhood's narrow alleyways. Children approached tentatively and then ran away. The houses here had been built thoughtlessly and carelessly, with no regard for structure. It was heartbreaking to see the disorganization, the poverty, and the hardship of life in the refugee camp. Guy kept quiet about where he came from when they entered Ramzi's grandfather's house, although he was sure they would have welcomed him anyway. Ramzi's family was very warm and hospitable. They were eager to share what they had, even if it was not very much. Guy and the visiting group followed the family up the crooked stairs to the roof, which was the only place in the house where they could all sit together. They ate on mattresses the family had placed on the floor.

Standing up on the roof and looking out over Ramallah's "skyline," an uneven collection of houses with Palestinian flags flying from nearly every roof, Guy thought this was something every Israeli should see. He felt like he was in a different country under different skies, even though he was 20 minutes away from Jerusalem. There was such power in the stark contrast between the simple, poorly built houses and the pride expressed by all those waving flags. He could feel the people's thirst to have their own place and be recognized. It was a proud city, but a sad one.

As they drove back to Jerusalem, Barenboim and the other musicians spoke about how easy it would be and how little it would cost for the Israeli government to provide Palestinians with better living conditions. The whole visit in Ramallah lasted only two and a half hours, from the concert to the meal at Ramzi's grandfather's house, but Guy went back to the happy city of Tel Aviv with his unforgettable memories of the sad city of Ramallah. There could be no happiness without sadness, and vice versa, but why did the two emotions have to be concentrated and separated in this territory?

Tyme Khleifi

I was born in Jerusalem and lived there until I was five years old. After that we moved to an area east of Jerusalem and very close to Ramallah, because my parents wanted my brother and me to join the Friends School in Ramallah, which is considered to be the best in Palestine. My mother used to work for the British Council and commuted to work every day, which was always difficult. However, as soon as the Second Intifada started, it became almost impossible. The daily journey to and from work took her several hours because she had to wait at many checkpoints. She was tired of spending so much time on the road, so eventually she quit her job and we moved to Ramallah.

Although they don't have an especially musical background, my parents have always listened to classical and Arabian music, so I grew up with music. When I was seven years old, they received a letter from the newly formed National Conservatory of Music in Ramallah (now the Edward Said National Conservatory of Music) inviting young students to enroll. When the conservatory first opened, they only taught violin, piano, and oud. I didn't even know what a violin looked like, so my father explained it to me. A Palestinian music teacher who lived in Jordan then came to our school to show us the violin. I liked the instrument and its sound, so I decided to try it out. That's how it all started.

My first teacher, the same man from Jordan, was very good with kids, and made lessons fun. He made me like the violin even more, but he was unable to teach at an advanced level, so I didn't really get anywhere with the instrument. Generally, the teachers at the conservatory came from Europe or the United States. Because of the problematic political situation in Ramallah, they would stay for a maximum of one year, and this was usually interrupted by frequent visits back to their countries. As a result, the conservatory had to find new teachers regularly, and my musical education was unstable. I had a series of nine teachers in five years. There were times when I thought it was pointless to continue. I had little musical motivation, and did not gain much from my lessons in general. In fact, the conservatory was not always able to provide a violin teacher, so I sometimes didn't have one at all. I didn't want to give up just because I had no teacher, so I decided to be patient.

The first time I started learning seriously was when I was eleven years old, and professor Edward Said arranged for a violin teacher to come to Ramallah from Chicago. This violin teacher also had to travel back and forth to the US because she had other commitments. I had a good five months with her after a long dry period. As soon as she came, she commented on my playing, and said, "Okay, this is ridiculous. You're not allowed to hold the violin like this, let's start only with the bow." She concentrated mainly on technique; we worked on my bow grip, for example. Unfortunately, she too left eventually, and after that we got another teacher who came from the Golan Heights. I thought that because he didn't come from abroad he might stay for a longer period, but sadly he only stayed for a year.

In May 2003, a group from the newly established Barenboim–Said Foundation came to Palestine. One of them was Julien Salemkour, Mr. Barenboim's assistant at the German State Opera and the director of the Foundation's activities in the West Bank at the time. He had visited us in 2002, and I enjoyed the harmony class he gave then. I assumed that he would not return either, though, so I was surprised to meet him again and to meet two other musicians he brought with him from Germany: Anna-Sophie Brüning, a violinist, and her husband, Johannes Brüggemann, an oboist.

At the beginning, the Barenboim–Said Foundation started a project in Ramallah in partnership with the conservatory, and that was how I first started studying with Anna. The conservatory had another violin teacher, though, and I was already studying with her when Anna arrived. At first I studied with both of them, as I was officially a student at the conservatory, but after a few months I decided to study with Anna Brüning alone. I studied with Anna for about two and a half years: the longest time I had ever stayed with one single teacher. Of course, Anna had commitments in Germany and had to leave the country regularly, but she always made up for lost time. She was my first steady teacher.

Two years later, the Barenboim–Said Foundation became completely independent. Gradually they formed an orchestra; they hired more teachers, including a cello teacher, which we had never had before. Johannes taught the oboe and Anna taught the violin and the viola. We had a chamber orchestra made up of strings, flutes, and Johannes on the oboe. After a few months we were able to give a small concert in Ramallah.

Through Anna and Johannes, I found out about the West-Eastern Divan Orchestra and its workshops. After meeting with my parents, Anna and her colleagues invited me to attend a Divan workshop as an auditor along with five other students from the conservatory. I had never heard a symphony orchestra before. I was shocked. I thought, "My God, people can actually play!" They were playing Beethoven's Third Symphony and Schubert's "Unfinished" Symphony that year.

I was happy to find out that I would be coming back the following year, in 2004, but again I was only invited as an auditor. The orchestra played Tchaikovsky's Fifth Symphony. I practiced the first movement before the workshop, and during the workshop I asked Mr. Barenboim if I could take part in the rehearsals. He said, "Of course, you are most welcome." After that I was motivated to practice harder, and I learned the other three movements so that I could play in all the rehearsals. Mr. Barenboim decided to invite me to join the orchestra on tour. I was only thirteen years old, so he called my mother to ask her permission to take me on tour; she gave him her blessing. It was my first experience with a big orchestra.

The fact that I have an Israeli passport means that I can travel from Ben Gurion Airport in Tel Aviv. When I travel with the Israeli Divan members they do not get hassled by airport security, but I always receive different treatment, and more time is spent searching me and my luggage because of where I live.

Leaving Israel is a big problem for me when traveling. At the airport they always ask me, "What kind of name is this?" I say, "Arab," and then they put a paper with the number 6 on my passport. There is a number system for security from 1 to 6 at the Ben Gurion Airport; 1 means they think you are not dangerous at all and 6 means that they search all your belongings, looking for bombs. They ask all sorts of questions. They see my address on the passport and ask me where this is. When I explain where I live and that it is in a Palestinian area, they always ask me to step aside. I speak a little Hebrew because I am exposed to it regularly, so I can answer the basic questions, but if it gets more complicated I start to ask, "What?" They say, "Great. So you can't even speak Hebrew . . ."

In general, returning to Israel is easy because they see my Israeli passport and let me in without a lot of trouble, but I will never forget the time my suitcase took a trip inside Israel because of where I live. I was on my way back from a Divan tour in December 2006 and was traveling with Daniel Cohen. Our trip involved a twelve-hour connection in London, but we decided to send our luggage directly to Tel Aviv. Our luggage had already arrived by the time we landed, but we couldn't collect it. We were told that our suitcases would remain at the airport before being sent directly to our homes. They didn't give any reasons for this.

They wouldn't send anything to an address in the West Bank, so we had both our suitcases delivered to Daniel's house in Netanya a week later. I was only able to get my suitcase two weeks after that because of the special trip I had to make to Netanya.

My family has always been open-minded. The Divan workshop was not the first time I had met Israelis on a personal level (other than at checkpoints). My father wrote a book together with an Israeli professor about Palestinian cinema, and they worked on it for several years. During that time we often visited the Israeli professor at her house and had meals together. My father was a film producer for a while, and directed films and TV series. He taught at Al-Quds University in Jerusalem, and is also a film critic, and he has always had Israeli friends who were involved in the film industry. He is originally from Nazareth, which is part of Israel now, and his whole family still lives there. So I was always kind of moving around.

I wasn't shocked by coming to the Divan. I guess it was the first time I had actually lived with Israelis for three weeks in a row. I had never experienced that before, but I didn't even think about it. I did meet people from certain Arab countries for the first time. I had visited Jordan, but I had never met people from Syria or Lebanon, or even Egypt. It was really interesting to meet them. We are all Arabs, so we kind of have a similar life, similar culture and traditions. I was curious to know how they live and how they think.

My family has been involved with the Divan in many ways. My uncle is a filmmaker, and he co-directed the documentary film *Route 181*, which we watched at the workshop in 2004. I hadn't seen the film before they showed it at the Divan. We watched it over two evenings, and both nights were very long, including the discussions that followed. Each part of the film lasted about two hours, and then we went on discussing it until 2AM or 3AM. It caused many people to think and form opinions—it was the usual thing: there were different opinions in the orchestra, and we tried to convince each other and discuss our ideas.

My mother started working for the Barenboim–Said Foundation when they began the music education program in Ramallah. She was not working at that point, and Julien thought that the foundation needed someone with her experience. Because I was studying music, we were all emotionally involved in the project. Her responsibilities for the foundation changed a lot in the beginning, because everything was new. The foundation opened a music kindergarten in Ramallah, and at first she was involved with its establishment. Later she started to be the local coordinator for this project, helping to find music students, organizing the teachers' travel to Ramallah, their teaching schedules, workshops and concerts. Now, she mainly organizes workshops for the Palestinian Youth Orchestra which take place once or twice a year.

In 2005, she organized the Divan concert in Ramallah: the concert hall, the broadcasting on ARTE, the production for the orchestra, the heavy security, the press, the arrival of the instruments, and everything else concerning the concert and its broadcast. It was demanding and challenging work. She was very nervous because we weren't sure if we would be able to come to Ramallah until the very last minute. Of course, when the concert did take place, everyone was thrilled. My family loved the concert. Most of my cousins, uncles, and grandparents were seeing an orchestra perform for the first time. My friends and most of the other people who came to the concert were very excited about it. Other people who didn't come were against it for various reasons, but most of the people who attended were positive and were very impressed to see a youth orchestra of a professional standard directed by Maestro Barenboim.

I was really too enthusiastic about everything; I was much too excited. It was all so great, I needed time to think about it and to digest the whole idea of playing at home in the big hall in Ramallah with the Divan, which is something I love. It was very emotional for everyone, especially for some of the people who were of Palestinian origin but were born in different countries and had never been able to visit Palestine before. This was also the first time musicians from other Arab countries were able to visit Palestine. Everyone had some sort of emotion provoked by going to Ramallah. There were many security issues, and the procedures for transporting the Israelis and non-Palestinian Arabs to Ramallah were complicated. To see that it did actually happen in the end and that we achieved the impossible was too exciting.

The orchestra didn't spend much time in Ramallah—only one day. I did manage to bring two friends home during that time, though, and one of them was Israeli. The entire Israeli group was required to stay in the hall for the whole day for security reasons, so we had to sneak out. It takes only two minutes to walk to my home from the hall: of course I would never have taken my friends across the city. We had coffee and *knafe* (an Arab dessert made with fried noodles, goat cheese, and sugar syrup), and my friends got to see my room. Then we went back to the hall and nobody suspected a thing.

Some of my friends in Ramallah have criticized the fact that I am friendly with Israelis—not to the extent that they would verbally attack me, but we have had a few arguments. Although I disagree, I can understand where they are coming from. Their criticism stems from their suffering under the occupation: the daily torments inflicted upon them by the Israeli army and the unpleasantness, to put it mildly, of checkpoints in general. Yes, it is emotionally painful, and I can understand this. But my opinion is that one has to overcome this. The pain is there, but I don't think the pain can be healed by pointing fingers and constantly repeating phrases like, "We hate you" or, "You hurt me." I don't think this is the answer. We have to deal with it in an objective and practical way, by discussing it, addressing certain issues, and presenting facts. At the same time, we have to listen, and try to understand different points of view: in other words, we have to start a dialogue.

There are social cliques in the Divan, just like anywhere else. Not everyone likes everyone else; not everyone gets along with everyone else. Groups are not only formed by nationality, many people simply stay with the people they get along with. English is my second language, and I do speak it well, but I'm not 100 percent comfortable with it. It's much easier for me to express myself in Arabic.

Journalists who interview us always want to know about how we live together in the workshop. I tell them that we can't only talk about politics twenty-four hours a day for a whole month. Sometimes we just want to go shopping; we don't want to watch the news all the time and discuss it. We are human beings; we do fight, but not only about politics. Sometimes I fight with my roommate about who gets to take the first shower. There's a personal, human level to this—it's not only about politics and identity.

Flying with the West-Eastern Divan Orchestra

It is the usual charter flight. The unsuspecting crew greets the boarding passengers with friendly smiles. We strap the celli into seats near the back of the plane and find space for all the remaining instruments onboard. Eventually everyone takes a seat, the pilot greets us, and we start to pull away from the gate.

The flight attendants begin with their explanation of the security procedures onboard. Now the fun begins. Nobody knows when it became standard Divan behavior, but the whole orchestra participates in the flight attendants' demonstrations.

The attractive blonde stewardess indicates the exit routes with her long, slender arms, and from the back of the plane I see a hundred pairs of arms practicing stewardess ballet. Undaunted, she holds up her demonstration seatbelt, opening and closing it to the sound of a hundred seatbelts clicking. Now she realizes this is a perfectly coordinated routine. She is a good sport; she is laughing, waiting for the next gag.

Donning the yellow life jacket available underneath our seats, she pulls on the red toggles on either side in order to inflate it. "Ssssss," hisses the orchestra in unison. The best is yet to come: when she dangles the oxygen mask from the overhead compartments, footwear of all colors and sizes appears, held aloft by their owners from shoestrings and sandal straps. She places the mask over her face; the shoes are held up to mouths and noses and there are groans of distaste. She completes the procedure to whoops, applause, and shouts of "Bravo!"

Alberto and Pablo Martos

As their names suggest, Alberto and Pablo are neither Arab nor Israeli. They were born in Granada, home to the Alhambra and a rich cultural history created by three of the world's major religions: Judaism, Christianity and Islam.

Young musicians from Granada and the rest of Andalusia make up about 20 percent of the West-Eastern Divan Orchestra, and visually most of them blend in perfectly. Their dark, curly hair and various shades of olive skin are genetic reminders of the region's diverse heritage. Often one cannot tell the Middle Easterners from the Andalusians. The Martos brothers' last name tells at least one small part of their family history: the fact that they are named after a place means they have a Jewish ancestor somewhere.

While there is not much Jewish culture to speak of in Granada today, there is a large and steadily growing Arab community, which Alberto and Pablo came closer to as they went to school and studied the cello and violin. Friends of theirs from school volunteered at an association for the integration of recent immigrants: Granada Acoge ("Granada Welcomes"). Most of these immigrants came from Arab countries, and Alberto and Pablo became familiar with their stories from what their volunteer friends told them.

During the Second Intifada, there was much discussion among their friends about the intolerable violence in Palestine, so the two brothers decided to join their friends and do something about it. Together with Granada Acoge, they organized a benefit concert to raise money for a hospital in the West Bank. They played chamber music, and some of their writer and poet friends read poetry. Some time later, they received a letter of thanks from the hospital, saying that it had been able to buy a new ambulance with the money.

Alberto and Pablo joined the Divan in 2004, its third summer in Andalusia. Both boys had already begun to have lessons at the Barenboim–Said Academia de Estudios Orquestales (Academy for Orchestral Studies) in Seville, an institution created by Daniel Barenboim and the regional government in 2003 to promote the education of young Andalusian musicians. The teachers at the academy were from the Staatskapelle Berlin, and flew to Spain once a month to give master classes. Pablo had violin lessons with Axel Wilczok, concertmaster of the Staatskapelle and one of the original mentors of the Divan workshop. With their cultural and musical backgrounds, the brothers were as well prepared as possible for the Divan.

On the other hand, there was nothing that could prepare them for what the Divan would be like, because there was nothing like it. They had a head start over many of the other Spanish musicians—for one thing, their English was good enough to have real conversations with the other musicians; and for another, they knew something about the conflict and were interested in knowing more. While the other Spanish musicians were socially and musically well integrated into the group, some of them felt out of place. They felt as if they didn't really belong to a project whose aim was to bring Israeli and Arab musicians together. Many of them knew nothing of this Middle Eastern conflict that one only read about in the news once in a while. It seemed too far away to touch their lives directly.

The Spanish role in the orchestra very soon became clear to Alberto. The year he and his brother became members of the orchestra, the idea of playing a concert in Ramallah came up for the first time. Barenboim and Felipe Gonzalez, the former prime minister of Spain, announced that it might be possible to go to Ramallah that summer, and they asked the orchestra members how they felt about it. Alberto definitely wanted to go, partly because he loved adventure, but this would be more than a simple adventure: it would mean a lot to him to go to this place to play. He and his brother felt a special connection to Palestine because of their contribution to humanitarian projects there.

In general, there was panic the evening the Ramallah idea was announced. There were so many different reactions, and people stayed up talking about it and didn't sleep all night. Tyme Khleifi was telling everyone, "Of course, we have to go, you'll love it! Don't be scared, it's not dangerous." The Israeli musicians were mostly speaking among themselves and with the Spaniards, and they were saying that there were people who would want to kill them if they went there. The Arab musicians, too, were mostly speaking among themselves and with the Spaniards. At that point, it seemed obvious to Alberto what the Spanish musicians were there to do.

Many times their function was not anything as profound as bringing people together in discussion; they were often just the natural, neutral link between people from different places. Being lively, outgoing, uninhibited people, the Spanish musicians made it easier for people to be together just to chat, or to play football, or to sight-read chamber music.

Being neutral was important, but it did not necessarily make them immune to disagreements with their colleagues, especially when it came to simple, decent human behavior. Alberto once witnessed an Israeli friend of his making a rude, unpleasant remark to an Arab musician who had asked her to do him a small favor. He had seen some animosity in her behavior toward the Arab members of the orchestra before, and had tried to overlook it, but this time he felt he had to approach her. He thought their friendship would be strong enough to withstand this small criticism, but she did not take it very well.

Group discussions were a study in human social interaction. On the one hand, it was fascinating to hear so many different points of view from so many different places. On the other hand, it often struck Pablo that many people who were otherwise very intelligent, intellectual, sensitive individuals could become so stubborn and narrow-minded when they began to talk about the Israeli–Palestinian conflict. These same people could be absolutely clear-headed in other situations, and here they would sometimes lose all self-control.

Pablo likened their reactions to the way watchdogs were trained: when the situation got tense, they reacted exactly the way they had been trained and conditioned to react at home. Alberto sometimes felt helpless trying to bring people back down to reality and objectivity; the others understandably felt the Spaniards were outsiders to the conflict, and had no authority to speak on these issues. On the other hand, at times like this, Alberto felt it was like when your mother told you that you were doing something not so good in your personal life. You would say to her, "What do you mean? You don't know what you're talking about"; but of course she *did* know.

Even if some of their colleagues did lose self-control while arguing, many of the same people kept coming back year after year. Those who did so became more and more open-minded, and began to learn how to speak to each other with more sensitivity and respect.

When the orchestra finally did go to Ramallah, in 2005—the year after the panicky discussions—Alberto and Pablo were sobered by their first direct experience on Israeli/Palestinian land. They landed in Tel Aviv with the Israeli group and then separated from them, traveling immediately with the other Spanish musicians to Ramallah while their Israeli colleagues went home for one night. The transition from modern, Westernized, well-equipped Tel Aviv to the walls, checkpoints, and ruins of the West Bank was quite depressing. The two brothers thought of contacting the people at the hospital that had profited from their benefit concert years before, but suddenly they felt too shy to bother them.

In his first year at the Divan workshop, Pablo had met Nabeel Abboud-Ashkar, who was also studying with Axel Wilczok. They found they had much in common and became very good friends, talking about their musical and professional ideas in relation to the human situation in the Middle East, and specifically in Israel and Palestine. Going to Ramallah with the orchestra for the first time convinced both Alberto and Pablo that they wanted to continue to be involved in humanitarian support for the region beyond their activities in the Divan workshop.

When Nabeel founded his conservatory in Nazareth in 2006, he enlisted the support of the Barenboim–Said Foundation in Spain to invite Alberto, Pablo, and their pianist Angel Jábega to perform and teach there. They extended their stay into a short tour, going to Ramallah as well to play a concert organized by Ramzi and his Al Kamandjati school.

Nabeel and Pablo felt they were in similar situations. Both were teaching music—Nabeel in his own school and Pablo in the Conservatorio Superior in Granada—and both felt an affinity with the German style of making music. They both wanted music to be as important and present in their own societies as it was in Germany, where they had both studied. In the winter of 2008, they even had their final performance exams on the same day in Rostock, where they were studying with Axel Wilczok.

Pablo was impressed by Nabeel's little violin students; they all played with perfect hand position and good posture, and they had such fun playing that they were moving with the music. "So Beethoven came here too," he thought, "he wrote for these kids too."

Pablo and Alberto had always played together since they were children, and they had played with many different pianists in a piano trio, but they had never played with Angel before. Their "debut" was in Ramallah, playing Manuel de Falla, and it was there that they decided they would stay together as a trio: the Garnati Trio, named after the city of Granada, or *Gharnata*, as it was called in Arabic in the thirteenth century. Angel taught at the conservatory in Granada, and had studied in Germany, too, and they all felt they had a similar approach to making music. Pablo felt the concert was one of the great and rare occasions in life in which human and artistic experience come together perfectly.

In Spain, there was more of a cavalier mentality about going to concerts. If you gave someone a ticket to your concert, they would say, "Thank you very much, I'll come if I can." That meant they would come if there was nothing better on television, or if they didn't have a date with a pretty girl. In Ramallah it was different; people were focused on their feelings and enjoying what was going on. They would come to you after the concert and say, "Thank you for the music. I had great feelings today."

The following year they returned, again with the help of Nabeel and Ramzi, and the financial support of the Barenboim–Said Foundation. They visited Nazareth again, and this time they were also accompanied beyond Ramallah by Mariam Said and Muriel Paez, the director of the Barenboim–Said Foundation. They performed in places they never thought they would visit as classical musicians: Jenin, Nablus, Deir Ghassaneh. The living conditions were depressing beyond description, and entering the checkpoint at Nablus was like entering a maximum-security prison. It was surrounded by barbed wire, and when the soldiers saw the trio's instruments they asked the musicians, "Why do you want to play here?"

Ramzi was just beginning to include Deir Ghassaneh in the activities of his Al Kamandjati program, and the trio was the first live classical music ensemble to perform there. The concert took place outdoors, in the courtyard of an old school. The piano there looked like it was about 150 years old, and the piano tuner came in vain, nearly despairing in an attempt to coax the ancient strings into an acceptable intonation. People started arriving an hour before the concert to get the best seats, and the little girls of the town were dressed in the clothes they would ordinarily wear to weddings. As the people were not accustomed to hearing classical music, the trio chose a varied program: they played the Turina piano trio and some Astor Piazzolla, in addition to Beethoven. Two Palestinian girls also sang some Arabian music.

The people of Deir Ghassaneh had been waiting for this concert for weeks: the only special thing they had the whole month was this concert. There was no theater, no café, no shopping malls like in the United States—just nothing. You could smell the audience's concentration; Alberto and Pablo understood how important it was to them and wanted to play their best, to give everything they could give.

In Deir Ghassaneh, in Nablus, and in Jenin, where the improvised concert hall was so full that people outside were pressing their faces to the window, Pablo felt the people in the audience were taking care not to breathe too loudly, as this might disturb the sound. He felt that they were slaves to the sound; they understood that sound was something very delicate. The trio could hear real, perfect silence in between the movements of pieces or within the music itself. In Spain, music was always performed in the midst of noise and had to compete with extraneous sounds, whereas in Deir Ghassaneh, the music was introduced into silence. The sound had more space here.

The human response was tremendously touching. After hearing the trio play Turina in Ramallah, a woman said to them, "Thank you for bringing us some Spanish music, light and life. We really need this life." She said she could feel freedom in the Spanish music, that that kind of feeling in this society and in this situation was very precious.

In Deir Ghassaneh there was a one-hundred-year-old man living alone in a dilapidated old house with a single chicken in a coop. He invited the trio to stay with him, saying, "Let's kill this chicken and I will make soup for all of you."

In Jenin a man came to them after the concert, nearly in tears, and said, "I will say nothing. Only silence can express what I feel about your music and the meaning of your coming here."

When they went back to Spain, they had a concert in a very nice hall, but Pablo felt it didn't give him anything like the feeling he had had playing in a little classroom in Deir Ghassaneh or Jenin. He felt he had done a good job after their concert in Spain. But music should be more than a good job.

The other funny thing about going back home was talking to people about the situation in the Middle East. Pablo's friends would start telling him what the situation was like with such conviction, even if they had never read a book about the Israeli–Palestinian conflict, let alone visited the area. Pablo himself felt that the more time he spent in Palestine, the more confused he became. How was it possible to have an objective point of view? Was there such a thing? To be truly objective, he felt, you would have to live in the library of a university and in the Middle East all at the same time. Nothing was 100 percent clear about this conflict; nothing was black and white. Every day you read about numbers of deaths on each side. On one side they called it terrorism and on the other they called it war, but it was all the same violence, the same sad result.

Alberto and Pablo remembered the terrorist attack in their own country very well, the explosion in the Madrid Atocha train station in 2004. The atmosphere everywhere had been extremely oppressive afterward; it was clear then that the conflict was not just in the Middle East anymore, it was at home too. It was their problem too, and it seemed obvious that education was the solution: "Send violins, not war planes," was Alberto's suggestion.

During their visit to the West Bank, they sometimes saw people sitting around on a boulder in the street from ten in the morning until eleven at night for lack of anything better to do. Alberto and Pablo could clearly see how this situation, this lack of hope, would breed violence. No human being with a good education and a decent salary would think of exploding himself in a bus; it went against human nature. Their Arab friends from the Divan would never even think of doing such stupid things themselves; they were too busy studying and working.

In the Divan they talked about all these things, but people were sometimes under pressure during the workshop, both socially and musically, and it could be difficult to get through to each other. Later, when Pablo was studying in Rostock and Alberto was studying in Berlin, they would run into other people from the Divan who were studying there too. They would all go out for a beer, just five or six of them, and end up spontaneously talking about the Middle Eastern conflict, with no pressure from any guest lecturers or politicians. There were always interesting conversations in the Divan, but the conversations they had with the same people in Berlin or Rostock were more interesting and more relaxed. Nevertheless, the workshop had made it all possible: for these people to meet in the first place, for them to study in Germany, and for them to meet again.

Pablo's favorite role in these conversations was that of devil's advocate. When the discussion would go in one direction, he would take the opposite tack, disagreeing constantly. In the end people would start to see more clearly how they really thought about things.

It was different being in Berlin, being far away from home and a little lonely. Then you were happy to see any familiar face, regardless of its origin—you would say, "Hey, Mohamed, hey Zohar, let's go for a beer," and that was when real personal contact would begin.

It is early April, and unseasonably cold; Alberto and Pablo are sitting in a *téteria*, an Arab tea salon, in the mostly Arab Albaycin quarter of Granada. They sip at their "Pakistani tea" and talk about their plans for the future, interrupting each other and finishing one another's sentences. They are no longer members of the Divan, but their connection to the Middle East is still strong.

"I really would love to forget all these problems forever," begins Pablo.

"And we will go there just to eat and to have fun," continues Alberto.

"But I see the situation is unfortunately complicated, and that's why I would love to be involved in these projects forever until the end of the problem. I would love to go again to Palestine to play and teach."

They are planning various projects: an exchange program between Nabeel's school and Pablo's students, a documentary film about the cultural bridge between Andalusia (including the Barenboim–Said Foundation) and Palestine.

Pablo explains how much support there is and has been in the past in Andalusia for Palestine. The bridge works "through the Barenboim–Said Foundation, sometimes through individual ideas and hope."

"And many people don't know that this bridge exists," Alberto adds.

Pablo continues: "Because, in Spain, most people think that the Barenboim–Said Foundation is to support an orchestra of foreign people, a very expensive two-week spectacle in Pilas. But it's not only that. This thing changed my mind, and now I'm changing the minds of many people."

INTERMEZZO

I have been on tour many times with Meirav Kadichevski, an Israeli oboist. She joined the orchestral academy of the Staatskapelle Berlin while I was playing there, and after a six-week European tour with the Divan in the summer of 2007 we found ourselves on another five-week tour with the Staatskapelle in China and Japan. Meirav and I often had a lot to talk about: the uncontrollable eclecticism we had in common, and our wacky metaphysical theories.

Both Meirav and I have always found it difficult to limit ourselves to one focused path in life. She once told me that when she played in a youth orchestra for the first time, the idea that most excited her was the possibility of trying everyone else's instruments. When we were in Beijing with the Staatskapelle, she went to the market and bought a variety of bargain orchestral instruments for her own amusement: the Meirav one-woman band.

Tours with the Divan are difficult and extremely tiring; all too often the orchestra arrives at the hotel after a concert long after midnight, and leaves early the next morning for the next city. Despite the relentlessness of these tours, there is a lot of collective energy that carries the whole group through the summer. After a concert, there is always leftover energy to celebrate at the group dinners organized by the staff.

While I was on tour with the Staatskapelle Berlin just one month after the end of the Divan tour, I realized I was suffering from a kind of energetic vacuum that I eventually termed "Divan withdrawal." There was no question that the Staatskapelle was a wonderful, world-class orchestra; our concerts with Barenboim were always inspiring. It was the time between rehearsals and concerts that felt so empty. After a concert there was no Arabian or Spanish music, there were no belly-dancing girls, no *unisono* cries of *Bravo!* at a meal if someone dropped a glass or a plate, no bathrobe parties in hotel rooms. People just went their own ways after the concert, like ordinary adults.

Perhaps I was regressing, but I felt unable to be an ordinary adult, and for several weeks I found myself wandering around Tokyo in a daze, waiting for something to wake me from the routine of rehearsals, sushi, and concerts. The Divan had spoiled me for other orchestras, even the very best. I was glad at least Meirav and a few other musicians who had played in the Divan were on tour with us; it made me feel less alone in my disorientation.

After we came back from our second mammoth tour in four months, we got down to the serious business of talking about Meirav's Divan experience. The year before, she had found an apartment on a street in Berlin-Mitte that quickly became known as the "Divanstrasse" due to the number of orchestra members who lived there. I went to see her there and we chatted about everything in her life that related to the Divan, which seemed to be everything indeed.

Meirav Kadichevski

It all started in Madrid airport in 2003. I was lucky I was there, because I hadn't wanted to go that year. Four years earlier, I had been eager to be accepted by the West-Eastern Divan Orchestra. In 1999 Daniel Barenboim was in Tel Aviv conducting the Israel Philharmonic, and he was holding auditions for his new orchestra for people in the Young Israel Philharmonic, where I had been playing. Mr. Barenboim, sitting in the big concert hall of the Israel Philharmonic with the conductor of our youth orchestra, asked me what my name was, and my conductor told him, "You can speak Spanish to her."

Mr. Barenboim asked me, "Why, where are you from?" and I answered, "Well, I'm from Israel, but my family is from Argentina."

"Your family?" he said. "Well, my family used to be apes! Now what are you going to play?"

It didn't matter what I played, because I played terribly, and he didn't take me that year. Ayelet, a violist from the youth orchestra who auditioned at the same time and did get accepted, said that Mr. Barenboim was eating falafel during her audition. She was nervous and shaking, and he was eating falafel.

In 2003 I was living and studying in Karlsruhe, Germany, where I had just finished a year of apprenticeship in the Southwestern German Radio Orchestra of Freiburg. I had heard about experiences in the Divan orchestra from my former youth orchestra colleagues, and so I decided to send an audition tape to the Divan and try my luck again. After receiving a letter that I was on their waiting list, I decided to make the best of my free time and take a vacation after a long year of studying. I bought a plane ticket to Israel.

Two weeks before the beginning of the Divan workshop, Tabaré Perlas called me and said that Barenboim wanted me to come and play. "*Now* you're telling me? No, I don't think so, I already made other plans," I said, and hung up. The next day Tabaré called me again and said, "Why don't you think about this a little? When else will you have the opportunity to play with such a great conductor?" So I gave up on my summer vacation plans (not imagining how many summer vacations I would later be sacrificing for this project) and said, "Okay, okay, I'll come."

I flew back to Israel to have at least a few days at home before traveling to Seville for the Divan workshop with the other Israeli musicians. I had known some of the Israeli musicians, like Ayelet, from my days in the Young Israel Philharmonic, but there were some people that I met on the flight for the first time. We all flew to Madrid from Tel Aviv and spent one night in a hotel, before flying to Seville the next morning. It was there, in the Madrid airport, that I had my first encounter with the Arab musicians of the orchestra.

We were standing around in the check-in hall getting nervous, because we knew we would all have to play for Barenboim again as soon as we arrived in Pilas; so we all got our instruments out and started practicing right there in the airport. Ayelet came over to me with another oboist and said, "This is Mohamed, your colleague." Mohamed looked at me and said, "Yes, we've met before, in Moscow."

At first I was confused, and then, a moment later, I remembered that I had gone to Moscow in 1996 with the Young Israel Philharmonic and nine other youth orchestras to play with the conductor Valery Gergiev at the Youth Olympic Games. There were ten youth orchestras on stage together in one enormous agglomeration (I was sitting in a section of forty oboists!) playing Tchaikowsky's *1812 Overture* and Mussorgsky's *Pictures at an Exhibition*. One of the orchestras there was the Cairo Youth Orchestra, and Mohamed was there with them. One of my Israeli colleagues had played with him before and had introduced us at the time. Seven years had passed since then, but thanks to Mohamed's phenomenal memory he recognized me right away when we met again in Madrid.

In general, I had always been terrified of Muslims. I thought they all wanted to kill me, so everything about them scared me. Mohamed was a very smiley guy, though, and I didn't feel any aggression coming from him. When we arrived in Pilas, we started talking while we were waiting for our auditions. We discovered that we could talk for hours about so many things. It was incredible how much this Egyptian Muslim had in common with me. Just the fact that we had both followed the same path of playing the oboe and studying music gave us so much to talk about: reeds, oboists, music, musicians, orchestras. Eventually these discussions led us to culture and religion, too.

We found lots of similarities between our religions and our cultures. We are still sometimes surprised to find how similar things are in our cultures—the food for one, the language for another. Many of our words are nearly the same, but are just pronounced differently. Later on, we developed a standard response (one of our many little jokes) for every time we discovered such a similarity: "What?! You say *básal*? We say *batsál* [onion]! So . . . why do we have a war?" And then we burst out laughing.

Talking to him about religion was so interesting and eye-opening, because I could ask him all the questions I had never been able to ask anyone before. He told me things I had never known and never could have known before about daily life as a Muslim, and what it actually meant to be a Muslim.

I would ask him what it was like living in Egypt. His family life and history were quite different from mine, of course, but his religion was not as different as I had thought it was. This religion, which I had believed was about killing anyone who is not a Muslim, actually shared a similar logic with Judaism, a basically humanitarian way of thinking. We both came to the conclusion that religion had been distorted by people seeking power over other people. We both thought this was wrong. Religion has been subjected to so much manipulation and abuse, but its original intention has always been to support people and give them spiritual guidance, not to cause suffering.

In the beginning I was uncomfortable with Mohamed's religiousness, because I had such fearful associations with Islam. I knew he was religious, but there were no visible characteristics of it as there were with Orthodox Jews, so it was difficult for me to conceive of his religiousness until I saw him praying one day. He took out his prayer rug, which he took with him everywhere, and went down on his hands and knees. When he did what I had always seen Muslims do on television, a sudden flash of fear ran down my spine. After the initial shock, though, I thought, "Okay, I trust this guy, there's no *real* reason to be afraid."

We spoke, and still do speak very freely and openly about such things, and it has helped me dismiss the old ideas I had about Islam. This shock of realization made me decide to open myself to new experiences and truths, and I think this happens to most people who come to the Divan and personally get to know people from the "other side." They start to question all the associations they had, which were usually based on second-hand information. Once people have their own first-hand information and experience—it erases everything else, including the fear of the unknown, and this process is quite enriching.

I remember going to a bookstore in Israel with my mother after I had met Mohamed and thinking, "I'd like to buy the Koran in Hebrew to be able to read and understand it myself." My mother wanted to buy me some books as a present, so I found the Koran and put it in a pile with a few other books. When my mother came to see what I had chosen, her reaction to the Koran was, "Come on, don't take that. Take any book, but not that!" Since she was the one buying the books, I thought, "I'll buy it another time, when I'm alone."

My ancestors originally came from Poland, Lithuania, and the Ukraine, and both my mother's and my father's families emigrated to Argentina in the 1920s due to worsening anti-Semitism in Europe. My parents were born in Argentina, as were my mother's parents. My mother's father was a passionate Zionist, and for many years head of the Zionist organization in South America. My father's sister emigrated to Israel in the 1950s, as did my mother's family in the 1960s, but both my parents were still studying in Argentina at the time, so they stayed until they finished their degrees and got married. In 1976 they followed their families to Israel, and, like all immigrants, went through the integration program in an "Ulpan," a place where they learned Hebrew with other recent immigrants. When I was born two years later, they still spoke Spanish with me in the beginning; my very first words were in Spanish. As soon as their Hebrew was better, they spoke only Hebrew with me. My parents wanted a purely Israeli daughter, not an immigrant child. They felt they had no other place outside of Israel to be Jewish and to feel accepted, and wanted me to be a native speaker in a place where I could feel accepted. I have never studied Spanish, but many years later, I happily discovered that I could speak it just from having heard it spoken in the family.

My father told me recently for the first time how much anti-Semitism there was in Argentina when he was young, and how he had had to fight to survive there. He told me of the time when he was playing on the basketball team of the Jewish community against other teams in the area. If anybody said anything against the Jews, my father's team would beat them either on the court or on the street to show them how strong they were. If you showed weakness, he said, they would eat you alive.

Such existential fear is deeply rooted in the hearts of many Israelis. Survival instincts and emotional reactions tend to blind us, preventing us from seeing other, more peaceful ways for solving problems that arise. I would like to believe that humanity is slowly coming to the conclusion that violence just creates more violence. In order to solve problems, it would be more efficient to talk to people or at least to ignore them, showing them that violence is not the way we choose to communicate.

My parents never questioned the idea of living in Israel when things were tense, or even during times of war. They didn't want us to be one of those families who left because things were too difficult.

Speaking to Palestinians in the Divan, I learned many things that were not written in any history books and that suddenly made me question whether what I had always considered obvious and self-evident was actually true. It was challenging for me to understand that Zionism, which I had always associated with protection, progress, and the Jewish culture I had grown up with—something that united my family and my people—could be a frightening thing for someone else, something associated with aggression, destruction and exile. It then struck me that any Palestinian group that I had associated with fear might give a Palestinian the same sense of security as Zionism had always given me. I could suddenly comprehend, without in any way accepting the measures being taken by such a group, how things might feel on the opposite side. One side's hero is the other side's terrorist, it just depends where you are looking from.

What we learn at school as history is in many cases subjective, or distorted to accommodate a certain narrative. Facts are hidden, proof is destroyed, other situations and events are emphasized, and interpretations are made. We then grow up believing that these versions of history, recent or ancient, are the ultimate truth.

There was never much talk of the conflict at home with my family, and we never had much contact with "Oriental" culture or people, neither with Israeli Arabs nor with Israeli Jews originally from Arab countries. My family was clearly oriented toward European culture, and all of my friends were of European or American origin. My mother seemed uneasy with "Oriental" culture; I had the feeling, growing up, that we were not "like that."

I was born in Tel Aviv and raised in a nearby town called Kefar Saba, which is five kilometers away from the West Bank, although we never went in that direction; we always went in the other direction, toward the beach. When I was two years old, I moved with my parents to Placentia, California for three years, due to my father's work. When we came back to Israel, we lived in Jerusalem for a year before going back to Kefar Saba. I remember feeling scared walking around the streets of Jerusalem as a child. The atmosphere felt tense. One memory that has stayed with me is the sight of a neighbor girl at my open window saying, "Be careful of kidnappers in the streets!" That scared me even more. It was more than twenty years later that I decided to look at this city with new eyes and slowly let go of these fears.

When I was eight years old, my father got another contract to go back to California for three more years. This second time, I noticed that I didn't have as many close friends in California as in Israel. A lot of it had to do with the way people lived; in Israel everyone lived in big apartment blocks and the kids would all play together outside, visit each other's apartments, and spend the night sometimes. In California, most people had separate houses with their own gardens and things were spread apart, so you had to make an appointment to play with other kids, and your parents had to take you there.

There was another Israeli family living in our neighborhood in Anaheim at the time. The mother of the family was a recorder teacher. Since I didn't have much of a social life, and was spending too much time watching television (at least four hours a day!), my mother suggested that I start taking lessons with her in addition to my other after-school activities of gymnastics, dancing and art. My parents enjoy classical music, but never listened to it much at home. For my tenth birthday, my recorder teacher gave me a cassette tape of Mozart's Clarinet Concerto and Concerto for Flute and Harp, which was the first recording of classical music I had ever owned. I loved it, and I loved playing the recorder, even if I never practiced between my lessons!

When we came back to Israel, I joined a recorder ensemble. Suddenly, playing music became a social thing. There were so many people my age playing other recorders and making harmonies together, and it was great fun. I started going regularly, and it became one of the most pleasurable activities I had. The people in the group also became my best friends. I felt bound to them in a very special way, beyond the normal friendships I had with other children. We gave concerts and even went on tours to Europe. When I got older, though, at the age of thirteen or fourteen, I was ready for a new challenge, in the form of a new instrument. I didn't want to play the flute or the clarinet like so many other kids I knew, and due to my age I hadn't even considered playing a string instrument (most string players start much younger). One day I was in the car with my parents, trying to find the right instrument, when they suddenly thought of one whose name they couldn't remember; they only knew that it was a wind instrument with a little reed and a beautiful sound. I asked my recorder teacher about it, and she said, "Oh, that's an oboe." It took another year, though, before I began to take lessons with an oboe teacher who my recorder teacher managed to bring to our conservatory in Kefar Saba.

Going to school in California, I had gotten used to a different kind of discipline; in Israel the kids would scream and the teachers would scream back, and there was not much mutual respect. I hated it and would sit in the classroom holding my ears. After I complained to my parents, they found a traditional, religious school for me to go to, where the discipline was more to my liking and I had the chance to deepen my knowledge of the Jewish religion.

My parents were not religious; they were only traditional in a very liberal, purely symbolic way. They celebrated the high holidays, but also ate pork and did other "forbidden" things. I learned much more about Judaism in school, but I can't say that it brought me any closer to it. A few years later, I was even repelled by it. It made no sense to me, and I felt I didn't belong to it. Since then, I have gone from complete denial of the Jewish religion to a search for the things in it that do have meaning for me, along with ideas from other religions.

I have often spoken to an Egyptian friend of mine from the Divan about my ideas on religion. We have both questioned life together, asking ourselves whether the religions and cultures into which we were born were the right ones for us. He came from quite a religious Christian family, and was just starting to question his own religion and culture. He had moved to the United States and begun to examine the ways of his native country, Egypt. We would speak about culture, about relationships and ethics. For me it was incredible to have these conversations with someone from such a different background. We sometimes had the feeling that nobody else would even understand what we were talking about.

My own father had often disagreed with my views about culture. When I told him I didn't think that Judaism was necessarily the right way for me, he said: "We were born into the Western world and into Judaism, and that's what we are and how we should be." I personally think it would solve a lot of our problems if every person in every country lived in a different country for a while: a worldwide exchange program. It would surely open up everyone's horizons.

Of course, a lot of people feel comfortable in their own societies, in their own groups, even in the Divan, and forcing people to be together could end up creating problems instead of solving them. In the very beginning of the workshop, in 1999, they made people have roommates from different countries, but it made many people feel uneasy. I think you should let people go at their own tempo.

You can try to make them understand why such a thing would be interesting, but it's not something people can be convinced of or coaxed into—it's just something that happens. You can only create the possibility for it to happen. There are some mixed rooms in the Divan now because people want to be mixed. But if people feel uncomfortable being together, then it's not a good way to create understanding. When you inflict ideas on other people, you are eventually bound to fail.

Some people take time to open up when they first come to the workshop. First they see that they can sit next to people from "the other side" in the orchestra, and then sit with them at lunch, and then speak to them. It's a natural process. People who are aware of it can try to take the first step to talk to others and let things happen slowly. It has become obvious to those who have been coming to the Divan for many years: "Of course I don't have a problem with you because you're Syrian, but I could have a problem with you if you're not a nice person." Once you break the ice, you understand that, beyond the fact that someone speaks a different language, looks differently and grew up in a different culture, we are all the same spiritual beings. Underneath the outer shell we are all alike, we are all equal and we are all just as important as any other. This is the level on which we communicate when we make music together.

One thing I started doing after I first went to the Divan was to "jump" out of myself and look at things from the side. During any conflict I might have in the orchestra, I would either jump to the other side and see how someone on that side might see me, or jump to the outside completely and see how both sides looked from there. It changed my whole way of thinking, and has become completely automatic since then.

What I called jumping was actually an attempt to shift my consciousness to a completely different position. Normally I would see things only through my own eyes, but by jumping I was trying to really understand the situation through these other perspectives. That was when the solution would become clear, both in personal and national conflicts: I would imagine what it would be like if I were, say, a Palestinian, and then explore my feelings about my people, my feelings toward my family and myself, my worries, and things would become logical. Suddenly I would understand why people reacted the way they did, even when I didn't agree with them.

I can't say that my experiences in the West-Eastern Divan Orchestra have always been ideal. I have had both the best and the most difficult times of my life there. When you spend such an intense period of time with so many people on tour, many personal conflicts tend to arise. But I can certainly say that I have learned some very important lessons from dealing with these conflicts.

One of the lessons I learned is that we either see others as we see ourselves, as people with needs and passions that are no less legitimate than our own, or we see them as something blocking our path. When we see the others as human beings with the same hopes, fears, demands and worries as our own, we know to treat them with the same respect with which we would like to be treated ourselves. On the other hand, seeing others as obstacles leads us to be completely indifferent to their suffering and leads them to be equally indifferent to us. It was a shocking thing for me, altruistic as I try to be, to discover how easily I can forget other people's needs without even noticing, on an almost daily basis!

One time, just after the Divan workshop was over, I was in Israel, sitting on the beach and talking to a friend about how special the orchestra is, trying to explain to her how it was possible for me to have Arab friends. She would say things like, "The Arabs are so aggressive," and "We have to kill all the Arabs." I had to take a deep breath, calm myself down, remind myself that she was my friend, and slowly explain my opinions.

While we were talking, a group of guys started playing football in the middle of the beach. The ball would hit other people sitting nearby, but the guys who were playing really didn't care. The only thing they cared about was enjoying their game. You couldn't go up to them and tell them to stop, either, because they would have become aggressive. Even the lifeguard didn't dare to interrupt. They were just a bunch of macho guys with no respect or sensitivity for other people; they were real bullies. I pointed to them and said to my friend, "Look, *these* people are aggressive. *My* friends are not aggressive!" Since then, I think she has begun to open up to the possibility of having Arabs as friends, but until she has her own experiences, nothing I say can really change her beliefs.

The nice thing about the Divan is that it's developing in a way that none of us could expect. No year has been like any other year; each summer is different. In 2005 we went to Ramallah. I was afraid to go there with the orchestra, since it was a time of much political tension and it was possible that we would face aggressive resistance. At the same time, I was really excited about it. I thought, "If I'm going to die, this might as well be the way for me to die. If I have to die playing in Ramallah, let it be so, because if there's anything meaningful in what I'm doing, it's to go and play there." It was actually so easy to go in the end, but it was exhilarating because of the way it happened. We had to split up into an Israeli/Spanish group and an Arab group while we were still on tour. The Israeli/Spanish group flew to Tel Aviv and the Arab group to Amman, and we went through different checkpoints to meet in Ramallah. The night before the concert, we stayed in Jerusalem, missing our "other half" and eagerly awaiting the next morning.

The rest of the story was really like a Hollywood action film: early in the morning we got into armored German diplomatic cars and drove down the mountain from Jerusalem. We passed the wall that was being built, and a few settlements. I had never seen settlements before—as a civilian I would never willingly go to a settlement. Then we arrived at the checkpoint and just passed right through it. The guards didn't even check the Spanish diplomatic passports we had received for this special event; they just said, "Okay, go," because we were in diplomatic cars. And suddenly we were on the other side, and Barenboim was there with his wife saying, "Hey, how are you doing?"

As soon as we passed the border, many policemen on motorcycles came and escorted us. We made much more of a spectacle than we would have if we had just gone in normally (I'm sure nothing would have happened to us that way either). When we got to the hall and met our colleagues again, we were all extremely excited. After the rehearsal was over, we Israelis unfortunately had to stay in the hall for security reasons while the others went into the city.

While we were waiting in the gardens of the hall for the concert to start, some of the Palestinian security officers who were there to protect us started playing backgammon with us Israelis. I went up to one of the armed security guards by the wall and wanted to take a picture with him. He could hardly speak any English, but somehow we were able to communicate, and in the end he gave me a card with his mobile number on it, invited me to his house, and told me that his mother would cook for us!

It was not the usual classical music audience at the concert; you could hear phones ringing, and once in a while people would go in and out, but I don't think there was any discomfort in the audience. By going there, we were saying, "We are here for you and we support you." There was some discomfort in the orchestra, though, because on both sides of the hall there were big "Freedom for Palestine" signs. These made some of the musicians uncomfortable, since they believed that we were only there to make music, and not to make a political statement. While playing, we all concentrated on the music, as we would have in any normal concert situation. It was over so quickly, and all of a sudden we were in the cars again, driving away after hardly having had a chance to say good-bye to our friends. It was very dramatic; every time I see this part of the concert in the documentary film about the Divan, I still burst into tears.

Most of the Palestinians I've met are very passionate about their fight, and that's understandable to me. That's what happens when you are repressed for a long period of time. I remember how I felt when I was in the army—I also felt repressed. You forget who you are, you start to lose your identity; so you do anything you can to keep it.

I was eighteen years old and not very eager to do my mandatory military service. Going into the army meant nearly two years of not playing music or dancing. I used to talk to my father about looking for ways to avoid it; after all, age is so often taken into account in the classical music world, and these were two important years I would lose when I could be developing musically. He said, "No, just do it. You'll close doors if you don't do it, you won't be able to get a job in a government agency or in any company that works with the government." At the time I was not very rebellious; I also had very little understanding of the political and humanitarian situation in our region, and wasn't yet really interested in gaining any knowledge of it. I also saw how enthusiastic so many of my peers were about their military service. The general belief is that the army is there for our survival, and that every citizen should do his or her part to serve the country. Although I am now sure there are better ways to serve a country than joining the army, this managed to convince me at the time. I tried to get into the army band, but there were no positions available, so I ended up doing office work, running errands and making coffee. I did what I had to do, and in the army that meant following orders without questioning, even if I didn't agree with them.

In the army the hierarchy is very clear. Someone who had a higher ranking than me had the right to tell me what to do, regardless of his intelligence or capabilities. I couldn't pass my frustration on to any lower-ranking soldier, though, since I myself was at the bottom of the ladder. So, whenever I could take a minute off, I would go to the toilets, lock the door and start hitting myself on the wall, jumping around and stretching my limbs, causing myself pain just to feel that I was alive. I wanted to feel my body, myself, because I felt mentally erased. That was my experience of repression, and it was only for one year and nine months; I knew when it would be over.

The summer of 2006 was a difficult one for the Divan workshop. A week before it began in Pilas, war broke out between Israel and Lebanon. I remember the uneasiness and the mixed feelings I had, feeling how people around me in Israel were united in their hatred toward Hezbollah and Lebanon in general. Together with my worries for the citizens of northern Israel, including my own family, I would think of my Lebanese friends from the Divan and worry about them and their families. Hearing on the news that all the exit routes from Lebanon had been bombed by the Israeli military forces, I suddenly burst into tears, thinking that my Lebanese colleagues would not be able to come to the workshop. I was surrounded by hatred, fear and anger, and the thing I longed for most was to be with them, hug them and show them my compassion; to know together that things could be different, that mutual understanding could still exist. During that week before the Divan, I had quite a few discussions with my family and friends about what I saw as a highly excessive use of force and violence. I felt very alone with my opinions at that time, and was very happy to finally arrive in Pilas. Unfortunately, many of the Arab participants decided not to take part in the workshop that year. I was quite disappointed by this, but of course I respected their decisions. I understood that they were living in a different cultural–political situation from mine and were subject to different kinds of pressures. For the first time I realized how lucky I was to be able to freely voice my opinions and follow my beliefs, which was not the case for some of my colleagues.

As we came close to playing our first concert of that summer's tour, Barenboim and Mariam Said came to us after a rehearsal in the bullfight arena in Seville with a suggestion for a declaration of the orchestra's anti-war beliefs. All of us—Israelis, Arabs and Spaniards—were in a rage of talking and arguing after Barenboim read us the declaration. Everyone had his or her own opinion about what the declaration should be like, or if we needed one at all. We were arguing in the buses all the way back to Pilas, and it took us quite a long while to calm down. In fact, we didn't really calm down, eventually we all got tired of arguing, went to the local disco together and danced the night away until the subject came up again the next day.

Terrible things have happened in the past, but I believe that if we understand the past, learn what there is to learn, and then let it go (including all personal and collective trauma), we have a greater chance of making things better for ourselves. "We will not forget and we will not forgive!"— a very popular slogan in Israel—only keeps us buried in our own suffering, leaving us no chance of moving on with our lives.

As Barenboim likes to say, every concert starts from zero. Every day is new. Yesterday's concert belongs to the past, today things are different: maybe the hall is new, the acoustics are different, my reed has changed, I slept well, I slept badly, and so on. My body is constantly changing, my cells are constantly being created and dying. Life is change, and so is music; that is why music is so touching. It's there and it's gone, it's the flowing dance of existence. Clinging to the past and to old ways and ideas might give me an illusion of security, but it just keeps me from discovering new ideas and from developing in ways I might not even be able to imagine right now.

For me, being brave does not mean following orders, going to war and killing other people. For me, being brave means questioning, looking for my own answers and letting go of attachments that create the illusion of security in life.

Fighting fire with fire accomplishes no long-term results. Explosions and violence in our region only shock people, bringing temporary respite from more violence, and then the problem comes back again. It's like trying to treat a sick patient by focusing on the symptoms: you can bomb yourself with chemicals, but it won't cure the illness unless you analyze the problem and search for the reason why such an illness has developed.

I often feel very small and powerless against the many outside forces controlling the world. I feel that there is so much I would like to change, but how can I, small and peaceful as I am, have any effect whatsoever on such a big and, at times, very cruel and violent world? Changing the whole world is impossible, and who am I to say what's right or wrong or who should do what? What I *can* do is take responsibility for myself, designing my inner world in the best way for me. When I change myself, I can affect my immediate surroundings.

By seeing how differently people could react to a certain situation, I came to the conclusion that *I* create my reaction to a situation; the situation does not create my reaction. If I can learn to control myself, I can choose my reaction to each situation. Everyone is basically responsible for his or her own reactions, but people tend to blame other people or situations for their own problems—"You made me angry," or "Something made me fail"—and they express anger toward this thing. The real solution actually lies on the inside, and it begins with acceptance of oneself and of the other. If I could really accept my own weaknesses and work on them, maybe I wouldn't feel the need to go around telling everybody else what they should or shouldn't do.

When a difficulty arises I can either run away from it, ignore it, resist it, or look it straight in the eye and find a way to transform it into something positive. As absurd as it may seem, I can even enjoy discomfort if I choose to do so; it's just a matter of decision. It's fine to cry and be sad about painful situations in our lives. Grieving and mourning contribute to healing, and are much healthier than suppressing emotions; but afterward, I believe we should choose life, growth and development.

One of the most valuable lessons I ever got from my oboe teacher Gregor Witt (of the Staatskapelle Berlin) was when I once came to him depressed because things were not going well for me at the time. After spilling my heart out, near tears, he finally said to me, "Well, feeling sorry for yourself sure won't help you!" I was shocked! How could he be so unsupportive?! I felt slapped in the face by one of the people I admired most. I later understood that it was just my ego that was hurt. My teacher was right. As soon as I started looking at my problems (the musical ones and the personal ones) objectively, without attaching any emotions to them, my mind was clear and free to see the solutions, which then popped up vividly.

I have learned a lot from Barenboim about drawing parallels between music and life, and thinking about these things has made me understand that certain rules apply to many things, like the rules of nature. If nature has its rules and we are part of nature, we must be affected by these same rules. In nature, everything is connected to everything else. Nature does not know the borders that we human beings have drawn on our maps, and it follows that my own well-being is connected to that of my surroundings.

Unfortunately, I don't see any possibility of completely doing away with military forces in Middle Eastern countries at the moment. It takes time to understand that military solutions are not successful long-term solutions. It took Europe many wars with a lot of pain, destruction and loss to understand this, but I hope we will eventually reach the same conclusions in the Middle East and every other war zone in the world. It's all a question of education and eliminating ignorance.

I often feel that we're fighting the wrong war. We fight other countries instead of fighting ignorance and aggression. Real strength comes from knowledge. People's own ignorance causes them to be afraid. Any chance I have to speak my mind and tell people about my experiences, I do. It's my own personal fight against ignorance. I feel that there's a greater meaning to my life than just going to do my job, whatever that may be. I feel a lot of responsibility that I would sometimes prefer to ignore but can't.

Accepting and letting go of fear and pride makes it possible to forgive, which is the only way to step out of this vicious circle of physical and mental violence. Perhaps the fact that we experience mutual forgiveness and acceptance together with our so-called national enemies, at least on a personal level, is what makes us, the members of the West-Eastern Divan Orchestra, so loving with one another on a human level. We are like lovers making up after an emotional fight, rediscovering each other. Over the years we have grown to be a family. In the many orchestras I have played in, I have never felt anything like it. Like an addiction, it has become a part of my life that I cannot live without.

INTERMEZZO

I first met Hassan Moataz in July 1997 at the orchestra academy of the Schleswig-Holstein Festival in northern Germany. He was one of only two Egyptian musicians in the youth orchestra, and a very talented cellist at fifteen. Hassan was an exotic novelty for the rest of us, who came mostly from Europe and the United States. I was part of the older kids' clique, and since he spoke almost no English at all, our communication was limited to smiling at each other during sectional rehearsals. I didn't see him much during orchestra rehearsal, because I was in the first stand and he, being so young, was near the back. It had never occurred to me until then that classical musicians could come from Egypt; I had always had many musician friends from different countries at Juilliard, where I had studied, but most of them were from the Far East or Eastern Europe.

At the end of the summer, awards were given to a handful of students, and I found myself standing on the stage with Hassan at the ceremony. I received an award for chamber music performance and he received a scholarship for the most promising young musician. While we stood there, I wondered whether our paths would ever cross again. At the time I was planning to return to the United States, maybe to study in San Francisco. If I had done so, rather than staying in Germany as I did, we might never have met again.

The next time I saw Hassan was in the summer of 2006 in the cafeteria in Pilas. This time we were able to converse in English, and Hassan told me that he was now the principal cellist of the Cairo Symphony Orchestra, and that he was married to a flutist named Reham who was also at the workshop. Their two-year-old daughter, Hala, was at home with Reham's mother in Cairo. He said he was very happy to see me, and even though we now had a common language, we both still just stood there with big silly grins on our faces. In my mind I was traveling back through time to the summer of our first meeting, trying to put together the image of the quiet, shy, skinny teenager with the successful young man standing before me who was now a husband and father. His face had filled out, but the broad, beaming smile was still the same.

Every time we saw each other that summer, we would revert to these smiles, our original form of communication. We were playing in the same orchestra again, and this time the hierarchy was reversed: he was in the first stand and I was in the last, being a non–Middle Eastern, professional substitute. The first time we met, he had been the "foreign" element in an otherwise predominantly European, Asian, and American group. Now I was the foreigner in this group of Middle Easterners.

Hassan told me how he came to play the cello, something he had never been able to explain to me before. He was the youngest in his family; his sister was ten years older and his brother was eight years older. He grew up listening to his sister play on an electronic organ. She had never had lessons but could play every Egyptian melody by ear, and Hassan began to try to play too. When his parents noticed that he was musically talented, they sent him at the age of nine to the Cairo Conservatory, where the teachers told him that he should play the cello. Hassan had never even seen a cello before and thought he would rather play the violin, but he accepted his destiny and was pleased when he met his teacher, a strict but good person. His teacher showed him the instrument and promised him that if he didn't like it, he could switch to another instrument. His offer was unnecessary, though, because Hassan soon grew to love both the cello and his teacher, who became his first musical role model.

Hassan continued to study in Cairo while visiting master classes abroad with various renowned cellists and taking part in youth orchestras like the one in Schleswig-Holstein. In 1999 he attended the first Divan workshop in Weimar and had lessons with Yo-Yo Ma, who was at the workshop that year. Hassan felt very lucky to be in the presence of such great musicians as Ma and Barenboim; he also had the good fortune to play the orchestral cello solo in the slow movement of Schumann's Cello Concerto when Ma performed it with them.

I soon met Hassan's wife Reham as well, a beautiful, warm, sincere person. I began to ask her about their lives, and she helped me fill in the events of the previous nine years, explaining how they had come to be a part of the "Divan family." Reham's father was an engineer working in Jiddah, Saudi Arabia, when she was born, and when Reham was twelve years old they moved back to Cairo. Her parents had always listened to both Western and Arab classical music, and she grew up singing and loving music. When they moved back to Cairo, Reham began to sing in a children's choir at the Cairo Opera House, where they sang Arab classical music, which she loves to this day. Soon afterward, she auditioned for the Cairo Conservatory as a beginner and, remembering a recording of one of Mozart's flute concertos her father had often played, she decided she wanted to play the flute.

She was accepted as a student, but was assigned to study the bassoon. The bassoon, Reham felt, was a poor substitute for the flute, and she went to speak to the director of the conservatory to ask him to reconsider. There were no places available to study the flute, he said, but she insisted, and he eventually relented. Hassan was in her class at the conservatory, and by the time he came to the Schleswig-Holstein Festival in 1997 they had fallen in love.

When Hassan attended the first Divan workshop in 1999, they

were already engaged, and the following year they got married. Around this time Hassan began to play classical Egyptian music on the cello, which required a completely different technique from European classical playing. Hassan enjoyed the challenge, though. He had to learn to play quarter-tones with great precision, to use a much slower and wider vibrato, and to soften his left hand, which was much more rigid when playing Western classical music. Soon he was being hired to play just as much Egyptian as Western classical music. After their marriage in 2000, Hassan had to stay in Egypt to earn some money for their new flat and their new life, but he encouraged Reham to go to the Divan workshop without him. She auditioned and was accepted. She continued to go every year afterward, until their daughter was born in 2004, the same year that Hassan became the principal cellist of the Cairo Symphony.

In the beginning, Reham had thought of the workshop as a wonderful musical opportunity, not necessarily anything more. Egypt was officially at peace with Israel, but when they learned about the Egyptian–Israeli wars at school, it was emphasized that Israel was still the enemy. There were Israeli tourists in Cairo, Sharm El-Sheikh, and Alexandria, and this was accepted. Nevertheless, there was still ample anti-Israeli sentiment among Egyptians. Both Reham's father and her uncle had fought in wars against Israel, but her family supported her participation in the workshop.

Her first year in the Divan was difficult, but she quickly realized that she had to rethink the ideas she had had about Israelis. They were not monsters, people to be put indiscriminately in the category of "enemy"; they were human beings, and they even had many things in common with her. Reham soon became friends with some of her Israeli colleagues and kept in touch with them from Egypt.

She stayed at home in 2004 and 2005 to take care of her baby daughter Hala, and returned to the workshop with Hassan in 2006. Before the workshop began that summer, a lot of e-mails had been circulating among the Arab members of the workshop regarding the Lebanon War, and many of them decided not to go. There is a belief in the Arab world that music is something to be enjoyed at celebrations, but not when people are suffering; to make music with "the enemy" while a war was raging was truly unthinkable for some. Hassan and Reham, both practicing Muslims, did not see anything wrong in going to the workshop in 2006. They were musicians, and as musicians, Reham believed they could do what governments could not manage to do: live together as human beings, listening to and accepting each other. In addition, Reham missed her friends from earlier workshops and simply wanted to see them again. They were more than friends, really. As everyone says who has been to the Divan, they were more like family.

In a 2007 symposium of the Salzburg Festival, Reham and other members of the Divan spoke about their involvement in the orchestra. She began to speak about her religion, and this was fascinating for me, because I had not heard many people in the orchestra speak openly about their religions. Three of the world's main religions are represented in the orchestra: Christianity, Judaism, and Islam. However, apart from the pork-free and seafood-free menu options in the cafeteria, religion is a personal issue that is not much discussed.

Early in 2008, Reham went to Berlin to study with Claudia Stein, principal flutist of the Staatskapelle Berlin, and participate in the German State Opera's orchestral academy. Claudia was Reham's mentor at the Divan workshop, and Claudia's daughter Elisa was the same age as Hala. Elisa was enrolled in Barenboim's music kindergarten just around the corner from the opera, so when Reham came to Berlin, Claudia used her connections in the kindergarten to secure a place there for Hala. In Cairo, Hala had attended a German kindergarten and was already learning to speak German. Hala became best friends with Elisa; the two of them played together in one room of Claudia's apartment while Reham had her flute lesson in another.

I went to see Reham on a cold day in February in the Moabit neighborhood of Berlin, where there are just as many storefront signs in Arabic as in German. I picked up a box of baklava from my favorite Lebanese bakery and went up to Reham's apartment. When she opened the door, a beautiful little girl with two black braids above her ears appeared from behind her. Hala, now four years old, was supposed to be at kindergarten, but Reham had come down with a cold and was too sick to take her there, so Hala entertained us by showing us her drawings, occasionally jumping up and down on the bed while Reham and I talked.

Reham told me that it had become important to her in recent years to feel that her actions put the principles of her religion into practice, and she had begun to search for a mention of coexistence between hostile peoples in the Koran. While searching, she came across the writings and speeches of a new religious leader in Egypt, Amr Khaled, a young man who had begun to preach to Muslims of all ages and varying degrees of piety about the importance of coexistence. He spoke about Islam in a different way than she had ever heard before; he brought out what she felt were the main points of the religion. The prophet Muhammad, he insisted, did not say that Muslims should not interact with other peoples; he said that they should live in peace with other peoples. Muslims should not let their own beliefs melt into those of the others; they should protect their beliefs and allow the others to live according to their own.

This was exactly what Reham felt she was doing in the Divan workshop and in Berlin, now that she was living here. She was seeing her Divan friends often; more and more of them were coming to Berlin to study, creating their own year-round society.

One morning not long after visiting Reham, I went to the Philharmonie to hear the dress rehearsal of the Verdi Requiem performed by the Staatskapelle Berlin and Daniel Barenboim. From where I sat, I could see Reham two rows in front of me with Hala on her lap, sitting next to two Israelis and an Egyptian, all of them from the Divan. Before the concert, everyone fussed over adorable little Hala, who sat perfectly still during the entire eighty minutes of the Requiem, entranced by the music.

Hala has inherited her mother's porcelain-fair skin and delicately pointed chin, her father's rounded nose, twinkling eyes, and infectious smile, and their common love of music. She will grow up as an Egyptian Muslim, but also as a child of the Divan; she is already used to being fawned over by her parents' Israeli friends. Reham told me that her Divan friends made it much easier for her to be away from home, and perhaps Hala will feel at home wherever there is music and one of the many languages she will someday speak: Arabic, German, and English, at the least.

Another "Egyptian Divanese" I had met before my first visit to the workshop was the oboist Mohamed Saleh Ibrahim. Like Meirav, I too had met him only once and very briefly, in the green room of the Philharmonie after I had played a concert with the Staatskapelle Berlin. It was early in 2006, before I had anything to do with the workshop. About half a dozen Divan musicians were standing around in Barenboim's room to congratulate him and talk about the coming summer. I was introduced to each of them; the whole thing lasted only a few minutes.

When I got together with Mohamed on Friedrichstrasse in Berlin more than a year later and mused over when and where we had first met, the answer shot out of him: "In the Philharmonie."

It had been difficult to catch up with Mohamed; he had been jetting back and forth between Europe and Chicago, where he lived with his wife. I finally tracked him down with the help of some mutual friends. He happened to be passing through Berlin between European tours, and was about to meet his Israeli friends Mor and Ayelet for a Chanukah dinner. He invited me to join them as well. Unfortunately I had other things to do that evening, but we sat together for nearly two hours in an incongruously prosaic Starbucks while Mohamed spoke about his extraordinary life in music and the Divan.

I had known Mohamed as the clown of the orchestra: a compact, mischievous Puck with a talent for making faces and maintaining a general atmosphere of hilarity in his vicinity. I also knew him as a wonderful musician, a magician on stage who could spontaneously find and express a new truth in the phrase he had played the night before, and the night before that, and so on. If these two facets of his personality were seemingly incompatible, I discovered yet another while we spoke: a deeply serious and spiritual one. "I can see God even more clearly than I can see you," he told me with neither presumption nor irony.

He proceeded to tell me parts of his life story, including his years in the Divan. I was astonished to hear that most of his extended family at home in Cairo considered music something sinful. His parents had always supported his musical career, and his father had been a wonderful amateur musician, but it was difficult for him to shut out the feeling of disapproval he felt from the strict, devout members of his family. While listening to him speak, I began to understand the strange marriage of the sublime and the ridiculous in his personality and playing. He recounted his hilarious and tragic story effortlessly, as if each episode were a book on a shelf before him, interspersing the tale with his infectious, high-pitched laughter, that sounded like a reed being tested without the oboe.

Mohamed Saleh Ibrahim and Friends

Mohamed was twelve years old when he was accepted to study oboe at the Cairo Conservatory. When he chose the oboe he didn't know that you had to buy new reeds all the time for this instrument. His family was not wealthy and he was too shy to ask for money; instead of asking he would just save the money his father gave him for lunch and not eat in order to be able to buy reeds. It was a sacrifice that made him appreciate playing even more. He worked hard, and after only five years of studying he auditioned for the position of co-principal oboe, and was accepted at the age of seventeen as the Cairo Opera Orchestra's youngest member. During his first year in the opera, he was also still in school and enrolled in the conservatory; he would go straight from school to theory and harmony lessons, and from there to a performance at the opera. He was nearly fainting from exhaustion all the time. After the first year it became easier, when the repertoire began to repeat itself: *Tosca*, *La Traviata*, *Aïda* (which they played so often he eventually learned it by heart), *La Bohème*, *Swan Lake*. The Bolshoi Orchestra would sometimes come to Cairo without a first oboist, so that Mohamed could join them to play Swan Lake.

Even though he was already playing professionally and had become quite well known in Cairo, he wanted to continue to learn, and he started his postgraduate studies in 1999, the year the Divan began. Mohamed had seen Daniel Barenboim only in videos, but this was something amazing, something new to him.

The conductors they had at the opera in Egypt were mostly Egyptian, not from abroad. Mohamed was eager to meet such a great conductor, of course, but the fact that he would be playing with Israelis interested him just as much.

It would not be the first time he had met Israelis; there was an American summer chamber music course for young people from the Middle East (and other places) called Apple Hill, and they held auditions in Cairo every year. Israel was so close, and yet its people were so far away; the very difficulty of encountering an Israeli in person was tantalizing to Mohamed. His curiosity to discover the people beyond the desert separating them drove him to audition for the program every year, beginning in 1995, but he was finally accepted only in 1998. It seemed absurd, and made him feel sorry that America was somehow closer to Egypt and easier to get to than Israel.

Mohamed's father had fought in the war against Israel in 1973, but he believed that going to war was just an order from the government. You wouldn't decide to go to war on your own. He told his son, "Go, *habibi* [darling]—go meet these people. You are a totally new generation."

He met his first Israeli friends there, Asaf Maoz and Doron Alperin, and his first Palestinian friend, too: Ramzi Aburedwan from Ramallah. It was paradise for forty days, playing together without any pressure and meeting people from different places without asking any uncomfortable questions. Every day the staff organized a different kind of activity: an ice cream night, a lake trip, a football game, a sunrise hike. It was fun all the time. After he came back to Cairo, he got a letter in the mail with photos from an Israeli girl. It was the first letter he had ever received from Israel, and it looked like someone had opened the envelope; but it didn't matter, it felt like a gift.

Since e-mail was not yet very common in 1998, Mohamed didn't keep in touch with the other friends he met at Apple Hill, so it was a lovely surprise to see some of his friends again in Weimar at the

Divan workshop. They had thought they might never see each other again, and there was a lot of excitement and hugging when they found each other. One Israeli horn player from the summer before at Apple Hill came over and kissed Mohamed, and it felt just like his brother kissing him.

After the reunions, the work began. Mr. Barenboim was dressed all in black for his first rehearsal with the orchestra, and Mohamed felt a burning intensity, an "energetic scariness," as he put it, in this person before him. His eyes seemed to ask Mohamed, "What are you doing here?" when he played the oboe solo in the beginning of Beethoven's Seventh Symphony. Mr. Barenboim's assistant, Sebastian Weigle, had conducted the first rehearsals, and Mohamed had played the solo very nicely. Now Mr. Barenboim was here, trying to harvest all the beauty possible in the music, using all the energy he had to make Mohamed play as he knew it should be, and it was intimidating.

After Mr. Barenboim stopped him several times in a row, Mohamed asked him what was wrong with his solo.

"Can you play it *piano*? More *piano*?"

Mohamed squeezed himself together, playing as softly as he could.

"Do you know the meaning of the word *legato*?"

Mohamed got angry.

"Of course I know what legato is, it's like this," and he drew an arch in the air. Everybody laughed. What Mohamed called *legato* was the slur connecting one note to the next in printed music; that was the word they used for it in Egypt. That was not what the Maestro meant, of course. He meant that Mohamed should play *legato*, the Italian word for "bound"; he should bind the notes of the phrase together so that one would melt into the next. He patiently explained the real meaning of *legato*, and slowly the solo got better and better, and the orchestra was impressed. Mohamed felt so many spaces in his brain opening up—this man made him pay attention to so many things: sustaining the sound, working with his breathing, playing *legato*. After rehearsal the Maestro came and hugged him, and seemed friendly. He said, "Don't be tense, it was fine, it was good!"

After rehearsal later that day, when everyone was outside talking, Mohamed met Ayelet for the first time. Ayelet was with a group of her Israeli friends, including Mohamed's friend Doron. Mohamed was the first Arab musician to approach the group and the first one Ayelet had spoken to. Mohamed was a funny guy, and he was Doron's friend already, so Ayelet felt comfortable with him. They asked each other where they were from, how old they were, and somehow the topic wandered to their parents and how old their fathers were, and then they realized that their fathers had fought against each other in Sinai in the 1973 war, the Yom Kippur War. They went on asking each other questions, and figured out that their fathers had been in exactly the same area of Sinai. Luckily both had survived.

"It may be a cold peace between our countries," Mohamed thought, "but we meet now and it's fine." Mohamed had never had a sister, but he began to feel that Ayelet was like his sister. Every time she saw him that summer, she would start laughing. "What, am I a clown?" he would say to her, doing his Donald Duck impression. There were serious discussions that summer with Mr. Barenboim, with Edward Said and Yo-Yo Ma, but mostly they remembered the music and the nonsense things they did. After their first conversation, they didn't talk much about where they came from or what it was like where they lived; they just stayed up all night with their friends talking and laughing and doing silly things. Mohamed began to invent his own words and they caught on quickly in the orchestra. Barenboim became "Burumburum," with an Arabic "rr." It wasn't nice to swear, so he developed his own variations on four-letter words: whenever somebody dropped something or tripped, you could hear exclamations of "Fush!" or "Shest!" One time Mohamed cooked *koshari*—an Egyptian dish made of rice, noodles and lentils—in the cafeteria kitchen for the entire orchestra.

At the end of the summer Mohamed told Mr. Barenboim how sad he was that he would never see him again. Nobody knew there would be a second West-Eastern Divan workshop. Mohamed hadn't known that he was capable of making more music; he thought he had reached his maximum. He told Mr. Barenboim he wanted to learn more, that he had no extra methods to achieve what he had now seen was possible. He wanted to learn to develop his *legato* playing, to make better reeds. Mr. Barenboim listened and was very helpful. He told Mohamed he would speak to Alex Klein, the principal oboist of the Chicago Symphony at the time.

After the workshop, Mohamed went back to Cairo to continue playing in the opera. He also finished his postgraduate degree that year, and then came the surprising and wonderful news that there would be a second Divan workshop. Mohamed was happy: it felt like going home again. The first year had been something like looking around a new apartment that you might want to move into; the second year felt completely natural and familiar—lived in. That year, Tamar Inbal came to play in the orchestra, an Israeli oboist so wonderful that Mohamed almost didn't want to play; it was enough just to enjoy her playing next to him. They traded off playing first oboe, she playing the first and second movements of Brahms's First Symphony, he playing the third and fourth.

Mr. Barenboim spoke to Alex Klein that summer and arranged for Mohamed to go and study with him in Chicago. Alex Klein was a wonderful person, oboist and musician, and he taught Mohamed important things about the way the reed vibrates and how the sound is produced. He showed Mohamed how to make better reeds and how to play *legato*. Apart from his studies, however, things began to get more difficult in many ways while he was studying in Chicago. His father, who had always supported his musical career and helped him forget the rest of the family who did not, passed away the first year he was in Chicago. At that time, Mohamed was grateful in more ways than one to have contact with Mr. Barenboim. Before Mohamed's father died, he saw some pictures of Mohamed with Mr. Barenboim. Mohamed's father told him, "This guy loves you; I see how happy he is when he hugs you." In addition to the musical trust and deep respect he had for the Maestro, Mohamed felt that in him he could touch the feeling of his father. Even if Mr. Barenboim might not feel the same way, Mohamed still had his own private love for him, his own attachment. They even had similar physiques: Mr. Barenboim was the same height, the same shape; he was like an Israeli copy of his father. Mohamed felt something like his father's hug when Mr. Barenboim hugged him.

The year of his father's death, the Intifada began. For a while it seemed like there would not be a third session of the Divan. Finally it was decided that the 2001 workshop would take place in Chicago, and shortly afterward the director of the Cairo Conservatory announced that it would not be looked upon well if Egyptian musicians participated in the orchestra that year. During the Intifada, there should be no contact between Arabs and Israelis. The conductor of the Cairo Opera Orchestra had held Mohamed's job open for him while he studied in America, telling Mohamed he could keep his position as long as he wanted; now he was in danger of losing it. Worse yet, there was a position waiting for him in the conservatory as assistant teacher, and that was also at stake. Mohamed spoke to the director of the Cairo Conservatory and told him that Maestro Barenboim had introduced him to his teacher, who would be coaching the orchestra that summer. "What can I do?" Mohamed asked. "I'm studying here in Chicago—I have to go." The director did nothing to explain where the rule had come from, but he told Mohamed that he would have big trouble if he went to the workshop.

Mohamed would not let himself be intimidated. He went to the workshop—and lost his job in the conservatory, for good. The following school year was especially hard. He had no scholarship from the Egyptian government, no more salary; he ran out of money for rent and was too proud to ask anyone for help. In the United States, there was no family atmosphere as there was in Egypt. The mentality seemed to be: "If you need me, give me flowers, do things for me. If you have nothing to give me, I have nothing to give you." He had to move out of his apartment and had no place to go for a few days. He had packed up all of his belongings and put them in storage. It was winter in Chicago; it was freezing and snowing outside, and the only warm place Mohamed could find was the train. He got on and tried to sleep until the conductor came by and woke him up, asking him what he was doing there. Rather than answer him, he decided to go on sleeping to avoid confrontation. It was a miserable time.

He didn't know how he would survive, let alone how he would go on studying and improving as a musician. He had to find a job to be able to eat, and he began to work in a furniture store, carrying very heavy things. He nearly broke his hand working there and could barely play for some time. Around that time Mohamed went to see Mr. Barenboim when he was in town to conduct the Chicago Symphony. He asked Mohamed how he was doing with his studies, and he replied, "I'm fine." He was too shy to tell him how it really was and ask him for support, so they just talked about the Divan and the next summer. Mr. Barenboim told him about a plan to take the orchestra to Andalusia, Spain. He told him it was a very nice place. Mohamed asked him what it was like there, and he said there was a beautiful campus in Pilas with an Olympic-sized swimming pool. They began to joke about it.

"Will there be girls in bikinis?" Mohamed asked.

"Bikinis? They even have naked girls if you want!"

Even if there were no naked girls in the swimming pool in Pilas, it was a beautiful campus, as promised. All the musicians in the Divan wanted to do the same childish things together, no matter where they came from. The swimming pool, suffering from disuse all day while the musicians were in rehearsal for hours at a time, was closed at night, and the fence surrounding it was padlocked. Of course, somebody found a hole in the bushes where there was no fence, and everyone else followed, splashing around in the pool and making noise all night. One summer in Pilas led to the next, and Mohamed began to think of leaving Chicago and all his problems there.

In 2003 he met Meirav, and remembered her face immediately from a one-minute meeting in Moscow years before. She seemed so familiar to him, not simply because he recognized her face, but because he felt he knew her spirit. They talked about everything for hours and hours. She told him he was the first Arab and the first Muslim she had ever known. He was amused at her curiosity: she wanted to know how these Arabs behaved—were they smart, were they stupid, were they funny, were they serious? Mohamed felt as if they were catching up, as if they had known each other a hundred years ago. It was so easy talking to each other, and Meirav became a part of the clique that always gravitated around Mohamed, a core group of people who had been coming to the workshop since 1999 and were familiar with all his invented words and silly pranks.

Meirav and Mohamed became a good team in the orchestra, playing side by side and supporting each other. The concert tour was exciting that year: they went to an Arab country for the first time—Rabat in Morocco; and they went to London to play in the BBC Proms concerts. While they were in London, Mohamed finally got up the courage to speak to Mr. Barenboim about his dire situation in Chicago. Mr. Barenboim was concerned and told Mohamed that they were setting up a scholarship fund for students from the Divan who were studying abroad, and that he would be one of the students to benefit from it. Mohamed couldn't believe what he was hearing. "This is the happiest Santa-Claus gift I ever got in my life," he thought to himself.

Finally he could start to eat regular meals, lead a normal life, study properly. Thanks to Mr. Barenboim, he was able to finish his studies in Chicago and then come to Germany to continue studying with Gregor Witt, the principal oboist of the Staatskapelle Berlin who had begun to teach at the Divan workshops. Mohamed was eager to learn about the "German sound" and the German style of playing; he loved their way of playing. In addition, Meirav was already in Berlin, also studying with Gregor Witt.

It was not easy starting over again with a new concept of producing sound; his new teacher made him feel there was something wrong with him, that he was not talented enough. Meirav tried to help him see things otherwise and told him it was pointless to fight with a teacher, that he should take all the wisdom and experience Mr. Witt had to offer and forget about his bad feelings. She was having difficulties herself, though she thought he was a wonderful teacher; she, too, was having to start over and learn some basic things no one had ever taught her. One year before finishing her degree, she was learning new but very elementary principles of playing, and with these new techniques she couldn't even get through a C major scale without making a mistake. Lessons were a struggle, both with the instrument and with her teacher. One day Mr. Witt took her to have a cup of tea before her lesson, and said, "Maybe it wasn't such a good idea after all that you came to study with me." Her pride flared up and she said, "Well, I do think it was a good idea, and I'm learning more than I've ever learned before, and I want you to give me another chance." He gave her the lesson, and another chance, and it was the best lesson she had ever had.

Mohamed was difficult to convince, though. He felt his teacher was telling him: "My way or the highway." Mohamed wanted more flexibility and support. His approach to learning differed greatly, perhaps irreconcilably, from Mr Witt's philosophy of teaching. While the relationship to his teacher remained tense, his Divan friendships grew closer during his time in Berlin. He had spent his first year there living with German friends, and at the end of the year he had to look for another apartment. His German was not exactly fluent, and he didn't know where to start looking. His friend Asaf had been part of his close-knit circle since 1998 in Apple Hill, and was studying with Axel Wilczok in Rostock. Asaf was living in a three-room apartment in Berlin with Mor Biron, an Israeli bassoon player who had also been in the Divan since 1999. Mor had always been too shy to get to know Mohamed. Mor felt he was perhaps not popular enough, not extroverted or funny enough. So when Mohamed called Asaf to ask him if he could stay at their place for two weeks or so while he looked for an apartment, and Asaf called out to Mor in the next room to ask him if it was okay, Mor said, "Yes, of course! It's *Mohamed* . . ."

Mor and Asaf each had their own bedrooms, and there was a third room—a long, narrow room typical of Berlin apartments. They thought they would turn it into a salon or a living room of some sort, but they never managed to find any furniture, so Mohamed brought a mattress and slept in the empty room. He went looking for an apartment every day, and every day he had no luck. Finally Mor and Asaf said, "Look, why don't you just stay and we'll split the rent three ways?" And, just like that, two weeks became more than two years. The Odd Couple plus one.

Mohamed immediately took over the kitchen. He would go to the Arab market and buy an enormous bucket of *tahina* and fill it with fresh chopped herbs; he made his own falafel, sometimes for dozens of people at a time when they had parties. He would make *Milchreis* (rice pudding)—or *Roslaban* in his own language. Although his German vocabulary was otherwise limited, they always called it *Milchreis* in the apartment. He would take the biggest pot they had, a huge pot for making stew, and fill it with *Milchreis*. Afterward, in order to fit it all into their modestly sized refrigerator, he would transfer it to every single container, plate, cup, and bowl in the house and cover them all neatly with plastic wrap. Mor would stand in front of the fridge laughing—he had never in his life had such a well-stocked kitchen. Not even a girl's kitchen, not even his own mother's kitchen was so overstuffed with food.

"I know that we're gonna get hungry in the morning and then there is something to eat," Mohamed would say, explaining his logic.

In addition to cooking, he became the resident barber. Mor went to him exactly four times to have his hair cut. The first time it was fantastic. He thought, Wow, this is great, a hair salon at home! The second time he found it a little short in the front, but he had never made a big deal about his hair, so he thought, Okay, never mind. The third time, it was a little bit bad and he decided to stop letting Mohamed cut his hair. But then once he didn't have enough time to go somewhere else, and he was about to go on tour and his hair was definitely too long. That was the fourth time, and it was really terrible. He could hear Mohamed laughing and shaking while he was cutting his hair.

The kitchen and Mohamed's room were the nuclei of the apartment. Asaf's room was the biggest, and Mor's room was fairly large, too; Mohamed's room was about the length of his mattress, and so narrow that you could sit, leaning your back against one wall, and reach the opposite wall with your feet. Nevertheless, all the guests who came to the apartment—and there were many—went straight to Mohamed's room. He called it his yellow submarine. He and Mor would sit there for hours, making reeds together—Mor shared his secret reed-scraping technique with him—or watching movies. Sometimes, late at night in the middle of watching a movie, Mor would fall asleep on Mohamed's mattress, and Mohamed would tiptoe around him, turn off the light, and go to Mor's big room to sleep.

The two of them became brothers, doing everything together. For two years, Mor and Mohamed traveled together from Berlin to the Divan workshop in Spain. They played together in Mozart's *Sinfonia Concertante* for oboe, clarinet, bassoon, horn and orchestra, as soloists with Mr. Barenboim and the Divan nearly twenty times.

In 2005, the orchestra's recording of Tchaikowsky's Fifth Symphony won the Echo classical music prize in Germany. Mr. Barenboim did not have the time to attend the ceremony himself, so he sent Mor and Mohamed to receive the award in his name and in the name of the orchestra. The symbolism was perfect: an

Israeli and an Egyptian, two original members of the orchestra and outstanding soloists. Nicole Foster, a longtime staff member of the Divan workshop, wrote out a speech for them and they traveled to Munich together, to the awards ceremony in the Philharmonie am Gasteig.

After the ceremony there was a big fancy reception, and both boys were looking around wide-eyed at the female musical celebrities strolling past them: Anne-Sophie Mutter, Hélène Grimaud, Anna Netrebko. Mor watched Mohamed get up and go over to Hélène Grimaud, and saw her smiling and then laughing with him, and he was sure that if Mohamed had gone on that way for another five minutes, she would have gone out with them that evening. But no, they went back to their hotel by themselves—the most luxurious hotel they had ever stayed in. They each had their own huge rooms with bigger-than-queen-size beds. They said good night to each other and went to their separate rooms, and Mohamed sat on his endlessly spacious bed watching television for a while and getting bored. Then he picked up the phone and called Mor in his room.

"What are you doing?" he asked. "I feel so alone here!"

"So come over," said Mor.

Mohamed packed up all his things and went to Mor's room, where they felt quite at home together except that the room was much too large.

When they came back to Berlin with the trophy, they put it in their kitchen and kept it there for two weeks, until Mr. Barenboim returned to Berlin and they had to relinquish it. They didn't really want to give it up; it had become part of the apartment. Before it left the kitchen, they made a whole series of goofy photos with it.

The year of the Echo prize was also the year of the Ramallah concert: 2005. Mohamed had wanted to go to Ramallah very much, but he was scared because of the violence he had seen there on television. His imagination started to work on him. He would have loved to fly to Tel Aviv with the Israelis, but he was afraid of having his passport stamped there; he had enough trouble at home in Egypt as it was. On the other hand, he was afraid of traveling by bus from Amman, imagining that someone might bomb the bus. It was silly, he knew, but he couldn't stop his imagination. The week before the concert in Ramallah, they were playing Mozart's *Sinfonia Concertante* in London at the Proms, and somehow word got around to Mr. Barenboim that Mohamed was afraid of going. Mr. Barenboim confronted him about it, and Mohamed admitted that he didn't feel comfortable going.

"Mohamed," he said, "please don't fail me."

Don't fail me. Those words were so powerful. Mohamed said to himself: "Okay, if I die there I will go anyway just because of these words."

His mother called him a few days later to ask him if he really thought it would be safe.

"I am one thousand percent sure," he said. She said she trusted his judgment.

He traveled from Amman to Ramallah with the other Arabs, and the bus did not explode. The night before the concert they stayed in a hotel in Ramallah, and late that night Mohamed heard a Syrian violinist walking through the hallways, calling out people's names and sounding scared, saying, "What's going on here? Why is it so dark in here?"

He thought something had exploded because the power was out in the hotel and the air was so thick with humidity—it seemed like smoke from a bomb. Mohamed and a few other musicians came out, laughing and teasing him, breaking the tension that no one talked about but everyone felt.

The next day all the Israelis arrived at the concert hall for rehearsal: Ayelet was there with tears in her eyes, videotaping everyone's emotional outbursts at being reunited; Mor was there, nervous for different reasons—he had to fill in for a colleague who didn't come to Ramallah, so he was playing a different part than usual.

Mor didn't realize what was really happening until the concert started. There had been so many discussions and arguments about going to Ramallah that, in the end, people had started to speak about it cynically, saying, "Okay, fine, it'll be all right, let's just go." He hadn't expected to be so overcome by the fact of being there and playing the concert.

Mohamed didn't know how touching it would be, either. During his years in the Cairo Opera Orchestra, it was easy to start thinking of a performance as a job, to just get used to it. It was easy to forget how a performance could be considered the greatest gift you could give. Sitting in the hall in Ramallah, he was happy to be there, but he was even happier that the Israelis were there, too. He decided to make this concert his personal gift to Ramallah, "A flower from the center of his heart."

Mohamed had heard how many people would be watching the concert, which was broadcast live all over Europe. He knew it was a historic occasion, something he and many people would never forget. He felt, while playing the Mozart *Concertante*, that his energy might spread out over the whole world.

After they played Beethoven's Fifth Symphony in the second half of the concert, and the audience stood and applauded for an unimaginably long time, the orchestra played an encore: "Nimrod" from the *Enigma* Variations. It was the last concert of a long tour, and it was in Ramallah, and they were playing this unbearably beautiful music. It all started to well up in Mohamed's throat, and his breathing stopped, and suddenly he had to play his solo. He started to play and had to use circular breathing to get through the rest of the phrase—his breathing was so unsteady from emotion.

Mohamed is still grateful to the Maestro every day for creating all of this, for doing all these huge great things that no one else could even conceive of. Someday Mohamed will ask him to take a break, a rest, have a vacation. Maybe they could go together, Mohamed and Burumburum, to the bikini place.

Until then, he and Mor will go on eating *Milchreis* and watching movies together. Now that Mor is the second bassoon player of the Berlin Philharmonic, he has a nice big apartment with several rooms all to himself, and has given Mohamed the key to it so that he can stop by whenever he is in town.

They still always fall asleep on the same bed, though.

Asaf Maoz

My father was born in Poland and my mother in India. They both immigrated to Israel when they were between seven and nine years old, and they met while serving in the military. Both of my parents are Jewish; my mother comes from a city called Kuchin in Kerala, an entirely Jewish enclave of India. The people of Kuchin claim to be the missing half of one of the twelve original biblical tribes. In 1954 the whole population of the city, about 50,000 people, immigrated to Israel.

In 1998 I went to the Apple Hill Chamber Music Center in New Hampshire, where I came into contact with Arab musicians for the first time. The first two people I met there were Mohamed Saleh Ibrahim and his brother Mahmoud, a wonderful cellist. I became good friends with both of them, and eventually ended up living with Mohamed many years later in Berlin. Apple Hill was very different from the Divan; the program focused more on our individual development, and that summer became a turning point in my life. I had been a very quiet, shy person until then, and I think I grew up a lot during that summer.

Two summers later, in 2000, I went to the Divan workshop for the first time. Back then, people were not as tolerant as they are today (although I know "tolerance" is a word Mr. Barenboim doesn't like "because tolerance implies an underlying negativity.") There were divisions not just between Arabs and Israelis (and the few Germans who were there), but between the Arabs themselves, who came from so many different countries. They were all completely separate. The Egyptians were the biggest group of Arabs, and they came with a chaperone who did not allow them to learn too much about us Israelis.

One evening we were having a discussion with Barenboim and Edward Said, and the Egyptian chaperone was sitting in the room with us. After about an hour and a half of discussion, some of the Israelis started to raise interesting questions about social customs in Egypt. At that point the man from the ministry told all the Egyptian girls to leave the room. We didn't understand why, because we were not asking any political questions at all. We were just interested in knowing what it was like to be a young person growing up in Egypt; we knew nothing about Egypt besides the pyramids and the Passover story, even though it was right next door to us. At some point our discussion did turn into a provocative political argument, led by one of the Syrian musicians. The chaperone then ordered all the Egyptian boys to leave the room too, because they might be influenced by this Syrian. We found it ironic that he was concerned that they would be influenced not by Israeli ideas, but by Syrian ideas! After that, there were far more Israelis in the room than Arabs, and we decided to stop the discussion because there was no point in talking about things by ourselves. It was very shocking for us to see that something like this could happen, because in Israel you can say whatever you want and nobody forces another opinion on you.

I didn't know anything about the Divan before I came, except what some of my friends had told me—that Daniel Barenboim and Yo-Yo Ma had been there the first summer; that alone sounded amazing. But when I came back to the workshop for the second and third times, I came because I actually liked the people I had met.

When the workshop was in Chicago in 2001, the atmosphere was different; I felt it was not as nice as it had been in Weimar. I didn't like all these American rules they imposed on us: having a curfew and not being allowed to drink on campus. I'm not such a big drinker, but forbidding alcohol altogether changes the social atmosphere of the group. I was over twenty-one and legally allowed to drink, but we older musicians couldn't hang out with the younger musicians in a bar because they were not allowed to go in. In addition, our housing was on the campus of Northwestern University, which was sprawling and impersonal in contrast to the cozy, closely knit atmosphere of the Belvedere School in Weimar. In the summers of 2003 and 2004, I went to the Verbier Festival instead of the Divan workshop.

At that time the individual players of the Verbier orchestra were on a higher level, and during the six weeks of the festival we played six different programs, as opposed to only one concert program all summer in the Divan. It was the best orchestra I had played in until that point, but I remember complaining that our sectional rehearsals, which were led by musicians from the Metropolitan Opera Orchestra, were not as thorough as the ones we had had in the Divan with teachers from the Staatskapelle Berlin, one of whom was Axel Wilczok.

In 2004 I had finished my studies at the Tel Aviv Academy, and taught and freelanced in Israel for four years. I decided I wanted to seriously improve my playing, so I went to Germany to study with Axel Wilczok: he was probably the best thing that happened to me in all my years in Germany. He is a wonderful *mensch*, and his personality was always a comfort to me. Before going there I had never studied German, so conversation was difficult in the beginning, but his musical demonstrations were always crystal-clear and beautiful. He never once played with a bad tone, like some other orchestral players I had had lessons with. I admired him for that.

When I began to study with Mr. Wilczok he said that I should come back to the Divan, and since I actually missed some people from the workshop, I decided I would. To be honest, coming back was not easy. Many people I had known earlier had become closer to each other over the years, so I came as an outsider even though I already knew most of the people. When we started to play, though, I was amazed at how good the orchestra sounded. As an ensemble it had made enormous progress. We played Mahler's First Symphony at the BBC Proms in London that year, and it was one of the best concerts of my life. That summer, 2005, was very powerful in general: we played Wagner for the first time, we went to South America, and we went to Ramallah.

My fear of going to Ramallah was not of the people there in general; I was afraid because I thought people would not understand what we were doing there and might try to harm us. The night before we left for Ramallah, we were staying in a hotel in Jerusalem, and a reporter came to interview us. People from the orchestra started shouting and crying. The questions were not particularly provocative, but the tour had stopped and we had had the chance to talk about things with our families; some people's families were not all that happy about what we were going to do. This interlude at home made people react differently than they would have if they hadn't seen their families.

The decision to play Wagner in the orchestra was difficult for me. The issue came up because some people from the orchestra asked Barenboim if we could read through it in rehearsal, and I can't deny that it was intriguing at first. Before we started to play the Prelude and *Liebestod* from *Tristan und Isolde*, Barenboim said: "I'll just explain a little bit before we play." We thought, "Well, it's a two-page part for us, so how much is there to explain?" Then he started to talk about the harmonies. He sat down at the piano, playing the unresolved chords in the Prelude, and at first we didn't understand what he was talking about. Then we started to see that he actually saw the entire work as a single arc. It was fascinating because afterward, when we played it, it was clear that we were all trying to follow and realize what he had just spoken about for an hour and a half.

After this first rehearsal, though, it became something of a gimmick to play it as an encore, and I didn't like it. Playing Wagner with a bunch of Israeli kids does symbolize something, especially with someone like Barenboim, who had performed the same piece in Israel with the Staatskapelle Berlin. We knew that if we performed Wagner with the Divan, no matter where, it would be all over the news in Israel again. I was not afraid of bad publicity for myself, but I was concerned that we, as a group, would be taken for kids who didn't respect the memory of our own people. That was why I thought it was wrong to play it over and over again as an encore (besides the fact that I think it's just a very long encore!). I especially didn't like it when we played it in a German city, in Wiesbaden.

The Wagner issue was the first time that we were divided into exactly three factions in the orchestra. For us Israelis it was a big deal; the Spanish people didn't care one way or another; and the Arabs were talking to us in the evenings, trying to understand what our problem was. I remember discussions with Nassib Al Ahmadieh about Wagner's music and the Holocaust. There were sleepless nights; people were shouting, saying they would never play Wagner. Most of it was just hot air.

After the first Wagner discussion, I called my father and asked him if it would bother him if I were to play Wagner. He said, "I don't know, let me think about it." My father is not a musician and has no background in classical music, but ever since I began to play the violin, he has listened to nothing but classical music. The next day, I spoke to him again and he said, "I've thought about it and it's okay; it won't bother me." That gave me some peace of mind. Somehow it was very important for me to get the approval of my family in this case. My father's parents had been forced to flee from Poland to Russia and back to Poland during the Second World War, and I kept thinking that if they were alive, I would have had to face a very serious conversation with them. On the other hand, when I played the entire *Tristan und Isolde* in Bielefeld as a member of the orchestra there, I never called to ask my parents what they thought about it. The thought never crossed my mind.

I have never lost my Israeli or Jewish identity, but after living in Germany for five years and playing in a professional German orchestra, Wagner seems less burdened by events of the past. Wagner is just another composer, although my paternal grandparents might have hated me for saying so. I went to one of the best musical high schools in Israel and never heard a note of any work of Wagner in my four years there. We had the best music teachers, but Wagner was not part of the curriculum, which is a shame because his music is part of the literature I should know as a musician. I eventually voted in favor of playing it in the Divan, because I felt it was important to play this music with a master like Barenboim.

The next year, we played the Prelude and *Liebestod* again, and, strangely, nobody said a word, as if we had jumped over a fence and we were now free. That year, Waltraud Meier came to sing Beethoven's Ninth Symphony with us, and one day she joined us in Pilas while we were rehearsing the Wagner. She stood right in front of the second violins when she began to sing the *Liebestod*, and I was in the first or second stand at the time, so she was very close. Some of my friends who were sitting in the audience of the open rehearsal later told me that my mouth was hanging open while I played. I was in shock. I had goose bumps all over and was nearly crying. Of course I had heard of her before, but it was only after playing with her that I found out that she was one of the world's greatest Wagner interpreters, especially in this role. I found it even more touching that she, who had sung Isolde so many times with the greatest conductors and orchestras, was equally moved by playing with us, the kids of the Divan.

My parents are generally very tolerant people, and I was raised in a liberal way. The family of my father's parents died in the Holocaust, so it would have been easy for my parents to oppose my going to Germany, but they were very open to it. I don't know how much my family accepts the Divan nowadays. My immediate family is huge; we are over fifty people, and the last time I was in Israel I got into a big argument with one of my uncles, a professor of nuclear physics in Israel and a very religious right-wing person. We were arguing about the logic of giving up territories and the concept of a "complete" Israel, *Eretz Israel*. Later that evening, I overheard him telling my aunt, "He's playing in Daniel Barenboim's orchestra together with Arabs, so his political opinions have changed." It bothered me a lot to hear that, because he made it seem as if I had been brainwashed. My political views have not been changed by the Divan itself; after I went there I developed more of an interest in reading about the conflict, and my opinions changed because of the things I read. As far as my extended family is concerned, I am doing something naive and beautiful, but meaningless.

At my birthday party a few years ago, I gathered up my whole family, forty or fifty people, and showed them the documentary film about the Divan, *Knowledge is the Beginning*. I could see that they were a bit shocked; it's not very easy to watch, especially for somebody who has no background in classical music. Most of my family has served in the army, so they think of Ramallah as an enemy territory, and it was awkward for them to see us going there to perform. I was glad, not because I put them in an awkward situation, but because I forced them to think for a moment. They could form their own opinions: decide whether to agree with what we did, to think it was wonderful, or to decide it was bullshit. In any case, they had to think about it.

One of my cousins who is a few years older than I am came and asked if she could borrow the DVD so that she could show her friends that there was another way of thinking. She said she was very surprised and impressed that there could be coexistence between Israelis and Arabs without too much division. I was very proud of her, because she was the only one who did that.

I had always thought that, once I had an orchestra job, I would stop going to the Divan, but in the summer of 2008, after playing in a professional orchestra for a year, the Divan was the best thing that could have happened to me. It was wonderful to play again in an orchestra where people were emotionally involved and enjoyed making music together. Yuval Shapiro told me that he wasn't coming back to the workshop because he wanted other people to have the same experience, and maybe I should do the same; but it's hard for me to imagine my summer without the Divan. I love the people. I think it would be a wonderful thing if it were to become a permanent orchestra, and I would be the first one to join it. I hope that, if it does, it will not lose its spirit over time. When we play concerts I always have the feeling that everyone is trying to contribute everything they can. Whenever I play with other orchestras and don't feel this "Divan spirit" from them, I am so disappointed.

For the last three years now, it has become a tradition for me and my closest friends from the Divan to call each other in order to make sure that we are all coming, because if one of us is not coming, we know it will be less fun. I've had great conversations with many people in the orchestra, too many to name all of them. One of my closest relationships in the Divan is the one with my old Egyptian friend from Apple Hill, Mohamed Saleh Ibrahim. I lived with him for two years in Berlin, and during that time I got used to his special way of speaking English. Even now, I use words that I used to use with him every day, and people don't understand me.

Mohamed admits that his English is very bad, and yet with him I have had some of the deepest, most emotional conversations I've ever had. During the lowest period of my life, which happened to be in Berlin while we were living together, he was my closest friend, the one who supported me the most and lifted my spirits.

My parents came to visit me once while I was living in this crazy apartment with him and Mor. I was very happy that they would finally be able to meet Mohamed. They knew I was living with Mor, and then when I told them that my Egyptian friend had moved in too, they wanted to know who this person was. When they met him, both of my parents completely fell in love with him, because Mohamed is always so loveable. We were sitting in the kitchen having this funny conversation, and everyone was getting along very well. Then my parents got up to leave and Mohamed asked my father how they were traveling back to Israel. He told Mohamed that they had a flight from Munich. Then Mohamed asked how they would be traveling to Munich. My father, who can read English but doesn't have many opportunities to speak it, responded, "We're training." I looked at my father and said, "You're doing what?"

Mohamed looked at me as if I he couldn't believe how I could not understand my own father; in Mohamed's language it was completely obvious. "Training!" he said, "Taking the train!"

INTERMEZZO

The guest lecturers at the first discussion of the 2008 workshop in Pilas were Elias Khoury and David Grossman. They spoke primarily about identity and identification with characters in literature, but inevitably digressed onto topics such as the creation of the state of Israel and the Palestinian predicament. Grossman described Israel as a country at war; Khoury contradicted him, saying it was not at war but was in fact occupying land that belonged to others. Khoury put forth the notion that the occupation had not begun in 1967 but in 1948, and that the UN partition plan of 1948 had not been accepted because it was seen as a program of ethnic cleansing.

When the moderator opened the discussion to questions from the audience, a young Israeli musician who was at the workshop for the first time stood up, took the microphone that was given to him, and read in a trembling voice from a piece of paper he had written on during the discussion. He explained that he would otherwise be too nervous to speak in front of the people gathered in the rehearsal hall. "Mr. Khoury," he began,

> I want to ask you whether you are aware that there are people in the Arab world who have vowed not to rest until they throw me and my family into the sea. There is no one who will rescue us if we don't help ourselves. Maybe it's wrong or selfish to say so, but there are many other Arab countries and no other Jewish

> countries. There is no place for us to go. My grandmother was in a concentration camp; she still has the tattoo on her wrist. We were persecuted for thousands of years and now we have finally come home. Why is it only our fault that the Palestinians are suffering? What about all these other Arab countries? There are many extremely wealthy Arabs who could have helped them; why do we alone have to be responsible for the Palestinians?

When he had finished, one person began to clap loudly; most of the others remained silent. These words were clearly not the young man's own, even if he believed them and repeated them with conviction; they had been passed down from generation to generation. Khoury said as much when he responded to him, implying that the young man's language, a language of the collective, prevented him from seeing anyone else's suffering but his own: "I think the first step is to go away from the idea that you can dominate the other with your suffering. This competition must stop. We must think about a real human solution for a region where everybody is free."

There was a clear division in the auditorium that day between "old-timers" and newcomers to the workshop. The new orchestra members sat in a different section of the hall, near the front, and I sat in the back with about twenty of the more senior members of the orchestra. During the young man's speech, some of them exchanged exasperated looks that said, "Here we go again," as if someone had rewound time to the beginning of the workshop, back to the same confrontations and crises the "old-timers" had witnessed or gone through themselves years ago.

The young Israeli who stood up to speak to Khoury on this occasion became less and less vocal over the course of the summer. Eventually, there was a relatively relaxed discussion on tour where he told the orchestra that he had come to the workshop absolutely convinced of his opinions and unwilling to budge. "Three days here changed so much," he said. After just three days he could defend the opposite point of view better than he could defend his own previous opinions.

During the same discussion, Israeli trumpet player Boris Kertsman talked about a conversation he once had with violist Ramzi Aburedwan of Ramallah. Ramzi was in Berlin at the time, and he went with Boris, his roommate Bassam Mussad, and an Israeli trombone player to a bar to celebrate the trombone player's birthday. They had a few drinks, they danced, and Boris and Ramzi began to talk about politics. Boris became very passionate, speaking more from his heart than his mind, and Ramzi expressed his own very different opinions. Boris left the conversation with his opinions intact, or so he thought. The next time he spoke to another Israeli about the same political topics, he heard Ramzi's arguments interrupting his own thoughts.

The Arabs at the workshop had different personal barriers to overcome. For many musicians from Syria and Lebanon, there was a constant worry that the Divan was a form of "normalization," or acceptance of the status quo in the Middle East. Normalization meant recognizing the state of Israel rather than regarding it as "occupied Palestine"; this term not only denied the Israelis' right to exist, but implied impermanence as well. Normalization was definitely a bad word even in Jordan and Egypt, where there was an official peace agreement; in Syria and Lebanon, contact with Israelis was illegal. The Arab position was: "Eventually we will go back home." According to Amir, a Palestinian friend of mine from the workshop, Israelis were seen by Arabs as monsters; the general assumption was that these monsters were not there to stay.

There were so many things Arabs and Israelis could agree on, according to Amir. However, the one issue that nearly always divided them was 1948, the year of Israel's creation. Many Israelis agreed that the wars were bad, that the occupation was bad, and that living conditions in the occupied territories were reprehensible. Nevertheless, no Israeli he knew was willing to examine the problems that arose from the creation of the state of

Israel itself. As Amir put it, "My grandfather was kicked out of his house so that the grandfather of my Israeli friend could live there." How could one even begin to speak about these things?

At a public forum with the orchestra, a woman from the audience once asked Amir, "How might it be possible for those of you enlightened people who have taken part in the Divan workshop to go and educate those in your Arab countries who are taught to hate?" She seemed to be saying, "Why can't you 'nice' Arabs do anything about those morons at home?" At this Amir felt compelled to unveil the true nature of this question. "The reason I don't hate is because I haven't experienced war first-hand," he told her.

> I refuse, however, to go and patronize people who are living in the poverty of a refugee camp, and expect them to understand what I'm doing in the Divan workshop and the values of coexistence. Why should they? This is not about being an extremist or narrow-minded, it's just common sense. If you're living under occupation, you're not going to want to go and work with your oppressors.

Talib Zaki, another Arab musician from the workshop, told me about the process of learning to accept Israeli existence, even making Israeli friends, and then going back to a country where it was illegal to do so. It was fine to talk about these things here in Europe, he said, but the really bad thing about the Divan was that it sometimes made him forget that he shouldn't speak so freely in his own country.

Forty Days and Nights in the Divan: Talib Zaki the Violinist

I have been a member of the Divan for only four years, and I want to tell the story of how things changed for me because of this workshop. I don't like to make things more beautiful than they are; I just want to tell what really happened.

I went to the Divan not because I wanted peace but because I had heard from my colleagues at home that it was a good musical experience, and because I wanted to play with Daniel Barenboim. I didn't want to deal with these people, I just wanted to play and not make any problems. I thought, it's forty days, it will be fine.

Of course you can't be like this when you get there, you have to deal with people. It's like being at a football game. You can't just watch and not take sides and join in. In fact, that was how I first met people who were really from Israel. I was playing football with the guys in the Divan and I accidentally hurt Boris, an Israeli trumpet player. He got up and said, "I'm okay, it's fine, don't worry," and then I thought, "Okay, so they don't try to pick a fight where there is none."

The problem in our Arab countries and in Israel is that the media are so effective. When you see every day in the news what they are doing in Israel, you don't see any other perspectives. Of course, the Israelis are enemies for us, as we are enemies for them. We are at war, even if there has been no confrontation for twenty-five years. Just because Israel is our enemy, though, doesn't mean that

100 percent of Israelis are our enemies. There are a lot of Israelis who want peace, and protest against war, who don't want to hurt the Palestinians or the Arabs; they want to have a peaceful life. I don't want to discuss why and how they came to be there; they are there now and they don't want to cause more problems.

One of the things I learned about myself in the Divan is that I am not liberal at all. I do have some very good friends from the Divan now, though, and some of them are Israeli. A little story about Facebook, the networking Web site, might show you how strong our friendship is. When you join Facebook, it's normal to add your friends to your list as you see them come up. So I added two friends of mine, Israeli girls from the Divan who live in Berlin, to my friend list. Everyone can see who your friends are on your Facebook profile. They can also see what networks your friends belong to. There are networks for every country. After I added these friends to my list, they both joined the Israel network, which is perfectly normal, and you could see on my profile that I had two friends from the Israel network. You can't imagine how many people came to me and said, "How could this happen?" For my part, I didn't care. But it was uncomfortable, so I had to remove them from my friend list on the Web site. A few months later, both of them sent me a new friend request on Facebook, and they had both left the Israel network.

It goes to show that nobody can move alone. If you want to understand each other, you have to understand each other's problems. With my close friends, maybe I no longer feel that they are Israelis, I don't know. They also don't put up a show of being macho and having to fight to protect their land through denial of the facts. These people are some of my best friends.

Basically, you can't make your opinion of Israelis in general from the Israelis who come to the Divan. Most of them in the Divan are really open-minded and very clever people. You can divide them into more or less three groups. The first group is totally liberal and has nothing to do with their government.

The second group is a bunch of actors; in front of Barenboim or the television cameras they say, "Of course we're friends with them," but they mostly stay in their own group. And the third group clearly doesn't want to have anything to do with us and doesn't try: "We don't like them, we don't want them, we're coming here for the music."

I think the problem with the Divan is that it lasts forty days, not more. If it lasted longer, you would finally have a real experience. Usually what happens is that, in the beginning, you find people who are interested in getting to know you whether you are an Arab or Mexican—it makes no difference to them. Then there are other people who are aware that they are Israelis and we are Arabs, but they want to know more. In this short time you can't accomplish very much with these people. The process is like this: in the first ten days, maybe you sit together at lunch or at dinner once. Then, the next ten days, maybe you start to have short discussions. The real time to discover things and get to know people is the last twenty days, when we're on tour. It's not enough time.

In some cases, I believe in letting things be solved without any extra effort. If people feel that they *have* to speak with the others, they will not do it, or they will do it badly. But if it is without any feeling of Big Brother watching them, they can be more free.

It wouldn't help to concentrate on the way we interact, and it doesn't help to talk about politics. When you concentrate too much on things that don't need a lot of attention, you will destroy them. It's a bad idea to bring everyone together and sit down and say, "Let's speak about the Middle Eastern conflict in a difficult foreign language." It doesn't help.

It helps when you are lost somewhere on tour in Valencia and you find some Israeli colleagues and try together to figure out how to come back. It helps when you are hungry and someone else is hungry too, and you go and find something to eat together. I think it doesn't help to bring in some big names and let them speak.

I once met an Israeli before the Divan, in 2002, when I went to the Paganini competition in Genoa. He was an Israeli who was living in America. We went out in a group and we spent the night together. After a while, he finally asked, "Where are you from?"

I didn't know where he was from, because at the competition he was representing the United States. I told him, and then I asked where he was from.

He said, "I'm from Israel."

"Okay, fine," I thought. Then we spent the night having a lot of fun, not talking about anything deep, but it was fine. Just imagine, if we had started talking politics, it would have been a bad night, we would have disagreed about everything. That kind of discussion needs time. It's too late now to discuss what happened in 1948, who was right and who was wrong. I don't want to discuss this, although I share the Arab point of view.

The problem is how to deal with all this now. Maybe we need to have a very long session someday and try to deal with this stuff. I think it's not the best idea to meet in the Divan once a year and try to solve any problems, but it is a good thing to recognize how these people interact. For me, the Divan is a place to discover myself first and how I react to others. It helps to know that we sometimes believe many things that are not true. It helps to understand how other people think too.

In 2006, when there was war, some of us Arab musicians didn't go to the Divan, and when we came back something had changed. I don't know what, but something has been different since then. There was something in the air when we came back—there was less harmony than there was before. This surprised me because I assumed that the Divan Israelis knew all we Divan Arabs were against the war, and I thought they came because they were also against the war.

In December 2006 we went on tour to America, and we Arabs joined the orchestra after we had missed the summer tour, and on the first day everything was fine and everyone came and told us how much they missed us, but the next seven days after that were terrible. Two friends of mine from before the war didn't speak a single word to me. Of course, I can understand what happened with them, but their silence goes against the fact that I still speak with other friends of mine who are open-minded and support peace.

What could you expect, though, when you saw in the news that Israeli children were writing very bad things to Lebanese children on missiles that were directed against Lebanon? I was on the Arab side, so I don't know what they saw on television in Israel. I felt not very good about what I saw, but we have to learn to be more clever in this situation. I don't have a problem with my Israeli stand partner because there was a war. Maybe she didn't know anything about the whole thing; I don't have to think that she was responsible for what happened—I can decide how to think about it and how to act with her.

The orchestra is so famous now, and maybe that makes people think they want to participate because it's so famous, but they are not going to speak to these people. These last two years, I have the feeling that people in the Divan are no longer interested in improving the workshop. It seems like people come with a clear idea: either they are ready to speak to other people, or they are not going to participate in dialogues at all. It seems like there are fewer people who are in between, who want to see if maybe it's worth talking to these people.

Before, it seemed like there were more Spanish people in the orchestra who could speak good English, who made it easier for us to meet. With them, you had more opportunities to make contact. Now, the Spanish people who come don't speak enough English. It's really a problem.

I think this conflict can soon be solved as a peace agreement, but it will take at least eighty to a hundred years for people to be able to live together normally. Look at the Egyptian experiment: they have peace—never mind what kind of peace—and if an Egyptian meets an Israeli somewhere outside of their countries, there is no problem. If they meet in Egypt, though, there is no way for them to be good friends.

We are creatures of habit, and it is normal not even to think about what you believe when you hear the same thing repeated every day, several times a day, at home, in school, in the media. We learn to hate each other. I asked some Israelis, and they say it is the same thing in their country—most Israelis hate Arabs.

In the Divan I have met people who can really change the way I think, like Guy Braunstein. When I met him I learned from him that 80 percent of the whole problem can be solved just by being human. Guy is a very special person; you can't compare him to anyone else. He believes in something and doesn't care how the Israelis will feel about it. It is really hard for the concertmaster of the Berlin Philharmonic to be with the Divan for such a long period of time; it shows how he puts the Divan and this idea first on his priority list. Guy is really a human being—he has this humanity that we need in the Divan.

I was too lazy to use my mind before I came to the Divan. I had ideas that were planted in my head, and I didn't want to make any effort to change, but with the Divan, I used my brain a little bit more. I found out that maybe politics is a bad thing.

In the Divan, mostly I learned how to be a human being.

INTERMEZZO

Guy Braunstein is the concertmaster of the Berlin Philharmonic, but when he comes to the Divan workshop he takes a seat at the back of the first violin section. "I don't care where I sit," he once told me.

It is easy to imagine why many aspiring young musicians come to the workshop for the first time. It is far more difficult to imagine why the concertmaster of the Berlin Philharmonic would give up his summer vacations (when he could be playing dozens of solo concerts) to play for free at the back of the section in a youth orchestra. Granted, Guy did play several solo concerts with the Divan in the summer of 2008: Haydn's *Sinfonia Concertante* for violin, cello, oboe, bassoon and orchestra. Immediately after the concerto, however, he took his usual seat in the seventh stand to play Schönberg's Variationen, Op. 31. It is probably also worth mentioning that all the soloists who perform with the Divan, including Waltraud Meier, receive the same fee as Barenboim himself: zero.

Guy is not the only professional musician in the orchestra. Over the years the number has grown: Mor Biron, second bassoonist of the Berlin Philharmonic; Ramón Ortega, principal oboe of the Bavarian Radio Orchestra; Nabil Shehata, principal bassist of the Berlin Philharmonic; and Mohamed Saleh Ibrahim, assistant principal oboist of the Qatar Symphony Orchestra—these are only a few of the musicians with prestigious positions. Guy, however, is one of the only musicians to join the orchestra after having already established his career.

On the evening before the Divan's concert in Oslo in 2008, Barenboim and Mariam Said gathered up the orchestra for a discussion on the rehearsal stage of the new Oslo Opera. Barenboim opened the discussion by saying that the orchestra was now nearly ten years old, and that this was a good time to reflect on the past in order to determine the way of the future. He invited the orchestra members to share their observations on the workshop's development and their wishes for its continuation. Guy was the first person to speak, but instead of contributing his thoughts he posed a question: "Why are we here?"

After some confusion, he tried to explain himself better: "I'm very curious to hear from everyone here why they go to the Divan and not to some other youth orchestra, like the Gustav Mahler Youth Orchestra, for example."

Many people, including Barenboim, tried to bounce the question back into Guy's court and ask him why he kept coming back, but Guy insisted on having his own question answered first. Nabeel Abboud-Ashkar responded first:

> When I come to the Divan, I am treated not just as a musician or a violinist who plays this well or this badly. Regardless of my musicianship, there is a separate part of my personality that is taken care of here. Sitting here in this discussion, we are all equal regardless of our individual levels of playing. This is a very good feeling because there are wonderful musicians in this orchestra and less experienced musicians. It is actually a dream for someone like me to sit next to you at a stand . . .

At this Guy made a barely audible, self-effacing remark. Nabeel continued:

> This would not be possible in other places, and this is just one of the special aspects of this orchestra. Another one is the fact that we

> feel committed to it; this orchestra has literally changed our lives and opened doors as no other orchestra could have done.

Waltraud Meier, who was to sing the first act of *Die Walküre* with the orchestra the next day, spoke of her own motivation for coming to the workshop; she had first performed Beethoven's Ninth Symphony with the Divan in 2006, and had been coming back every year since. "I'm so happy to be an honorary member of this orchestra," she said, and there was an enthusiastic round of applause.

> I can tell you why I want to come back every year. I think you're not aware of how you make music. You're a totally different orchestra from any other: you're not playing for a living but for your lives. When I'm with you on stage it is so different, it is a totally different energy. This is what your stand partner is feeling too; he feels you have the same wishes, the same ideals. All that comes together in one idea when you play, like in Beethoven's Ninth: *Alle Menschen werden Brüder*, all men will become brothers. We have a long way to go in that respect, but keep up that ideal! When you play it, you describe it while playing it. I want to thank you for giving that to me because I feel it every day. That's why you're so different and I always want to come back.

After hearing such heartfelt answers to his question, Guy had no choice but to explain his own reasons for being at the workshop.

Guy Braunstein

I had been curious about the Divan for years and wanted to go in 2004, but then I came down with a high fever and had to stay at home. I was very skeptical about the project; I thought it was just something that made waves without having any real substance. I wanted to find out what it was like for myself, though. The first time I was able to join the orchestra was in December 2006, on a short tour to the United States. I had spoken to Daniel Barenboim about going to earlier workshops and he knew I was interested, so when they went to the States he asked me to come. The tour came at a very bad time for me, when I was extremely busy and tired; I only had four days free, and the last thing I wanted to do was get on a plane to the States and have jet lag. Daniel nagged me about it, though, so I said to myself that I would go only once, just for him, and in a funny way this turned out to be the case—although I have been back twice since then.

Even though I slept much less than I ordinarily would have in four days, I came out of the tour with so much energy that it lasted for a good two months. I was totally hyperactive. There is an atmosphere in the Divan that you don't get anywhere else, and that was the reason I came back. I didn't come back for Daniel; I really did only go for him the first time. When I came back it was because of the people I met there. I go to the workshop now for purely selfish reasons.

I don't have much experience with youth orchestras, but I haven't found this special atmosphere anywhere else. In spite of this complicated political situation we're in, the people in this orchestra produce the best music you can hear anywhere. There is more dedication here than in most places; maybe it's to prove a point. And when Daniel comes, he seems to totally ignore the very special situation we're in. It's just business as usual, and he screams at everybody who plays the wrong dynamics; maybe we make such good music because of the combination of his demands and the adversity we face.

The starting point of this orchestra is of course very different from a professional orchestra. This orchestra makes enormous progress from the first rehearsal to the first concert, which is nothing like what you experience in a professional orchestra. It's one thing to be able to learn everything very quickly and without any resistance, but if you have to take your time and learn slowly, you can learn more in the process. The problems you face are different, the process is different. The process we go through here is exactly what is missing in professional orchestras: in the Divan, we are developing an identity from nothing, from Dead Sea level. I am not talking about the level of playing, but the musical identity. The Berlin Philharmonic has its own identity at the first rehearsal of any program; the starting point is already very clear. You can try to bend it north or south, but the identity will remain. In the Divan, we build a new identity for each piece we play. The process is much longer, but more flexible in a way.

The workshop is the one time in the year when you don't run to see the news; you create your own news. During the year between workshops, you do read the news and you see it's heading toward war with Iran. There are three Iranians in the Divan now, and I met two of them last summer already. When I read everything being said about Iran on the Internet, all I can see are their faces, and I think: "What the fuck are they talking about?" Since last year I've been dreaming about playing in Teheran. When I met these Iranians we started fantasizing about playing a concert there together. I still hope I'll be the first Israeli to go there, rather than the air force pilots.

When I came to the Divan for the first time, I was disappointed to see that the Arabs were so much more curious about meeting us Israelis than most Israelis were about meeting them. The Israelis are less eager to mix—they sit with the people they already know; there is so little curiosity on their part. I wonder if it has to do with the fact that they just know each other much better, or whether the Israeli "propaganda machine" is working overtime. In Israel, the propaganda has to be more sophisticated than the methods that used to work in the former USSR, but nevertheless it works. In Israel propaganda is made for the customer who feels sophisticated, beyond the influence of it; but it still shapes you in a way. I've caught myself being susceptible to the propaganda too.

A good friend of mine from the States is the most liberal person imaginable; he doesn't consciously believe in any separation or difference between races. Nevertheless, when he goes uptown in New York late at night, if he sees a group of black men standing around he crosses to the other side of the street. This is the result of exactly this kind of very sophisticated propaganda. I grew up totally unprotected from this, even though I try to resist it and be aware of it. Nobody is 100 percent protected from prejudice.

The Divan doesn't solve the world's problems; nobody thinks it can or does. When people start discussing the problems of the Middle East they have to start by *not* saying exactly what they think; otherwise they wouldn't be able to start at all. Mostly, though, the kids in the Divan don't sit around talking about how to solve the conflict; they talk about the usual things kids talk about: cars, football, and sex. They talk a lot about sex; it's normal.

The first stage of any conflict, accident, or calamity is denial. If you slip on a banana peel and break your arm, the first thing you think is: "What if I could rewind time? What if I hadn't slipped on that banana peel?" You don't want to accept that it has happened and you can't undo it. Most of the Middle East has never gotten past this stage in relation to the Israeli–Palestinian conflict. Most Israelis are somehow hoping that the Arabs will cease to exist someday, and most Arabs are hoping that the Israelis will cease to exist someday. This is not going to happen. After breaking your arm, you can't rewind time and suddenly be able to see the banana peel before you step on it. Now that Israel exists as a country, there is no going back to the way things were before. Both peoples are there to stay.

Let's face it, as classical musicians, we don't have much of an influence on anything. How many people in this part of the world play or listen to classical music? But if other professionals—doctors, scientists, footballers, car mechanics, whatever—would "Divan" themselves, then we'd be getting somewhere; then we could start to make a difference. What if there were a great taxi driver exchange? If you took all the drivers from, say, Jerusalem, and exchanged them with all the drivers in Amman, who knows what would happen? With the existence of GPS, it would be theoretically possible. Taxi drivers talk to everyone.

Of course the Divan has an effect on the musicians in it, but it has an effect beyond that too. People who come to the concerts of the Divan in Madrid, London, Paris, or anywhere else, probably either come to see the sensation—monkeys from enemy countries putting on a show—or they come to see Daniel Barenboim; but if they watch and listen carefully from the beginning to the end of the concert, it will have some kind of effect on them. It has an effect on the families and friends of us musicians. The Divan by itself is almost nothing. It is the best orchestra in the Middle East, and it goes to show what Israelis and Arabs can do when they get together; but it has to be the start of something much bigger.

There have been a lot of attempts to make peace in the Middle East, and most of them were not very sincere or honest. People from many fields have tried to solve this problem, but it seems to me that the Divan is almost the only thing that is working. So many things have happened over the years: the First Intifada, the Second

Intifada, settlements have been built, walls have been built, military operations have been carried out—and none of these things have been effective. On the other hand, Communism fell as a result of a domino effect that began with movements less significant than what this orchestra has become. I'm a real believer in the domino effect, and I wonder whether this orchestra might just become one of the dominoes that will end our conflict.

INTERMEZZO

On July 16, 2008, the Amman Symphony Orchestra gave a concert with a Lebanese choir in the Roman amphitheater in Amman, Jordan. The orchestra sometimes augmented its ranks by inviting musicians from neighboring countries like Lebanon or even Israel. Georges Yammine was one of the Lebanese musicians who performed with the orchestra that evening. Less than a month later, the West-Eastern Divan Orchestra was scheduled to perform in the same amphitheater; it was to be the orchestra's first appearance in Jordan.

After the concert by the Amman Symphony Orchestra was over, the musicians left the amphitheater and began to board the bus. Georges had one foot on the bus steps when he heard: *tok-tok-tok-tok-tok*—a succession of gunshots. He dove into the bus to take cover. When the noise was over, he looked out and saw blood on the street, women screaming and crying, and the young gunman, who pointed the firearm at his own head and then ran away from the crowd.

Six of the musicians were wounded, but only two were seriously injured: one was shot in the back and the other in the shoulder. One victim's cheek had been lightly grazed; a bullet whizzed by the ear of another. Georges had no time to panic; by the time he realized what had happened, it was all over and he was busy comforting the distraught musicians around him. Georges's first thought was that the gunman had perhaps mistaken the Amman Symphony for the Divan, or that he may have wanted to target the two Israeli musicians who had played in the orchestra that evening. The assassin's motives were later revealed:

the nineteen-year-old from a Palestinian refugee camp was against the secularization and Westernization of Arabic culture. Western classical music apparently fell into this category. The young man (who later committed suicide) might not even have been aware that Israelis were among the performing musicians.

The incident had not been in the international news, but the musicians in the Divan quickly found out by word of mouth, and many wondered whether their own Amman concert would still take place. About a week and a half after the beginning of the workshop, Barenboim announced that the Jordanian concert had been cancelled, and that the orchestra would be performing at the Ravello Festival on Italy's Amalfi coast instead.

The attack in Amman was an isolated event, and the gunman was not associated with any political movement, but it was another reminder of the instability of the entire region. If even the Amman Symphony could not perform safely in Jordan, what would it be like for the Divan? Jordanian pianist Karim Said was convinced that the majority of Amman's residents would be indifferent to the Divan's appearance, if it could go there someday. People didn't care much about classical music in Jordan, he said. That was why he went to London to study when he was only eleven years old.

Karim once invited me to dinner at his apartment in London, and though I offered to help with the preparations he insisted on doing everything himself. I stood back and asked him about his recollections of being the youngest member of the Divan workshop in 1999. Soon I decided to stand back a bit further, glad to be exempt from assisting his culinary preparations, which included doing yesterday's dishes, irrigating the kitchen floor while washing a fish, and chopping vegetables on a cutting board precariously balanced on the corner of a countertop. His handling of knives was a terrifying spectacle, and he seemed unmoved by my exhortations to avoid inadvertent amputations to his pianist fingers.

Despite the drama in the kitchen, the food was very good; Karim made a delicate ginger-lime cream sauce for the fish, complemented by a potato salad made according to his mother's recipe.

Karim Said

I was born in Amman and have a Jordanian passport, and I am also a Lebanese citizen. Although I spent my early childhood in Jordan, I went to Lebanon often, once a year at least; my maternal grandmother lives in Beirut, which is where both my parents grew up. On the whole, my family is more closely linked to Lebanon than to any other place, although they have happily settled in Jordan. The only thing that reveals my Palestinian origins is my dialect in Arabic. That's what most Palestinian families seem to do—they keep their dialect alive. Almost nothing else suggests my origins. You would never be able to tell from my name, for example, where exactly I come from.

My father was born in Cairo, because his parents had gone there to join Edward Said's branch of the family (Said was my grandfather's first cousin). My father's family had had a successful business in Cairo, but one year after he was born they had to leave the country because of the revolution. It was then that they moved to Beirut, right next door to where my mother lived.

After the 1982 Israeli invasion of Beirut, my parents fled to Jordan. My mother is an English teacher and my father is a businessman, and they both spoke to me only in English until I was six years old. They wanted me to be a native English speaker. After that, they started to speak Arabic with me as well. It has proved to be a blessing; I've been traveling alone since I was nine years old, and it would have been impossible without being able to speak

English. My parents and I still speak a mixture of languages—about half Arabic, half English.

My father is a very serious amateur jazz musician. He plays the guitar and drums, so I was introduced to jazz very early. My musical education began with him teaching me the drums, but at five I started taking piano lessons. Neither of my parents really liked classical music very much. We had exactly two classical music CDs at home: Mozart's Flute Quartet and Vivaldi's *Four Seasons*. Everything else we had was just pop, rock, and jazz. I loved classical music, though, and my piano tuition was strictly classical. I was very lucky to have started with my teacher, Agnes Bashir from Georgia. After the first Gulf War, many musicians from the former Soviet Union who had been living in Iraq came to Jordan, and she was one of them. She was a fantastic teacher, and I had a very structured education with her, although I did play jazz on the side. My father taught me jazz harmony, which meant that I was trained at a very young age to think in chords, and this still helps me now.

I am the only person in my family who has chosen a musical career, although there were many amateur musicians in the family. Edward Said and his late sister Rosemarie were both pianists, and his sister Jean still plays the piano as well. In fact, his immediate family was incredibly serious about classical music, I believe, although none of them made a career out of performing it. It is well known that my late great-uncle managed to find time to play recitals regularly, and I regret not having attended any.

Uncle Edward told us about the first Divan workshop. I was only ten years old, far too young to go, but he helped to get me invited as an observer. I heard from the administration of the Divan workshop that my audition tape had been lost in the post, but they decided to invite me anyway. I was very lucky. I did not have a clue what this workshop would be about. I didn't really care, either; to me, it seemed like an adventure to travel, to meet older musicians, and to meet what seemed to be a strange breed of people called Israelis. I did know that there would be Israelis there, but I didn't know what that meant. I remember everything happening at the last moment, so there wasn't even enough time to talk about it at home. It was more a matter of the essentials: getting a visa, getting ready, practicing, making sure I prepared something to play for Mr. Barenboim, and so on.

I received a lot of attention in the beginning, because everyone likes a cute little boy who apparently plays well. I enjoyed the first two years immensely. There was probably just as much partying as there was work, and there was always Arabian music being played at night. There were quite a few people in the orchestra who were excellent Arab musicians as well. I couldn't play Arabian music, nor did I want to, but I would occasionally improvise some jazz on the upright piano in the canteen. I would often sneak out of my room at night to go to these parties; since I was the youngest one, I was put to bed early by a treacherous female German housekeeper. A few years after the second Divan workshop in Weimar, I went back to the same boarding school for a piano competition, and the same lady greeted me. She remembered me, and they had even kept a newspaper clipping with my photo in it. They obviously liked me somehow, even if I gave them trouble at the time.

I was forbidden to speak to reporters that first summer by one of the various adults responsible for me. There was, however, a sneaky German-Palestinian journalist who told me he had permission to interview me early in the morning, knowing I would be awake and without adult supervision. My supervisor found out about it later, and she got very angry with the reporter. Around the same time, I had discovered the word "bitch" for the first time, because everybody was saying it. Some of the people there who were twice my age or older didn't speak such good English, and they would apply it to men and women alike. It didn't seem like such a bad word, because everyone was using it. When I saw my supervisor later on, I asked her, "So, did you find out where this bitch is?" She was shocked, to say the least, and this was my first severe scolding at the Divan. Unfortunately for me, there were many to follow by all sorts of people.

The ping-pong table was a major part of the first Divan workshop, for some reason. Everyone would gather around the table in the evening; even Mr. Barenboim played once. He also played football with us. I was too small to play back then, so I was given the job of nurse. I had to take it seriously, so I wore a mask and pretended to treat people when they fell. I think I didn't really know who Daniel Barenboim and Yo-Yo Ma were when I was ten years old. Later, as I grew up, I became more aware of who these people were in the music world. Yo-Yo Ma was such a nice person; we got along well, so I asked him to help me with my sight-reading. He said, "Sure," and he got out the Chopin Cello Sonata and played it with me. I'm not sure whether this piece was my choice or his, but in any case, it was much too difficult for me at the time. He would say, "Just follow the left-hand line here," and so on, giving me advice.

I remember going to the Buchenwald concentration camp with the orchestra that summer. While we were there, Mr. Barenboim sat me down on his knee and said, "Do you know why you're here? You're quite young and you probably shouldn't have come, but do you know why you're here? You're here because it's important for this to never happen again, and young people should see this too."

That first year we were also taken to Bayreuth to see a performance of *Die Meistersinger*, with Mr. Barenboim conducting. Somehow they managed to get tickets for some of us, even though it was notoriously difficult to get tickets for performances at Bayreuth. Maestro Barenboim invited me to sit in the orchestra pit on a little footstool next to the podium. It was the most uncomfortable thing imaginable, but I didn't care. Even though I didn't understand any German, let alone Wagnerian German, I was captivated for the entire five hours. It was the first opera I had ever seen. I've always cherished this memory; the effect this experience had on me is indescribable.

After the first workshop in Weimar, my family considered sending me to the Musikgynasium Schloss Belvedere, the boarding school for musicians that had hosted the Divan that summer. Because I was fluent in English, though, my parents felt it made more sense for me to go to England instead. In addition to the language issue, as beautiful as Weimar was, London was London. Everyone is at home being a foreigner in London, which is what I love about it. I feel most at home in London; there are millions of people here with backgrounds and stories more interesting than mine. When I was eleven years old, I left my family in Jordan to study at the Purcell School of Music in London, another boarding school for musicians.

I have gone to every summer Divan workshop except when it took place in Chicago in 2001. I have gotten to know the people from the orchestra extremely well. I'm generally not good at staying in touch throughout the year, but when we see each other in the summer it's like seeing family again. We live together for quite a long time every summer, considering the fact that we are essentially strangers.

When I started going to school in London, I met my late great-aunt Rosemarie. She was a top historian in London and a specialist in Middle Eastern and Persian Gulf history, as well as a musicologist. She raised my awareness and educated me. I received quite a thorough education in the history of the Middle East through her. She armed me with facts, which are always useful for staying calm in discussions about politics. She also taught me how to separate the personal from the political, how to present myself rationally in a political debate, which gives me more confidence. It's easier to walk away from a difficult discussion if someone starts shouting and screaming hysterically. The debating skills I learned from my aunt have proved to be very useful at the Divan.

At the first workshop in Weimar, people were just people to me, which was nice. I knew where people came from, of course, because of the language I spoke with them. I also have quite a good ear for dialects in Arabic, and even at the age of ten I could tell where all the different Arabs came from. I noticed that some Egyptians couldn't always work out where we were from at first, because people from Palestine, Jordan, Lebanon, and Syria probably sound similar.

People who don't know me often mistake me for an Israeli in the Divan, and this was true at the very beginning as well. Back then, I simply made friends with people I liked. Only later did I begin to find out about their political views. When I grew up and went on talking to the same people, I found out that the people I liked were sometimes completely on the other end of the political spectrum. It was very interesting; I could discover that I really didn't like what they were saying, but I learned how to make the distinction between the person and the words in practice, exactly as I had been taught to do in theory. This is something many people can't do. The Divan made me realize that you don't have to agree with a person in order to like him or her. I suppose that this was easier for me than it might have been had I grown up in a refugee camp, for example.

Whenever I talk about politics in a group discussion in the Divan, I am always aware of the fact that I'm not an actual participant in the orchestra simply because I play the piano, a non-orchestral instrument, and I was often too young to contribute anyway. I have always gone to the workshop mainly to have lessons with Daniel Barenboim and Cliff Colnot, his conducting assistant at the Divan, and to learn from their orchestral rehearsals. I don't generally like to draw too much attention to myself in discussions, because I feel that I'm not actually contributing a great deal to the collective, as opposed to my colleagues in the orchestra. Arguing with people about sensitive topics as an outsider seems inappropriate in general.

When I do talk about politics, however, it is usually one-on-one, and I choose my discussion partners carefully; they are people who I know are not going to get personal. I usually like the people I'm talking to. I'm not trying to convert anyone; I'm not on a mission. I'm not comfortable if there is any sort of personal confrontation, and I think many people feel this way. Others may not actually talk about politics at all. As an observer, I think, how stupid. For once in your life, you're face to face with Israelis, or with Arabs, and you're not going to talk about certain things? How fake, how unnatural!

On the other hand, I sometimes ask myself what the point is in discussing politics at the Divan. What is actually going to happen as a consequence? People are almost inevitably going to get upset, and it is probably going to be unpleasant. And then the conversation will be forgotten the next morning as soon as the rehearsal starts. So, what exactly will be achieved?

Great-Uncle Edward's death was such a loss for the people who joined the orchestra later. He knew exactly how to deal with musicians in this situation, since he was a musician himself. He had a unique combination of qualities. The Israelis could see that here was a Palestinian, one of these people who are often described as inhuman, crazy etc., yet they were very impressed by him, as anyone would be. There has been a big hole in the workshop since he died. It is wonderful, however, that his widow Aunt Mariam continues to work with us.

I am very sad that he is no longer with us to witness how far his hard work has taken us. Obviously the orchestra has developed immensely since his death. When he was alive, it was not yet as important as it is today, neither internationally nor musically. The first workshops were comparatively provincial; back then, it was little more than a youth orchestra playing in a small concert hall after a summer course, and now it's a first-class, nearly professional orchestra. The nature of the Divan has changed over the years. In one way, it's weaker without Uncle Edward, because when he was involved the leadership was more balanced. There has been no replacement for the lectures he used to give and the discussions he used to lead.

I remember one occasion that demonstrated Uncle Edward's effect on people. Barenboim and he received the Principe de Asturias prize in Oviedo, Spain. I was there to play in a concert before the awards ceremony. During his stay, Uncle Edward visited a university to give a lecture, and as soon as he walked in, before even saying a single word, the audience gave him a standing ovation that lasted several minutes.

I go to the Divan every summer to make music more than anything else, and over the years I have witnessed a world-class orchestra being created by a master. Many people would give anything to be able to witness the rehearsals I have witnessed, to hear one of the world's greatest conductors telling an orchestra exactly what he thinks about the most basic musical principles, as well as what you would expect to hear from a great conductor. The music is truly above all in the workshop, because we're all helpless; there's nothing we can do about the conflict in the Middle East. I have no doubt that what my late uncle and Mr. Barenboim have achieved will go down in history, but I am also certain of this orchestra receiving all the musical recognition it deserves as a great orchestra, regardless of the nationalities involved. I feel its sound is unique, and I am proud to have grown up alongside this orchestra.

INTERMEZZO

The violinist Yasmin is one of the millions of stateless Palestinians in the Middle East. She is also an unassuming but captivating personality in the orchestra. Everything about her is gentle: her walk, her delicate yet assured soprano voice with its Arabic dynamics and intonation, her seductive yet placid feline eyes. I had never personally spoken to Yasmin before the end of the 2007 tour, but those great, curious eyes wide enough to take in the ever-broadening world of the Divan hinted to me that she had stories to tell.

She came from a society I could only imagine. Without the slightest tinge of resentment, she explained to me that there were certain things Palestinians could not have in the country where her family now lived. As trite as it may seem, her story more than anyone else's made it clear to me just how privileged I am. Perhaps it was because we had much in common; it was easy for me to identify with her in most other ways. We were both modern, independent young women, musicians, foreigners living in Europe for professional reasons. That was where our similarities ended, though: my American passport made it very easy for me to go almost anywhere in the world, whereas her lack of any passport at all made even short trips complicated.

The Divan was capable of changing Yasmin's destiny, even if it could not grant her citizenship. As a "citizen" of the Divan, she was able to perform in Europe, the United States, South America, and Ramallah, a place she would otherwise never have been able to see.

Yasmin of Palestine

My father is Palestinian. His parents fled from Akka (now Akko) in 1948 and thought they would go back in a few months, but of course that didn't happen. I don't have a passport and I am not a citizen of any country, although I've lived in the same place all my life. I have a Palestinian refugee document. Where I live, I have a temporary residence ID card, which says that I am a Palestinian from Akka. My mother is a citizen and has a passport, but she cannot help me get one.

My parents are not musicians: my mother is a pediatrician and my father is an architect, but they both like music very much. My mother used to sing and my father used to play the guitar a little, and they were the ones who sent me in this direction. I started to play the violin when I was nine years old, after my father heard about a music school for children in our city.

I don't speak the Palestinian dialect, and neither does my father, since he was born outside of Palestine. We speak Arabic just like our neighbors at home. There are only a few words I say that people can catch me on, that let on that I might be Palestinian. It's like that on both sides, though: the Palestinians make fun of my accent, and at home they sometimes say I have a Palestinian accent when I say certain words. I don't know exactly where I belong. Sometimes I try to fake it; I try to speak like the Palestinians when I am with them, and like my neighbors when I am with them.

My father's family has preserved some Palestinian traditions: the food, the stories about my grandfather's farm with lemon trees. There is always interest in meeting other Palestinians. When you are at university and you hear there is a new Palestinian there, you always ask where he comes from in Palestine.

I auditioned for the Divan in 2004. I knew that the Divan was a very good orchestra; I had heard about it from people who had played in it. I was excited about the cities we were going to see on the concert tour, but I didn't know anything else about the orchestra, what this project was for, who we were going to meet. We were not told what it was all about. I don't remember knowing that there would be Israelis there.

I arrived in Pilas with my friend from home, and the first time we heard someone speaking Hebrew, we said, "What's that? That's not Spanish." Then we started to hear these strange names. Then we heard that they were from Israel, and we saw how many of them there were; there were more Israelis than Arabs that year.

We went into shock and didn't really recover from it all summer.

Just imagine you are twenty-one years old, and for sixteen or seventeen years of your life you have been told: "Israel is your enemy, you have to destroy it." You study it in a school, where the uniforms are even the same color as soldiers' fatigues. You see news of the Middle Eastern conflict on television, you talk about it with your parents, you see how much they are depressed about the situation, you see in the news how many children are killed by the Israeli army, and then boom: you're face to face with your enemy. What would you do? You wouldn't be happy. I thought, "What should I tell my parents when I go back?"

We never see Israelis where I come from, so for us they were like aliens, like people from outer space. We knew about them only as people that you cannot see who cannot come here, who come from a place you cannot go to, and when you see them for the first time you think, "Are they real?"

The first year, I didn't make Israeli friends. I made friends from other Arab countries. I didn't know what to talk about with the Israelis, and I think they also sensed that in me. There were also many people who came to the workshop for the first time that year. Since then, many of the same people from that year have been invited again and again, and I think it's good, because we got used to each other; it's much better now. At the end of the workshop, we were not as shocked anymore, but still, most of the discussions would end up in fights. We were very separate.

We talked about going to Ramallah that year, but we couldn't go in the end. I was so excited about going, but at the same time, we would be going with Israelis, and I wasn't sure of my opinion of that. All of these subjects were new for me. I couldn't form an opinion or make a decision about something I had just started to think about for the first time two or three weeks earlier. I could not put it in the same place with something I had been studying and living all my life. All this talk about *ta'ayosh* ("coexistence" or "cohabitation") was new for me.

This was also the first time I met Palestinians from Palestine. For me that was very interesting. When they spoke about crossing the checkpoints, it was like the biggest fairy tale I had ever heard. I thought, "What? You wait for four hours or a whole day and you miss school or a violin lesson. Why?" Then you see how they deal with the Israelis: more naturally. They speak with them and they know how to deal with them, and they can be friends. Or not, if they don't want to. It's more natural behavior than it is for us. It's not like the other person is from outer space.

I still remember when I first met Nabeel Abboud-Ashkar, because he didn't speak to me in Arabic. He thought I was Spanish or something, although I think I look very Arabic. He asked me in English where I was from, and after that we spoke in Arabic. Then I asked him where he was from, and he didn't know what to say. He said, Palestine.

"Where from Palestine?"

"Nazareth." He shrugged his shoulders. "Israel."

This was very strange for me. "What?!" I thought, "Decide where you are from!"

I didn't understand these things at the time. We knew there were Arabs living there, but at home we never even say the word "Israel." We say "occupied Palestine" even on the news and in books. We don't differentiate between one area and the other. The first time I heard this term "Palestinian territories" was in the Divan.

These people spoke Hebrew also, and they hung out a lot with the Israelis. Most of the Arabs were not hanging out with Israelis, but the Israeli Palestinians were. We didn't really understand how and why that was happening. I remember talking to Nabeel about these things once, and he told me that the question of identity was very difficult for him. He was raised in Israel, he has many Israeli friends, he lives there, he speaks the language. Even in discussions with the orchestra, you cannot tell from his opinions whether he's Israeli or Palestinian.

The workshop was the first time I really started to think about where I belong. Before, I would always say automatically, "I'm Palestinian." In the Divan, some of the Israelis would ask me, "Where are you from?" Usually it would go like this:

I would say, "Palestine."

"But where in Palestine?"

"Akka, Akko."

"But how did you come from there?"

"No, I was born in an Arab country."

"But you're saying you're Palestinian."

"Oh yeah . . . well, I don't know how to explain that. I'm a Palestinian who has lived all her life outside of Palestine."

When I started thinking about this, I realized that of course I will always have my Palestinian roots and be a Palestinian, but that I am also a citizen of the Arab world.

When my parents found out I spent the summer with Israelis they asked me, "Really? What are they like? Are they good musicians?" It was more my mother who wanted to know. My father was more distant, but he never told me not to go back.

I speak to my parents about everything but I always feel that, at a certain point, it's too much for them. If I had never gone to the Divan and somebody came to me and talked to me about all these things, it would not be the same. I would still have my old ideas; you have to experience these things to change something in your mind, your personality, your spirit. Just talking about it to others is difficult, because what they're living is something totally different from this experience.

The whole summer of 2004 I was still really uncomfortable and stressed; I didn't know how to deal with this situation. In 2005 it started to get easier. Sharon Cohen was my stand partner for part of the tour, and we started to talk a little more, or just to not be afraid of trying. If I saw some Israelis in town somewhere shopping, I would talk to them about clothes or something. I started to be more relaxed about doing everyday things with them, seeing them as people, not necessarily as *Israelis*.

When Mustafa Barghouti came to talk to us, he showed maps and explained things about the wall that was being built. He was talking about reality, but the Israelis couldn't see it. There was a big discussion with him, but everybody was waiting for this discussion to end so we could begin the real one just among ourselves outside the main hall. There was a lot of confrontation, but I found out that the Israelis listened when we talked. Of course they were defending their situation and the things we felt were wrong, but they listened to what we had to say.

I think these discussions brought me closer to reality. I don't think I was living in reality before. I think at home, we live in our own world, our own bubble. It hurts sometimes to have these discussions, because what you hear is not the same way you see it; but it made me start to think about the *real* solution. I started to think, "Okay, this is the situation. It's like that: we're here, they're there, what could the solution be?'

I think this happens for the Israelis too, that they are brought closer to reality by our discussions. Every year I feel less tension in the discussions. There is still tension, of course, and there always will be, but the people who come every year are developing a method or a way to think about these things. You learn how to keep inside you the things that are not so healthy to let out, and you think about what the solution might be.

In 2005 we started to talk about going to Ramallah again. When it looked like it was really possible for the orchestra to go there, all the Arabs met with Mariam Said. We were in Wiesbaden to play a concert, and the next day we had to decide where we would go. There were plane tickets to go anywhere, and you just had to decide whether you wanted to go to Ramallah or to go home. We were going back and forth: "Yes we'll go, no we won't." We were so afraid.

Some of the boys were concerned because they had not done their military service in their native countries yet, and they were nervous that someone would find out they had gone through an Israeli checkpoint. Other people were concerned about where our original passports would be: if you get your passport stamped by Israeli immigration, you can forget about going home all your life.

That was the main issue, and we sat with Mariam asking what the arrangements were. She told us that we would go from the Jordanian side, so we would not be going through Israel itself, even though we would enter Palestinian territory through an Israeli checkpoint. Everybody was afraid, but then, one by one, people started to say, "Okay, I'll go"; and then finally, the whole group said, "Okay. We'll go."

My worst nightmare was that they would take us to jail or ask for the original passports, that we might be kept there, and God knows what would happen. You never knew what might happen—I was going to a place where nobody in my family had ever been. The moment I made the decision to go, though, I thought, "I will go now, but I will not think about what will happen later." I didn't tell anyone at home that I was going. I didn't want anything to affect my decision, like the fact that they would be afraid for me. So I said to myself, "Okay, I won't tell them. I'll go and come back and then they will know about it."

We had wanted someone to take our passports to the Spanish consulate or embassy in Ramallah. But then in the bus, when we were already at the Allenby Bridge, only one minute before going through the checkpoint, they told us we had to take them with us. We asked why—we didn't want to go; we were afraid.

Mariam Said and Muriel Paez told us, "It might sound silly, but try to look relaxed when you go through the checkpoint. Smile if you can." We tried, but I was so nervous. My identity document was in my handbag, and I put it through the X-ray machine and then the soldier wanted to search my bag. I told Muriel, "Please, he cannot search my bag, the document is in there."

She went and talked to him, but he searched through my bag anyway. Then he asked me something about a bottle of shampoo or something I had in there, but he didn't find the document.

Then we were on the other side and I started crying. We were very tired, and things are always more extreme when you're very tired. I started crying and I couldn't stop. It was a very strange feeling being there. Nothing in the world feels like that—nothing you can experience is like that. It was like going to Never-Neverland. It is a place you imagine all the time and they tell you about all your life, and you don't even think about the possibility of ever going there: it's impossible. It's *impossible*. And suddenly you are there. We were looking at mountains and trees, and it was just a normal landscape, but we were looking at it like we had never seen mountains or trees before.

When we had just crossed the checkpoint and we were going to the bus, one of my friends said, "Guys, can you believe we are here? We're actually in Palestine?"

I told him, "No, I need time, I can't believe it. It's impossible."

We went to the hotel and Mr. Barenboim was waiting for us. Then we went on a tour, if you can call it that—we went to the Qalandia checkpoint and I saw the wall and took a picture of it. I was so shocked. I felt angry and I wasn't happy at all. It was humongous; it was something you would never want to see every day. Then you saw the difference between one side of the wall and the other. On this side it was all trees and nice, and on the other side it was a disaster. There was a watchtower at the corner with an Israeli soldier in it, looking down at us. It felt very strange. I thought, "This is Ramallah, this is Palestinian territory: Why are you here? The wall is not enough?'

I felt good playing the concert, though. I know that the Israelis didn't feel good about the "Freedom for Palestine" signs in the concert hall. I think they weren't 100 percent convinced, but it was so brave and noble of them to come and be there. For me, also, it was a sign that I was doing the right thing, that I hadn't made the wrong decision to come.

After the concert, there was a woman waiting for me. She had the same family name as I did, and she was originally from Akka. We didn't know each other, but she had heard that there was a Palestinian girl in the orchestra with her family name, and she came to the concert to find me. She hugged me and she was crying. We couldn't figure out exactly what relation we were to each other; after all these years we couldn't find our common relative.

My family at home saw on the news on television that I was there with the orchestra. They said, "What? She's in Germany—she told us she was in Germany!" Then of course they understood that I couldn't tell them.

It was a great joy for them. My mother was on the phone with all my aunts, saying, "You have to come, Yasmin is on the television, she went to . . . *a place!*" They met and watched it together. They only saw it on the news; they didn't see the whole concert live. They were in shock and they were very happy at the same time.

When I came home they wanted me to tell them all about it. It's really a privilege to have Palestinian origins and actually be able to go to Palestine to visit!

The workshop is only three weeks or one month a year, and your experience there cannot be equal to your experiences the rest of the year, of course. You go back to the same situation in your society and you cannot describe the experience to everybody, you cannot fight everybody. Some Palestinians at home say, "How could you go there and play with Israelis?!" There are some clashes about it. They still cannot totally understand it.

You try to express your feelings, your opinions about this when talking to people at home, but very carefully. Sometimes you may shock the other person, and then they don't want to listen to you anymore. Sometimes, even before you start to talk, they don't want to listen to you because they have their own ideas.

It's a shame because it's difficult when you go back to the Divan in the summer. You have to "click on" again and start from the beginning. Every year it's easier, though, because you start to have really nice friends. You only meet your friends. You miss them and you want to see them again.

At the end of 2005, I didn't have really close friends yet, but it was much, much better than 2004. It still was not totally spontaneous, though; we still had the lines we drew for ourselves and for them. Then, in 2007, something changed. Many of us Arabs didn't go to the Divan in 2006, and I missed some people, I really missed them. We saw them in New York in December 2006, and then when we came back in 2007 it was good, it was normal. I missed some of them very much and was happy to see them, and we became much closer. The friendships I have now are the ones I made in 2007. I knew most of these people before, but we were not close friends until then.

Now, four years after my first Divan workshop, I'm studying in Berlin and most of the time I hang out with my Israeli friends from the Divan, because they all live on the same street where I live. The whole Divan is in Berlin now, more or less, thanks to Mr. Barenboim!

I still think the Israelis in the Divan are very different from other Israelis. I met some in another workshop, and they were very different. I was at a chamber music course in Malta; it was a Mozart festival and it was fairly small. There were Palestinians and Israelis there, and some people from Malta. I was accompanied by an Israeli pianist who was very nice, but another Israeli guy there asked me where I was from, and at that moment I decided to say, "Palestine."

I always have this dialogue in my mind: "What to say, here or there, quick!" Every time somebody asks me where I am from, I have this gray color in my mind: "Uh . . . I don't know."

So that time I said Palestine. He said, "Where in Palestine?"

I said, "Akko," pronouncing it the Hebrew way.

He said, "I'm sorry, but that's not Palestine."

His friend made him shut up, at least. From that I learned that not all Israelis are able to hear what we have to say, like my friends in the Divan.

Other people were just curious. They had the same experience that I first had meeting Israelis. One day we were with a group of Israelis at a jazz club in Berlin near the Hackescher Markt, where they had a jam session every Wednesday. Bassam and I were there with an Israeli pianist who brought some friends of hers we didn't know. At the end of the evening, a guy came to me and said, "Hello, I'm so-and-so."

I said, "I'm Yasmin,"

He said, "I'm from Israel. Where are you from?"

I told him.

He said, "Wow!! It's the first time I've ever seen someone from there," and he was looking at me with big eyes, and then he started asking things like, "What do you do?"

I said I was a violinist. He said, "You study *music*?"

I understood exactly what he was thinking. It was the first time he was seeing somebody from my country. It was the same for him as it was for me.

You always have conflicts with yourself. You never get rid of that; there's always something telling you this might not be wrong, but . . . part of you thinks of all the massacres, the children dying, and on and on. The other part of you can go out and have fun with them because they're just people. Even when we're together, we don't speak about these things most of the time; we try not to.

Where I come from, people sit at home watching the news, cursing and shouting: "No, we don't want peace!" I think, okay, go and live there. Then say, "We don't want peace."

That's the main thing I've learned from this. I see Palestinians from Palestine, how they're suffering, and of course they want peace. But you cannot feel that until you experience it directly.

Sometimes we talk with Bassam or other people here in Berlin about the conflict. We say, "This is the solution, they should do this, they shouldn't do that." Suddenly I realize that we shouldn't be allowed, I think, to theorize about the solution when we're not living there. If you really want to know how the Palestinians from the occupied territories and the Israelis feel, and what solution they want, you have to go there and live there with all this tension and be forbidden to go out. Then you can think about what should be done.

All Roads Lead to Rome

About two weeks after the 2008 Divan tour, I was in Rome rehearsing with a piano trio for a concert commemorating the terrorist attacks of September 11, 2001. The program was a wild mixture of ensembles and compositions; a special international orchestra had been assembled for the event, and most of us were staying in the same hotel. I was only playing with the trio and not in the orchestra, so it was not until my third day in Rome that I met some of the other musicians. Late that morning, I opened the door of my hotel room and found myself face to face with Nabih Bulos, a Jordanian violinist from the Divan. My first thought was that I was simply confused. I had been on tour with the same one hundred people for six weeks, and I was used to "seeing" people on the street from the orchestra, only to discover upon closer examination that they were strangers. After I stared at him for a moment, Nabih did not transform into a stranger, and I burst out laughing in astonishment. "You! Here?!"

He was less surprised; he had seen a concert program with my name on it, and had only wondered if there were another Elena Cheah out there who played the cello. An unlikely prospect, but one never knew. He told me that Feras Hattar, a Jordanian violist from the Divan, was also in Rome for the same concert. Nabih and I went across the street to have an espresso, enjoying the happy coincidence of our playing in the same concert in Rome. I had not yet had time to begin suffering from Divan withdrawal in the short period since the end of the tour, but I was still thrilled to see my two colleagues.

I had only started to get to know Nabih during the most recent Divan tour. When the orchestra decided to go to Ravello rather than Amman, Nabih's hometown, it was too late to find accommodations for the entire orchestra in Ravello. The closest hotel with enough space for all of us was in Salerno, an hour and a half away on winding mountain roads too narrow for the buses that took us to Ravello. We spent three days rehearsing and performing in Ravello, which meant a total of nine hours spent on the bus for trips back and forth. On one of these bus trips I started talking to Nabih. At that point I already knew he was a funny guy—he had a seemingly endless repertoire of comic, skillfully crafted vulgar expressions, and was famous for his fascinating party trick of progressively flexing and releasing each individual abdominal muscle, making a vertical ocean wave of his belly.

We talked the whole way from Salerno to Ravello. According to Nabih, there were "stars" and supporting roles in the Divan. The stars were either people who gave interviews at all the press conferences and stood up to contribute something to nearly every discussion, or they were musical stars: the soloists of the orchestra. He didn't fit into either of the "star" categories of the Divan; he played more of a supporting role. Like most people, he was there for the music. When someone once suggested that the Divan print a statement of purpose in their concert programs, Nabih vehemently opposed it. "I really disagree with any kind of statement," he said. "Part of the appeal of this orchestra is that we don't get bogged down with words. I'm not here to make a statement but to play." Besides, how were you going to get over a hundred people from mutually hostile nations to agree on a single statement?

We talked a bit about his political views, but we talked more about our musical lives, and that was our main topic of conversation when we ran into each other in Rome. Like Nabeel Abboud-Ashkar, he had studied something else before "converting" to music:

economics. Nabih chose music over economics because it was something "you just can't bullshit your way through." He could fake his way through economics exams without having prepared, but he couldn't bullshit his way through a musical phrase. A piece of music had to be prepared and polished. Sincerity was required. Music created an international, bullshit-free zone. He was now preparing for orchestra auditions and wanted to know about my experience in professional orchestras, especially because I had willingly liberated myself from a tenured position—something one just *didn't do*, certainly not in Germany, anyway.

I was reluctant to tell him about my experience in professional orchestras because I now saw my entire musical history through the filter of my Divan experiences. It was unfair to look at things this way, of course, because the Divan existed for a maximum of six weeks a year: not long enough to develop the problems that beset people in their everyday lives. Things happened in the Divan that would be unacceptable if applied to a longer period of time, but the attitude during the tour was usually: "If we don't sleep for six weeks, we'll catch up during the rest of the year. If I have a big argument with my stand partner, I'll live with it for two more weeks." It was extremely difficult, if not impossible, for me to imagine ever re-entering a professional orchestra after having seen and heard what an orchestra *could* be, if only for six weeks.

Nabih and I both had evening flights the day after the concert, so we spent the whole day wandering around the city, from the Piazza del Popolo down Via Margutta, across Piazza Navona, past the Pantheon to Campo dei Fiori, finally stopping at Largo di Argentina to watch the cats lounging around on broken columns of former Roman temples. Nabih was a great talker, and together we must have left a film of words all over Rome, a thin stratum sprinkled atop this city with its endless layers from every epoch of European civilization. We floated from one topic to the next, orbiting around the central theme of the Divan, that great nebulous body that was more than just an orchestra. After nearly a year of asking people what the Divan meant to them, I found myself explaining to him what it meant to me and how it had changed me.

When I joined the Divan, I told him, I thought I would be an unbiased observer, but that soon proved impossible. It would have been like being a wallflower at the most exciting party in the world. Once I gave in and became a part of "planet Divan," I began to feel parts of myself coming together. That may sound like a trite thing to say, but the parts in question had a long way to travel.

I always felt equal parts native and foreigner wherever I lived, including the city where I was born: Pittsburgh, Pennsylvania. Even before I was born, some families in Nashua, New Hampshire, where my parents lived at the time, forbade their children to play with my two older brothers because they were "mixed": my father was Chinese and my mother was Jewish. In Pittsburgh, people did not explicitly forbid their children to play with us as far as I knew, but at the public swimming pool across the street, other kids would sometimes dance past us holding their eyes aslant and calling us "Chinks." I never thought we looked particularly Chinese, but my Chinese father was always with us on summer evenings and weekends, and that was enough ammunition for the neighborhood kids. There were no other Asians in the area, let alone racially mixed couples.

Music made us different, too. My brothers both played the violin, and my earliest memory is of lying on my mother's lap, watching my brother Dorian play the violin in our living room. Our house was always full of the sound of practicing, and I left school early every day so that I could practice three full hours in the afternoon and still have enough time to be a child. My brothers and I played in the Pittsburgh youth orchestras and lived in a suburb where nobody knew what classical music was. Explaining to our classmates that we had music lessons and played in a symphony orchestra on the weekend while they played football or video games was as bizarre as telling them that we disappeared into the forest once a week to practice witchcraft.

Nabih could relate to this. Playing the violin in Jordan was also a weird thing for a kid to do, one that didn't do much for one's popularity at school. It had all started for him when Queen Noor founded the National Music Conservatory in Amman in 1985. Shortly afterward she sent music teachers to schools to test the children's musical aptitude. Nabih was chosen as a potential music student, and it was recommended that he play the violin. "What's a violin?" he asked his mother. "It's, well, a box. With strings." Strange, he thought, but why not? He started to play the box with strings and he liked it. One day the lovely Queen Noor came to visit her music school and listen to the children play. Seven-year-old Nabih gazed up at her in awe when she went around the circle of little musicians, eventually stopping in front of him. "You're so beautiful," he gasped. "Like . . . like *Beauty and the Beast!*"

This childish utterance, which he instantly and embarrassingly regretted, was prophetic in a way; American films on television like *Beauty and the Beast* had helped Nabih learn to speak English fluently and with a perfect American accent. As he got older, it seemed obvious that he would go the United States to continue his education. One thing led to another: as he became more involved in music, he began to feel less a part of Jordanian society, and as he felt more and more out of place in his society, he became more and more involved in music.

It was not so different for me, even if there was no king or queen in my life. American culture had little to do with what we did at home and in our free time. The less I found in common with the other kids in my school, the more I sought refuge in my musical activities and with my musical friends. When I was eight years old, we moved to New Jersey and I enrolled in the Pre-College Division of the Juilliard School, where I met lots of other "weird" kids like myself every Saturday. Most of them were either Asian or Jewish, and there were even a few other mixtures like us.

My father emigrated to the United States when he was ten years old, and rebelliously renounced all the Chinese languages he spoke in an effort to become a real American. My mother came from an atheistic Jewish family that didn't even celebrate the high holidays for tradition's sake, like so many other "non-practicing" Jewish families. That meant that my brothers and I looked more different on the surface than we really were. We grew up speaking only English at home, apart from a brief attempt on my mother's part to teach us French, the language her parents had spoken at home. We had no religious education and no foreign "homeland." I was curious about my roots, though, and the friendships I made at Juilliard with Jewish and Asian kids were probably an unconscious expression of my curiosity.

When I was ten years old, I became best friends with an eleven-year-old Israeli girl at Juilliard. We were inseparable until I was sixteen, when we parted abruptly as girlfriends sometimes do. I was truly adopted by her family; for a while, I spent almost every weekend at her place. We went home to her Bronx apartment after Juilliard on Saturday evening; we ate together as a family, and watched and discussed the latest news about Israel. They had everything I thought I needed: an apartment in New York, an intellectual life that revolved around music, and a group to belong to. They celebrated the high holidays, spoke Hebrew, and ate traditional Jewish food. They belonged to a larger, collective identity, and included me as one of their own. They were also terrifyingly patriotic. My friend had come to the United States when she was seven years old, but at fifteen she still told people that she came from Jerusalem after living more than half her life in America. I, on the other hand, had moved from Pennsylvania to New Jersey at eight, but always said I was from New Jersey. Home was just the place where you slept and kept all your things . . . wasn't it?

My friend identified very strongly with Israel and the Jewish people. I soon realized that this would and could never be my world, this place where people were killing each other over a tiny piece of land. I, who had no emotional attachment to any place besides New York (a teenage infatuation, my adopted hometown) could not understand how anyone could be so fanatical about a place. At the same time, hypocritically, I had an undeniable desire to have come from somewhere specific, to belong somewhere, to speak the language and be familiar with the traditions and wisdoms of my ancestors, whoever and wherever they were on both sides—to have a connection to something culturally richer than shopping malls, baseball, rock and roll, or Hollywood.

The ties to an ethnic "homeland" had been severed on the Chinese side of my family by economic necessity and pragmatism: home was where you could make a living and get a good education regardless of your status in society. That was why my Chinese grandmother emigrated to the United States from Singapore with her three small children after being widowed in her twenties.

I never heard my Jewish grandparents talk about where they came from in Europe, and when I was young something indefinable kept me from asking them about it, even though I wanted to know. Later, when I would have had the courage to ask, they had already passed away. All I knew was that my grandfather was born in Poland and my grandmother in Belgium. My grandfather moved to Belgium as a young man, met my grandmother, and had a son with her there. In 1940, my grandparents fled to Portugal with their infant son, my uncle. There they waited ten long months for a ship to take them to America. I knew that my grandfather's family had been killed in concentration camps, maybe in Auschwitz, but nothing more.

With all these disconnected, untraced roots in my family tree, my childhood dream was to be a member of some kind of clan, any clan. It was an impossible dream, because there would never be a place for me and my kind, because there was no group that consisted of "my kind"—half-breed Chinese–Jewish Americans. I wanted to belong to one side or the other, not always to have to sit uncomfortably on the proverbial fence. Whenever I was with people who had their own culture, like my Israeli childhood friend and her family, or my Chinese and Japanese friends from Juilliard, I envied them their heritage.

That was of course an extremely naive thing to envy, especially in my Middle Eastern friends, whose heritage was often burdened by animosity toward an enemy. I realized this as I got older, as it became less important to me to belong to one club or another. Nabih, a Palestinian born in Jordan, seemed perfectly happy to be a citizen of the world rather than be labeled a "Palestinian" or a "Jordanian." The tendency to label was only one of the many problems in the region.

When I started playing in the Divan, two extraordinary things happened: one was musical, the other social. The musical miracle was the acute sensitivity of the musicians—a way of listening, understanding, and responding that I had never encountered in any other orchestra, professional or otherwise. If I had found this kind of musical kinship in any professional orchestra, I would never have quit. I felt I was coming home musically. I also found myself surrounded by people who were firmly rooted in their cultural "homelands" but were nevertheless trying their best to belong to something larger, something that extended beyond the borders of their small, troubled countries. They had exactly the kind of history and cultural security I longed for, and yet many of them were painfully but methodically shucking off the notions of "us" against "them" that they had inherited along with all the other traditions of their peoples. Their journey was the opposite of mine: they were approaching the point where I had started in life. They had a place to call home, and yet they had the courage to leave the protective sphere of their national identity, even if it seemed like an act of treason to some of their families.

For once in my life, being an outsider was an asset. As an outsider in the Divan, I saw how much all the musicians had in common with each other, whether or not they cared to admit it. It was like watching estranged relatives meet after decades of feuding. Sometimes it seemed they weren't sure whether to be amused or infuriated by their similarities. I empathized with their ambivalence. I may not have come from Israel, Palestine, any of the Arab countries, or Spain, but I did know what it was to try to unite two seemingly contradictory worldviews in one consciousness.

Now that I have spent three years watching my Divan colleagues try to create the intellectual space necessary to accommodate all their opinions, it is beginning to seem possible, and even comparatively easy, for me to retrieve and reconcile what I thought of as the incompatible aspects of my own personal family history.

By the time I drew this conclusion, Nabih and I were standing behind the railings in Largo di Argentina, watching a few well-fed cats bathe themselves lazily in the evening sun. It was already time for me to go to the airport. I had done so much talking myself, and yet I had not shared all my observations about the Divan with Nabih; I left out the ones I thought he would probably not want to hear. He was about to embark on a professional life in music. I didn't want to tell him that the West-Eastern Divan Orchestra was in every sense the greatest orchestra I had ever played in. I didn't want to tell him that it didn't get any better than this; that there was a reason professionals from some of the best orchestras in the world kept coming back every summer; that the Divan kids could teach most seasoned musicians a thing or two about playing together; that he would never find a purer spirit of music-making anywhere in the world as far as I was concerned.

I didn't tell him these things. I kept them to myself and said good-bye, wishing him luck for his auditions. As I sat in the taxi in heavy Roman traffic on the way to the airport, I wondered what would become of the Divan and all its members. I admired them all beyond description for their willingness to create a new "us," for wanting to eliminate "them": not the people, but the *notion*.

As Guy Braunstein puts it, the orchestra is on a journey, the longest journey imaginable, to all the countries in the Middle East. It is on its way home.

Appendix: Edward Said's Speech upon his Acceptance of the Principe de Asturias Prize

Oviedo, October 25, 2002

It is a tremendous honor to be awarded this extraordinary prize and to be able to share it with my dear friend and colleague Daniel Barenboim. I am grateful beyond words to the members of the Prince of Asturias Concord Prize for choosing us to receive this wonderful sign of recognition. And I would also like to congratulate the other recipients, whose outstanding achievements in the arts and sciences have similarly been recognized here today.

The world today is full of battling identities and nationalisms. They have filled the news for several years now, many of them the result of what happened when the great classical empires began to dissolve after the Second World War. All too often, inherited schemes of imperial partition such as took place in India and Palestine aggravated communal tensions even more than before, and seemed to have settled nothing. Muslim and Hindu nationalists still fight on, and Palestinian Arabs and Israeli Jews are still a long way from any kind of peace. The idea and the practice of coexistence and equality appears so distant as to seem foolishly utopian. Far from achieving and fulfilling themselves, identities in close conflict with others directly bring about the terrible violence of war and protracted conflict. Other, unrealized struggles for identity simmer away, nursing injuries and a sense of sustained injustice that often lead to outright belligerence.

In every case, though, both sides of the battle over identity consider that they have justice on their side. But where is justice? Is it to fight on and on even if one's power has grown well beyond that of one's opponent? Or is it to oppose unjust practices and keep calling attention to abuses of human and political rights? Or is it to take a superior position and pretend that identity is of no concern to you?

The underlying problem with all this is that it is impossible to be neutral or to look at such tensions from on high. No matter how detached we try to be, these are life-and-death matters for every human being in one way or another. Each of us belongs to a community with its own national narrative, its own traditions, language, history, foundational ideas, heroic figures. These provide the substance from which all identities are formed, although not all identities feel themselves to be embattled and under constant pressure. Moreover, it is true that no identity is fixed forever, since the dynamics of history and culture assure constant evolution, change and reflection. Worst of all is when either individuals or groups pretend that they are the true representatives of an identity, only they the correct interpreters of the faith, only they the real bearers of a people's history, the only true realization of a given identity, whether it be Islamic, Judaic, Arab, American, or European. From such insensate convictions come not only fanaticism and fundamentalism, but also a total absence of understanding of and compassion for the Other.

One of the especially attractive attributes of Spanish identity to me is that as a nation it has successfully negotiated the pluralism—and even the warring contradictions—in the history of its own complex identity. Spain's Islamic, Judaic and Christian histories together provide a model for the coexistence of traditions and beliefs. What might have been an unending civil war has resulted instead in the recognition of a pluri-cultural past, a source of hope and inspiration, rather than of factionalism and dissension. What was once suppressed or denied in Spain's long history has received its due, thanks to the re-creative efforts of heroic figures such as Americo Castro and Juan Goytisolo.

As a Palestinian born in Jerusalem, my national history and the society of my forbears was shattered in 1948 when Israel was established. Since that time—the better part of my own lifetime—I have participated in the struggle not just to bring justice and restitution to my people, but also to keep the hope for self-determination alive. Our modern history as a people has been full of unacknowledged suffering and continued dispossession. As an American living a life of privilege and study at Columbia University, where I have been incredibly fortunate in my career as a teacher, I came to the realization very early on that I had the choice either of forgetting my past, as well as the many members of my family who were rendered homeless refugees in 1948, or of dedicating myself to lessening the traumas of suffering and dispossession by writing, speaking, testifying to the tragedy of Palestine. I am proud to say that I chose the latter course, and with it the cause of a non-militaristic and non-imperial American policy. I have always believed in the primacy not of armed struggle but of rational argument, openness, and honesty, all deployed in the interests not of exclusion but of inclusion. How to reconcile the reality of an oppressed people, much abused and ignored as having no political and human rights, with the reality of another people, whose history of persecution and genocide unjustly, in my opinion, overrode the presence of an indigenous people in the march toward self-determination? That was the issue. It involved the cooperation of many people, many colleagues and like-minded friends, Arabs and Jews, and non-Arabs and non-Jews, whose passion for justice brought them together with the people of Palestine, suffering under Israeli military occupation for thirty-five years. That suffering, as well as the dispossession of the entire Palestinian nation in exile, cried out for acknowledgement and justice.

It has been a hard fight, and we are far from nearing its end. Daily sacrifices are made by courageous Palestinian men and women who go on with their lives despite curfews, house demolitions, killings, mass detentions, and land expropriation. But we are always in need of moral support; we need to grip the world's imagination; we need to show those who believe Palestine/Israel is the land of only one people that it is a land for two peoples who can neither exterminate nor expel each other, but must somehow approach each other as equals with equal rights to live in peace and security, together. It is therefore crucial for me to recognize the energy and dedication of those Israeli and non-Israeli Jews who have crossed the line of convention, conformity and assertive identity and acknowledged their moral involvement in a cause that in so many ways is also their cause. I should like to pay tribute to Daniel Barenboim, whose great musicianship has been offered as a gesture of the highest form of human solidarity to Palestinians and other Arabs.

Strange though it may seem, it is culture generally, and music in particular that provide an alternative model to identity conflict. I can only speak here as a Palestinian, but it has often struck me how impoverishing and constraining our life of struggle has been, simply because as a people deprived of citizenship we have tended to focus all our energies on the immediate goal of achieving independence by the most direct means possible. This is understandable of course. But there is what I might call the long-range politics of culture that provides a literally wider space for reflection, and ultimately for concord rather than endless tension and dissonance. Literature and music open up such a space because they are essentially arts not of antagonism principally but of collaboration, receptivity, re-creation, and collective interpretation. No one writes or plays an instrument just to be read or listened to by oneself: there is always a reader and a listener, and over time, the number increases. My friend Barenboim and I have chosen this course for humanistic rather than political reasons, on the assumption that ignorance and repeated self-assertion are not strategies for sustainable survival. Discipline and dedication have provided us with the motor to bring our communities together in concert, without illusion and without abandoning our principles. What is so heartening is how many young people have responded, and how, even in this most difficult time, young Palestinians have chosen to study music, learn an instrument, practice their art.

Who knows how far we will go, and whose minds we might change? The beauty of the question is that it cannot be easily answered or easily dismissed. Your acknowledgment of our efforts, however, takes us a great step forward.

Appendix: Mariam Said on her Involvement with the Barenboim-Said Foundation and the West-Eastern Divan Orchestra

New York, November 11, 2008

For a long time I was an attentive witness to the evolution of this project founded by my late husband, Edward Said, and Daniel Barenboim. Edward was suffering from leukemia and not feeling well after his treatment in the summer of 2003, yet he insisted that we go to the workshop in Seville – and we did. The orchestra was going on tour at the end of the workshop, and a concert in Rabat, Morocco was scheduled. Edward had been planning to go to Rabat. When he fell ill, it was suggested that I go in his place. Edward dictated to me what he wanted to say. I borrowed his pen and wrote it all down. It was his prized turquoise and silver 1912 Montegrappa. Afterward, I handed it back to him. He held it for a second and then said: "take it, it's yours." In retrospect, this was the moment that Edward passed over the reins of this project to me. Reading his message at that concert marked the beginning of my direct involvement with this endeavor.

When Edward died, it began to dawn on me that the project would not survive if I allowed myself to be merely an honorary symbol of Edward. I was determined to persevere with this endeavor no matter what. For this project to really succeed,

Daniel would need my support. Somebody had to represent the Arab side.

In 2004, I did what was necessary to assure the establishment of the Barenboim-Said Foundation USA. I also attended the workshop in Seville, participated in the discussions and joined the tour. I have attended the workshop every summer. My role is to organize and coordinate the discussions that take place during that time. At Daniel's suggestion, I began attending the auditions of the Arab musicians and accompanying the teachers on their auditioning trips. My principal job is to liaise between the Arab institutions and the foundation. I am the contact person for the Arab countries, and the Arab members of the orchestra rely on me for help and advice. I am also involved in the Foundation's musical education programs in Palestine/Israel (the Center and Kindergarten in Ramallah, and the Conservatory in Nazareth). I follow their progress and am engaged on many levels in their work. I try to visit at least once a year.

Our ultimate aim is to perform in all the Arab capitals as well as in Israel. To this end, I have been trying very hard to arrange for concerts in the Arab capitals. But because of the precarious political situation in the area, this has not so far materialized. But I intend to persevere. For the past three years, I have made it my crusade to show the film *Knowledge is the Beginning*, the story of the foundation and the orchestra, at universities and other institutions all over the world. I shall not tire of spreading the message of this humanistic endeavor in the hopes of breaking down the walls that separate people and undermine Arab-Israeli coexistence.